Sources of the River

TRACKING DAVID THOMPSON
ACROSS WESTERN NORTH AMERICA

Jack Nisbet

MAPS AND ILLUSTRATIONS BY
JACK McMASTER

SASQUATCH BOOKS
SEATTLE

To J. D. and to Claire

26 25 24 23 22   18 17 16 15 14

Printed in the United States of America

SASQUATCH BOOKS with colophon is a registered trademark of
Penguin Random House LLC

Cover design: Bob Suh
Interior design and composition: Cameron Mason
Cover map by David Thompson, "Map of North America from 84° West," 1804.
Map courtesy of the National Archives, Kew, United Kingdom.
Cover and interior: Oil on canvas painting by Paul Kane, "Boat Encampment,"
1849-1856. Painting courtesy of the Royal Ontario Museum, Toronto, Ontario,
Canada.
Cover calligraphy: Jack McMaster

Cataloging in Publication Data
    Nisbet, Jack, 1949–
        Sources of the river : tracking David Thompson across western North
    America / Jack Nisbet.
            p. cm.
        Includes bibliographical references and index.
        ISBN 1-57061-020-7 : Hrdbck.
        ISBN 1-57061-006-1 : Pprbck.
        ISBN 1-57061-522-5 : Pprbck. (2007)
        1. Columbia River Region—Discovery and exploration. 2. Northwest,
    Pacific—Discovery and exploration. 3. Explorers—Biography.
    5. Cartographers—Northwest, Pacific—Biography.
    I. Thompson, David, 1770–1857. II. Title
    F1060.7.T48N57 1994
    971.03'092—dc20   94-6478

Sasquatch Books
1325 Fourth Avenue, Suite 1025
Seattle, WA 98101

SasquatchBooks.com

CONTENTS

LIST OF MAPS

FOREWORD TO THE 2007 EDITION

David Thompson traveled far and wide in mid- and north-western North America. Even today, few people range over the continent as he did, from the northern boreal forest to the prairies and plains, from the Columbia Plateau to the Great Lakes Basin. Yet, whereas his contemporaries were heralded for their achievements in their lifetimes, he was not.

He was never offered a knighthood, as fellow fur trader Alexander Mackenzie, in 1793 the first European to cross the continent, had been in 1802. He was never made a governor of a territory, as Meriwether Lewis had been in 1807, a year after returning from his transcontinental expedition, or a superintendent of Indian Affairs, as Lewis's former commanding officer and fellow explorer William Clark had been in the same year. Unlike these men, he never had his portrait painted. The Welsh boy schooled in England before finding himself on the west shore of Hudson Bay in the midst of his teenage years was probably the best educated of this cohort of explorers, but his achievements were overlooked at least in part because he never managed to publish a book about his travels, as Mackenzie did in 1801, or catch the attention and travel under the auspices of a head of state, as Lewis and Clark had, at the behest of President Thomas Jefferson. Perhaps it was just as well, for Thompson's behavior as a cartographer, explorer, fur trader, and naturalist suggests that the mantle of public life would have sat awkwardly on him. Clearly, he preferred a book to a social gathering. And the book of nature was his favorite text.

Throughout the twentieth century, historians have tried to write Thompson's narrative of exploration and travel for him, working either from his twenty-eight years worth of field notebooks or from the four drafts of his narrative that fell incomplete at his death. In *Sources of the River*, Jack Nisbet succeeds by trying a different tack. He gives us a biographical sketch of the explorer at a human scale by setting his own perambulations and contemplations alongside Thompson's.

Thompson interested himself in the details of life—the way, for example, that the tangled conifers on the shores of Lake Wollaston (which bestrides the watersheds of the Mackenzie and Churchill rivers in present-day northern Saskatchewan) could be loosened from the rock on which they clung, slid down into the water, and carried away by the wind, looking for all the world like substantial islets. So captivating did he find details that the production of a sustained narrative of all his travels and explorations kept bogging down in endless revision. The trees, not the forest, kept his focus. Thompson thought big by accruing details until they formed a whole, not by sweeping generalizations. And he was curious about geography and the natural world, less so about politics, business, and personal ambition. Nearly our sole fur trader whose business interest did not dominate his working life, he represents a rare breed. The Columbia River was a world of wonders for him, not principally a route. It has been said often that he lost the race to the Pacific to John Jacob Astor's fur traders, but it was a race in which history, not he himself, entered him. He found the Columbia too engaging to treat it only as a thoroughfare.

Nisbet understands David Thompson. He gives us the man, the person, not the hero. Born in 1770 within a month of William Wordsworth, while fur trader and arctic explorer Samuel Hearne was struggling on the Seal River (in today's northern Manitoba) and Captain Cook was naming Botany Bay on Australia's east coast (one bay south today of Sydney's harbor), Thompson grew up and was educated at a London charity school to be a reader. We can assume that, either before he left England or after reaching York Factory on Hudson Bay at the age of fourteen and taking up his duties as a writer under Hearne's charge, he read the works of Baron

Lahontan and Louis Hennepin, the most widely read authors on North America in the first half of the eighteenth century, and of Jonathan Carver, whose *Travels through the Interior Parts of North America* (1778), which appeared in Thompson's London when he was eight years old, was the most commonly read narrative in the latter half of the eighteenth century about what would soon become the midwestern United States.

We know that Thompson copied for Hearne parts of his own journal of arctic exploration, which would appear posthumously as the *Journey from Prince of Wales's Fort* (1795). Thompson's book knowledge apparently whetted his appetite to know more: more geography that awaited exploring and mapping, more native people to meet who could help him read the land, especially its watery veins, and more plants and animals than could ever be surmised by Comte de Buffon, whose theory that both animals and people in North America were feeble and degenerate forms of their European counterparts Jefferson would famously disparage in his *Notes on the State of Virgina* in 1784. Nisbet gives us that curious David Thompson better than anyone before him.

And he also does so in terms of the locale. Thompson charted so vast an area of the continent that Nisbet's predecessors were always tempted to paint his achievements with a broad brush. But just as doing so does not suit Thompson's temperament, neither does it do his achievements justice. Despite his mobility, he was a man of place, one place at a time. He wrote as if he was always of the moment, not looking round the next bend of a river or trail, as Simon Fraser was in 1808 on the river that bears his name, or habitually negotiating to be handed from one native group to the next just to reach the Pacific, as one senses Alexander Mackenzie was from his *Voyages from Montreal* (1801).

And it is this particularity of time and place that *Sources of the River* captures so well. Nisbet does not pretend to intimately know all the watercourses paddled and mountain

passes traversed by Thompson. Instead, he concentrates on
the Columbia River and its tributaries on the Pacific Slope.
More than Cartier with the St. Lawrence, Coronado with the
Rio Grande, La Salle with the Mississippi, or even Mackenzie
and Fraser with the rivers that bear their names and which
they so disappointedly and quickly descended and ascended
(both realizing that the watercourses would never further their
purposes, for Mackenzie, of reaching the Pacific; for Fraser,
of offering a navigable fur trade route), Thompson's name
belongs to the Columbia. That the river is reduced today by
what seems an infinite series of dams to what seems an infinite series of puddles and reservoirs, as one writer scorn-
fully put it, makes all the more resonant Thompson's careful
descriptions of its fitful, snarling reaches when it was a freely
flowing deluge, rumbling out of the mountains, up north and
then bending extraordinarily southward to course through
the deserts of the Columbia Basin to the Cascades and the
ocean. More than anyone else in written form, Thompson is
the chronicler of that sinuous yet turbulent torrent, the dark
arrow that was also the lifeblood and, with its salmon, the
staff of life to so many peoples, and which took the explorer
through a multilingual world of Interior and Coast Salish dia-
lects, Chinook Jargon, Hawaiian, Cree, Iroquois, and French
and English.

If, from our twenty-first century vantage point, assaulted
as it is by the visual, David Thompson had a failing as an ob-
server of his time and place, it is that his chronometer was
his only paint brush; his maps his only sketchpads. Adding
hue, tone, and shading to Thompson's life and times on the
Pacific Slope, Jack Nisbet paints us the best portrait we have
of David Thompson. As we come to mark the bicentennial of
the explorer's years on the Pacific Slope, this new edition of
Sources of the River is thus fitting and timely.

—I.S. MacLaren
Professor of History and Classics
University of Alberta

AUTHOR'S NOTE

When David Thompson died in 1857, he left behind a wealth of written material in the form of journals, letters, reports, and four drafts of reminiscences about his life in the fur trade. In retracing Thompson's travels through the West, I have chosen to rely on his original field notes for the backbone of the story, both for chronological integrity and for the sense of immediacy they bring to his journeys. In many cases, I draw passages from his other writings to clarify or embellish events, and on such occasions I credit the source in order to make clear the perspective. Since, as far as we know, he did not begin keeping a journal until 1789, all selections previous to that time necessarily come from his memoirs.

When quoting from the original daybooks, I have retained Thompson's idiosyncrasies of spelling and punctuation as much as possible. Over the years he developed his own personal shorthand, using, for example, ⊙ for sun, dº for ditto, &c for etc., SRC for strong rapid current, and similar abbreviations for latitude and longitude. These few symbols I have written out for ease of understanding. Thompson was, for the most part, an excellent speller, and I saw no reason to modernize the few words that have changed since 1800. As for the names of places and peoples he visited, I have tried to follow current tribal usage and to render geographical locations as they appear on the most recent maps. Sometimes this means that a tribe name is spelled one way by Thompson and another way by me, or that a river changes its spelling when it crosses the border between Canada and the United States.

I have had a great deal of help on this book from the kind staff members of numerous libraries, especially the Archives of Ontario, the Fisher and Robarts Libraries at the University of Toronto, the Toronto Public Library, the Hudson's Bay Company Archives in Winnipeg, the Royal Ontario Museum, the Glenbow Museum in Calgary, the Spokane Public Library, the University of Montana Library, the Suzzallo Library at the University of Washington, the Rosenbach Library in Philadelphia, and the Habersham County Library in Clarkesville, Georgia. I also received encouragement, information, comments, places to stay, and extended tours from many individuals, and single out only a few of them here: Tom and Susie Bristol, Cary Cleaver, Ivan Doig, Charles Ferree, Harriet Huber, Nancy Hunn, Connie Poten, Ann Rittenberg, Terry Webster, Steve Zender, and Joan Gregory and all the people at Sasquatch Books. I want to thank them all very much. Special appreciation is due to John Stern for his insights, to Sean Peake, Hugh Dempsey, and Gene Hunn for generously sharing their files, and to Emily for being such a good sport.

Arctic Ocean

Mackenzie R.

Great Slave
Lake

Lake
Athabasca

North Saskatchewan R.

Fraser R.

Vancouver
Island

PACIFIC OCEAN

Columbia R.

Cascades

Missouri R.

Snake R.

Lake
Win

0   500 k
0   500 mi

DAVID THOMPSON'S TERRITORY

PAUL KANE, *BOAT ENCAMPMENT*. OIL ON CANVAS

PROLOGUE

U P ON THE hill, the March morning was seared with a frigid light that preceded the sun, locking the mud-frosty ground up tight. As I wound down the slope past the old town dump, a horde of ravens and magpies broke out of the black pines, and we sank together into the ocean of white ground fog that hugged the valley floor. My eyes followed the course of the local creek, bare cottonwood arms that led to the Colville River. Not a whole lot wider than a creek itself, the Colville meanders north for thirty more miles before dribbling into the Columbia River, and that was the way I was headed.

This was a route I had followed many times during the years I lived in northeast Washington, and I remembered again how much I liked this part of the country, with its open, piney hillsides and comfortable valleys. As I drove north the fog thinned, and I looked out over easy swales of farmland where lumps of stubble and umber muck shadowed the snow's receding face. The peat bottoms seemed impossibly rich for a place that receives less than twenty inches of rain a year. This rich dirt had been one of the first things the Canadian explorer and fur trader David Thompson noticed when he passed through this valley almost two centuries ago: "The ground of the day seems very fit for cultivation, black deep mould & the higher Ground a kind of black gray greasy earth." Thompson had been right. A couple of months from now, grain and alfalfa would be sprouting in that black earth all across the valley floor. The tamaracks in the hills would be budding out, matching the barley's yellow-green, adding depth to the mix of pine and Douglas fir. But even in high spring, the most visible feature of the landscape would be rocks. From the worn quartzite cliffs that ring the valley to the rubble piles left by small-time miners, you could always see the bones of this place.

It was still early when I reached the Kettle Falls bridge over the Columbia, and I rolled down my window to let in a blast of cold air as I crept along beneath the old steel trusses. Clouds of mist clung to the surface of the water, and a delicious turpentine smell seeped down from the wood-burning power plant up on the east bank. Over on the west side of the river, I could see the familiar slope of Bisbee Mountain, spotted with scrub maple and sumac. Along its ragged face, outcrops of dark quartzite have weathered into shades of fawn and chocolate, ferrous red and sulfur yellow, so that the hillside throws off an aura of heat and pressure and time.

At the foot of this hill sits Barney's Cafe, a rambling structure veneered from footings to chimney top with the forged colors of the local stone. I stopped in for a short stack of Barney's buckwheat cakes, sliding into an empty booth to gaze through one of the big windows at the river. Outside, in-air that hovered right at freezing, a waitress in a thin blue-sweater squeegeed away at the plate glass. When she was-done, I could see every faint burble on the Columbia's surface.

Barney's Cafe and the Kettle Falls bridge lie just below the Canadian border, about midway along the length of the great river: five hundred and fifty circuitous miles from its source lake up in British Columbia, another seven hundred down to the treacherous bar where its fresh water meets the Pacific. Many stories revolve around the site of Kettle Falls, which once divided the river so neatly. But the cascades for which this place was named have been silent for half a century, and the water framed by Barney's windows is now officially known as Lake Franklin Delano Roosevelt, the backup from Grand Coulee Dam a hundred miles downstream.

On this particular morning, the Columbia's surface seemed gray and ordinary, its current sluggish. Much more alive was the scene in Barney's parking lot, a huge asphalt rendezvous for vehicles from both sides of the border. While cars and work trucks came and went, I sat inside amid the breakfast clamor and thought about all the other traffic this stretch of river had seen. Fingers of great ice sheets had descended on this crossing several times, leaving behind scratches on the bedrock and spewings of unsorted gravel. The hooves of great camel herds had tromped past, preyed upon by big cats and bears and scavenged by nodding condors. Around ten thousand years ago, humans began filtering in, and through the millennia successive cultures appeared, shaped tools from the local quartzite, and faded away. In historic times the falls marked a summer fishing place; when David Thompson arrived here in the early 1800s, he found a large village of Colville Indians drying salmon in long cedar sheds. Succeeding traders beat down a portage trail for their canoes and fur packs, and built a small fort on a bluff above the river. White missionaries soon followed with Bibles and primers, and prospectors rushed in to grub for ore around every little cliff and outwash. Turn-of-the-century homesteaders plowed and planted, froze and flooded, dried out and blew out and burned out, and some still hung on.

I thought of my old neighbor Lynn Walker in the Colville Valley, one of the homesteaders still hanging on, and about a-piano I had once helped him move. His wife had just

inherited the big black upright from her mother, whose
mother in turn had ordered it from New York City in 1892,
then watched it come ashore many months later at the bus-
tling port just below the falls.

"You bet," Lynn had puffed as we tried to steer the out-
of-tune hulk through a narrow doorway. "This baby's been
around the Horn and up the river. Clipper ship to Astoria,
then mules around all the rapids, then a big sternwheeler
up to Kettle Falls. They used to race all up and down that
Columbia before the dams. Yes sir. They had this country
opened up like a can of sardines."

David Thompson was the man who began to open up this
country. Thompson was the first person to chart the entire
length of the Columbia River; he also explored its source lake
and the nest of tributaries that wind through the area we now
call the Inland Northwest—southeastern British Columbia,
western Montana, northern Idaho, and eastern Washington.
As he traveled he carried a compass, a sextant, and a business proposition for the native tribes he met. For Thompson
was not just a geographer out to map a river, he was also a
fur trader with the North West Company of Montreal, out
to expand its domain and convert the natives to its commer-
cial purposes. He was an agent of revolutionary change in the
region: its history turns on the moment of his arrival.

I first became acquainted with Thompson in the 1970s,
when I was writing a series of articles about the natural history of eastern Washington. In the Northwest Room of the
Spokane Public Library, I found a book he had written, called
A Narrative of Travels in Western North America, 1784–1812.
It was a story that sprawled across the continent, full of hair-
raising adventures and sharp descriptions of wild country. He
touched on subjects that ranged from the mechanics of the
fur business to details of natural history. He had a special eye
for the mosaic of native cultures he encountered, noting their
various characters and social customs even as he proceeded
to indelibly alter their future. During a long career that took

him from Hudson Bay to the Pacific, he never seemed to lose his enthusiasm for new country.

There was something contagious about the man's particular brand of curiosity, and I found myself making detours to walk a trail he had walked or to canoe a river he had paddled. Thompson wrote his *Narrative* after he retired, and several footnotes in the text referred to his original field journals. These I wanted to see, because from the time he crossed the Continental Divide in 1807 until he reached the junction of the Columbia with the Snake River four years later, he was moving through territory that had never been described on paper. Anything that he had to say about what he saw, no matter how casual, carries the weight of that first contact.

Scattered portions of his field notebooks had been transcribed and published in regional history journals, and I stitched these together, then fretted about what Thompson might have been up to during the periods that had not been transcribed. I ordered microfilm copies of some of his notebooks and began learning to read eighteenth-century script. At first his rough field notes bewildered me. Many entries contained more numbers than words—paragraphs filled with notations of distance and direction, pages dominated by column after column of astronomical observations. Sometimes he would get partway through one journal only to turn it upside down and begin at the other end, and sometimes he would write two versions of the same trip in different books. He capitalized most of his nouns and often seemed to be in too much of a hurry for punctuation, so that one thought piled into another. A few passages looked like he might have written them while standing up in a canoe. After a while, though, I got the hang of his style and started looking forward to the next page. As I read on, I became absorbed in the flow of his daily life, and began to get a sense of wonderful randomness bursting from the mind of an orderly man—one day he wouldn't enter anything more than the weather and what he had to eat, the next he might fill a whole page with the submarine habits of a water ouzel or note that bears make a humming noise when they lick their feet.

PANCAKES FINISHED, I wandered out of Barney's and over to the river, picking my way along the rocky bank toward a stunted yellow pine that stuck up from a ledge of fractured rock. I knew this tree well, as a favorite perch for raptors, and-once had almost put my pickup in the river trying to focus on a rough-legged hawk that had landed in its broken top. It was a fat, ancient tree, its bark broken into rough jigsaw plates. The rays of morning sun drew a deep orange cast from the trunk.

Straight across the river rose the hill where fur traders who followed Thompson had built their first small trading post, and where Catholic missionaries later established St. Paul's Mission. The hill juts out into the river, terminating in staggered bluffs, and its height commands the bay that broadens out upstream. A big black-and-white enlargement of this part of the river used to hang in Barney's cocktail lounge, taken with a box camera in some year before 1940, when the gates of Grand Coulee Dam first closed. In the photograph the bay was no longer a bay, but an extensive mud flat that spread out beneath the bluffs. From the base of Bisbee Mountain, a series of tall blocks of quartzite stepped across the river toward Mission Hill, and their path created the falls. For eons the waters of the Columbia's upper half had plunged-over these ledges, hammering scores of pocks and craters into the rock below. Churning pools at the bottom of the twenty-foot drop inspired French voyageurs to name these falls La Chaudière (The Boiler). Rocks and boulders swept over the edge were tossed about with tremendous circular force, polishing certain potholes as smooth as the inside of a cooking kettle.

I leaned against the yellow pine and looked across the river, trying to imagine the scene that greeted David

Thompson when he first arrived on the opposite shore: the spectacle of many families gathering for the season's fishing, the shouts of spearmen below the pounding falls, the smell of-split salmon hung up to dry. It had been late June, and the explorer had sampled some of the first of the summer chinooks, then boated across the river with the Colville chief and climbed Bisbee Mountain in search of cedar wood for a-canoe.

From behind my head I slowly became aware of a faint noise that seemed to be coming from inside the tree. It was a series of anxious creaks, like the joints of a chair coming unglued. The sound was vaguely familiar, and as I tried to place it, a chorus of sneezy whines circled overhead and a phalanx of nuthatches landed in the top of the pine. The birds went directly to work, spiraling around the trunk from top to bottom as they probed crevices in the bark for insects and pupae. Insects. Bark beetles, that's what the noise was: the pincer jaws of soft-bodied larvae boring their galleries between the bark and sapwood of the pine. And now these masked bandits were coming after the beetles and all their kin; each quick yank meant another morsel of food. It was the kind of small event that David Thompson might have noticed as he tramped toward his next destination, sextant in hand. There was something appealing in the notion that a man who had traveled tens of thousands of miles would stop to watch a flock of little birds, would still bend down to finger the soil in the Colville Valley.

A lumber truck rumbled across the Columbia River bridge, then downshifted to toil up Mission Hill. Above my head the nuthatches skittered around the trunk and bare limbs of the yellow pine. Just beyond their reach I could hear the creak of bark beetles chewing away inside the old tree, gnawing at the edges of time.

CHAPTER ONE

IN THE COUNTRY OF SAUKAMAPPEE

1700–1787

D AVID THOMPSON WAS born in London of Welsh parents in 1770. His father died when David was two, and at age seven he was sent to the Grey Coat School near Westminster Abbey, a charity school that aimed to "educate poor children in the principles of piety and virtue and thereby lay a foundation for a sober and Christian life." He spent seven years there, and though several of the textbooks he studied from had been published almost a century before, he apparently received a solid grounding in the basic skills of his day, including geography, algebra, navigation, and the workings of the tides. In his free time he read such popular adventure stories as *The Arabian Nights*, *Robinson Crusoe*, and *Gulliver's Travels*, and on outings he walked to London Bridge and St. James's Park. Thompson would later write that he had been given a "mathematical education" in preparation for service in the Royal Navy, but as his graduation neared, England was signing the peace treaty that ended the American Revolution, and the Navy no longer needed large numbers of new sailors. He probably would have wound up in the merchant marine had not his headmaster received a letter from the secretary of the Hudson's Bay Company, which sometimes recruited young clerks from orphanages and charity schools and was looking for four students to serve apprenticeships in the North American fur trade. Only two upcoming Grey Coat graduates were considered eligible; one of these ran away, the other was David Thompson.

In May 1784 Thompson sailed from London aboard the Bay Company's *Prince Rupert*. They crossed the North Atlantic, then spent a month weaving through the summer icebergs in Hudson Strait; by the time the ship traversed Hudson Bay and docked at Churchill Factory on the western shore, it was early September. Supplies for the trading post were unloaded and furs from the warehouse taken on as quickly as possible. Two weeks after arriving, the *Prince Rupert* set sail again, trying to beat winter ice-up in the strait. She left behind a fourteen-year-old boy who, as far as is known, had never before been out of London; he would receive no word from home until the arrival of the next supply ship a year later. Thompson recorded memories of his early years with the Bay Company in his *Narrative of Travels in Western North America, 1784–1812*. In one draft of these memoirs, he described watching the *Prince Rupert* sail away: "While the ship remained at anchor, from my parent and friends it appeared only a few weeks' distance, but when the ship sailed and from the top of the rocks I lost sight of her, the distance became immeasurable, and I bid a long and sad farewell to my noble, my sacred country, an exile for ever."

David Thompson had been set down in a vast wilderness territory inextricably bound to the fur business. Ever since the beginning of the sixteenth century, natives along the North American coast had been swapping their beaver robes and other furs for the extra iron kettles and similar useful articles of European cod fishermen who put ashore in sheltered coves and river mouths. Pelts that had previously served as everyday clothes and coverings suddenly took on new value.

When Jacques Cartier sailed up the St. Lawrence River in 1535 in search of the Northwest Passage, he met canoeloads of men, probably Micmacs, waving furs on sticks. During the trading session that followed, "they bartered all they had to such an extent that they all went back naked without anything on them; and they made signs to us that they would return on the morrow with more furs."

By the end of the century, the French had established a colony on the St. Lawrence, and European gentlemen and military officers had developed a taste for expensive beaver hats fashioned from the skins of these New World rodents. In the ensuing rush for pelts, French entrepreneurs set up shop in New France, importing wool cloth, iron utensils, firearms, and trinkets for exchange with the nearby tribes. Vigorous hunting quickly depleted the beaver grounds along the St. Lawrence, and intertribal warfare over who would control the trade disrupted the supply of furs coming in from the hinterlands. In response, some of the more adventurous Frenchmen took to the interior in pursuit of pelts, paddling with the natives in their birchbark canoes along aboriginal trade routes through Quebec's network of rivers and lakes. They moved north toward Hudson Bay and south across the Great Lakes into the Ohio Valley, where they began bumping into trappers from the British colonies.

The French soon found themselves squeezed by English interests to the north as well when the British Crown granted a charter to the Hudson's Bay Company of London in 1670, ceding it rights to all the lands drained by all the rivers that feed that huge bay. French traders, however, had already discovered the value of the thick pelts coming in from the cold northern regions, and chose to ignore the claims of Great Britain. The two countries and the tribes with whom they each were allied skirmished in the north and in the south until their spats grew into the long series of French and Indian Wars. When the British finally prevailed and the French surrendered all claim to New France in 1763, the

NORTH
ATLANTIC
OCEAN

Hudson Strait

HUDSON
BAY

Lake
Athabasca

Churchill
Factory

York
Factory

Saskatchewan R.

Lake
Winnipeg

St. Lawrence R.

Montreal

Lake
Superior

Lake Huron

Lake
Ontario

Missouri R.

Mississippi R.

Lake
Michigan

Lake Erie

Ohio R.

| 0 | | 500 k |
| 0 | | 500 mi |

EMPIRE OF THE EARLY FUR TRADE

Hudson's Bay Company expected to have the bulk of the northern fur trade to itself.

But it wasn't long before a new generation of "pedlars from Quebec" took over the business. Experienced French traders teamed up with Scots moving in from the depressed Highlands, Yankee opportunists from the American colonies, and Englishmen who saw potential on the Canadian frontier. By the time David Thompson arrived on Hudson Bay, several of these independent operators had pooled their resources to-form the North West Fur Company, headquartered in Montreal, and their upstart coalition was gaining strength.Up until this point, the Hudson's Bay Company had taken a conservative approach to its fiefdom, building forts at the mouths of the major rivers that feed the bay and relying on Cree and Assiniboine emissaries to ferry goods to the interior tribes and bring pelts back to the bay. Geography gave the Bay Company a major advantage, for ships docking at its posts on the bay's western shore were already halfway across the continent, right on the doorstep of rich fur country. In 1774 the company built a pair of inland posts, but the effort was expensive, and a series of difficulties delayed further expansion. The North West Company, despite the long distances from its port in Montreal, was far more aggressive. Organized into efficient brigades, the "Nor'Westers" forged across Lake Winnipeg into the prairies and penetrated northwest as far as Lake Athabasca, where they tapped into an enormous lode of prime pelts. They built a succession of new trade houses at strategic intervals and intercepted the native middlemen on their way east to Hudson Bay, treating them to rum and bartering for their choicest furs. They strangled the flow of pelts that had previously poured into the posts on the bay, and the Bay Company's profits were suffering when David Thompson landed at Churchill Factory in 1784.

Churchill was, by many accounts, a miserable posting. Thompson spent the winter "growling at the cold" and the summer "quarrelling with mosquitoes and sand flies." He learned to walk in snowshoes and shoot a gun, and borrowed books on history and "animated nature," but chafed at what he saw as the meager opportunities at the post. The London governors of the Hudson's Bay Company had sent along a glowing letter with the boy, recommending "that he may be kept from the common men and employed in the writings, accounts & Warehouse Duty . . . so that he may by degrees be made capable of business & become useful in our Service." Thompson was not feeling very useful, and his complaint that his penmanship was going to ruin for lack of practice won him the attention of the post's chief officer, Samuel Hearne. Hearne was working on a book about a journey he had made to the Arctic Ocean a few years earlier, and he allowed the new apprentice to copy out part of the manuscript that became *A Journey to the Northern Ocean*, a classic tale of resourceful travel under the most rugged conditions.

When the annual supply ship arrived in the early fall of 1785, it carried orders from London reassigning David Thompson to the supply depot at York Factory, 150 miles to the south. The boy made the journey to York on foot with two native couriers, called "packet Indians," whom the Bay Company employed to carry messages between posts. Their course lay down the muddy beach of Hudson Bay, with the drift ice and driven boulders of the sea on their left and a treeless bog on their right. Each man carried a blanket for cover and a gun for hunting; for food they roasted any ducks and geese they could shoot. Along the way they often passed clusters of polar bears lying on their bellies, heads together and bodies radiating out like the spokes of a wheel. The two couriers taught the boy to walk past the bears with a steady, direct step, eyes focused straight ahead. One afternoon they prepared to cross a fair-sized creek, and saw that

> on the opposite side of the ford was a large polar bear
> feasting on a beluga; we boldly took the ford thinking
> the bear would go away, but when halfway across, he

lifted his head, placed his forepaws on the beluga, and uttering a loud growl, showed to us such a set of teeth as made us turn up the stream, and for fifty yards wade up to our middle before we could cross, during this time the bear eyed us, growling like a mastiff dog.

Narrative

The couriers delivered their charge safely to York Factory, where he helped hunt geese and ducks in the surrounding marshes and learned to build snares for rabbits. In 1786 the Bay Company resolved to make a renewed push inland, and that summer young Thompson was one of forty-four men sent on an expedition to the interior to compete with the Nor'Westers. From York Factory, the group pushed west up the Nelson River, fighting its current all the way. There were tedious portages, where the canoes and cargo had to be carried around rapids. The current was often so strong that the three-man crews could not make any progress by paddling, and they would try to keep going by poling with iron-tipped rods. When that didn't work, they would stop, attach long ropes to the bow, and put two men ashore to haul the boat upstream while the third stayed aboard to steer. This was known as line-hauling, or tracking, and since Thompson was too inexperienced to steer a boat, he labored for days at the end of a tracking line, trudging through blistering heat and clouds of mosquitoes. "To alleviate this latter," he wrote, "the men make for themselves wide, loose caps of coarse cotton with a piece of green bunting in the front, but the sweat from toil and heat makes it unbearable in the day time, but serves well at night."

On the go fourteen hours a day, the brigade made its way to Lake Winnipeg and around its windy north shore to the-mouth of the Saskatchewan River. After a brief stop at-Cumberland House, erected twelve years earlier as a hub-for inland canoe traffic, the Bay men continued up the Saskatchewan. This great river flows east from the base of the

Rocky Mountains all the way across the prairies, making it a natural highway for the fur trade. As the canoes traveled upstream, they gradually left behind the dense forests of eastern Canada and entered the more open landscape that borders the Great Plains. David Thompson liked the change: "Every hour appeared to bring us to a better country, instead of dark pine forests the woods were of well grown Poplar, Aspen and white Birch and for the first time saplings of Ash. The whistling and calls of the Red Deer [elk] echoed through the woods, and we often heard the butting of the Staghorns."

The flotilla split up at the north and south forks of the Saskatchewan, with Thompson's party of five canoes ascending the south branch. About a hundred miles upriver, they spotted two adjacent trading posts, one belonging to the fledgling North West Company and the other to an independent from Montreal who had not yet joined the coalition. Here the Bay men stopped and selected a spot for their own house just upstream. It was a common practice throughout the history of the fur trade for rival companies to establish such close quarters, and they got along with varying degrees of amiability. In this case the newcomers were greeted warmly by the gentlemen in charge of both posts. One of them was French—"Every sentence he spoke or answer he made was attended by a smile and a slight bow, our men grave and stiff as pokers"—the other a Scot, who was happy to "have the pleasure of speaking english." (The Hudson's Bay Company imported almost all of its workers from England and Scotland's Orkney Islands, whereas most of the men from Montreal spoke French.)

The post that Thompson helped build that fall was named South Branch House. It was a large log building divided into three sections—the "Master's Room" on one end; a "Guard Room" in the middle, where the actual trade transpired; and three men's "Cabbins" on the other end. Here the apprentice's handwriting got plenty of practice, for the house master was illiterate. As clerk, or "writer," one of Thompson's

jobs was keeping the post journal, and in a careful, copybook
script he followed the standard Bay Company format, listing
the day's weather, the jobs the men were doing, who came
in to trade, food brought by the hunters, and any other arrivals, departures, or "unusual occurrences." On Sundays he
recorded only the weather.

Around the little trading post, Thompson began his education in the ways of Canada's vast prairies. Native hunters
supplied bison and elk meat, a welcome change from the constant diet of fish and fowl on Hudson Bay. The post had a few
horses, and it seems likely that the young clerk learned to ride
here, for he mentions traveling up to fifty miles away from
the trade house to find the hunters' tents. His duties brought
him into close contact with the Cree and Stoney Assiniboine
Indians who traded there, and he learned how to hand out
gifts of brandy and tobacco during the rituals of greeting, and
how to smoke the introductory pipe that always preceded the
actual exchange of goods for pelts. Although beaver remained
the backbone of the trade, the furs of other animals were accepted as well. At South Branch House that winter, the skins
included fox and wolf, lynx and wolverine, coyote and badger.

As soon as the snow began melting in the spring, the
natives left their winter camps to move out onto the plains
for their spring buffalo hunt. The Bay men sorted the furs
they had collected over the winter and built a wooden press
to squeeze the pelts into compact bales. An average beaver
pelt weighed a little better than a pound, and one pressed
pack, designed to be carried around a portage, usually topped
ninety pounds. Warm or wet weather would draw out the
smell of any unscraped fat, and the fur bundles often made
rancid traveling companions.

When the ice broke up on the river, the packs were
loaded into canoes, and Thompson floated downstream
with them as far as Cumberland House. There he passed
the summer mending nets and fishing for sturgeon while the
boats made their round-trip journey to York Factory. When

HUDSON
BAY

Lake
Athabasca

Nelson R.

N. Saskatchewan R.

CREE

Lake
Winnipeg

PIEGAN

Bow R.

BLACKFEET

S. Saskatchewan R.

ASSINIBOINE

Continental Divide

Missouri R.

SNAKE

0   300 k
0   300 mi

Legend
1. Churchill Factory
2. York Factory
3. Cumberland House
4. South Branch House
5. Manchester House
6. Saukamappee's Camp

THOMPSON'S EARLY TRAVELS

they returned with fresh trade goods, he joined a brigade
heading to the new Manchester House, midway up the north
fork of the Saskatchewan. Their trip west across the prairies
coincided with the migration of several buffalo herds crossing the river in search of fresh pasture, and for days the Bay
men-maneuvered their boats through swarms of bison dog-
paddling across the current, only their big heads visible above
the water. Undeviating in their course toward the opposite
shore, the beasts "often came against our file of canoes and to
prevent them coming on the canoes we had to shove them off
with the paddle."

When the boats arrived at Manchester House, Thompson
learned that his travels were not finished. The year before, a
Bay trader had made an excursion west to trade with a group
of Blackfeet Indians, and his trip had been so successful that

the company was sending him back with five men; the young clerk was assigned to go along and learn the Blackfeet language. When they set off in early October, Thompson's kit-consisted of "the clothes I had on, which was a cotton shirt, a blue cloth jacket and leather trowsers . . . another shirt, a leather coat, a blanket and Bison robe, forty rounds of ammunition, two long knives, six flints, a few awls, needles etc. with a few pounds of tobacco, and a horse to carry myself and baggage, which obliged me to walk the greatest part of the journey."

After about a month's march across the prairies, the men saw a line of brilliant white clouds coming into view on the horizon. Their guide said that these were the Rocky Mountains, but Thompson and the others found this hard to believe—at this time only a handful of white men had ever seen these mountains, and nothing in Thompson's experience had prepared him for the apparition of the east front of the Rockies rising from the plains. "As we proceeded they rose in height, their immense masses of snow appeared above the clouds and formed an impassable barrier, even to the Eagle." The furmen continued west, and near the foothills of the mountains crossed the Bow River, where they met a dozen "Peeagan" Indians on horseback. Thompson's "Peeagans" (now spelled Piegan in the United States and Peigan in Canada) belonged to the great Blackfeet Nation, along with two other tribes, the Bloods and the Blackfeet proper. The loosely associated bands of these three tribes lived a nomadic life, shadowing the seasonal movements of buffalo and the ripening of berries around the western plains. Their hunting territory extended from the Saskatchewan River south to the Missouri, with the Piegan bands tending to stay farthest west, along the foothills of the Rockies.

The Piegan scouts that Thompson's group had chanced upon gave the Bay men a hearty welcome and led them to a nearby camp. The elders who gathered to greet them said they were thankful the traders had come; according to

Thompson, they were especially grateful for fresh tobacco, which was "the great luxury, and like money commanded all things." The elders also were anxious to know how many animals the Bay men had seen on their way west, and were happy to hear that the buffalo had not already migrated north. After the exchange of news, three of the most prominent men invited the visitors to lodge in their tipis.

> The Peeagan in whose tent I passed the winter was an old man of at least 75 to 80 years of age; his height six feet, two or three inches, broad shouldered, strong limbed, his hair gray and plentiful, forehead high and nose prominent, his face slightly marked with the small pox, and alltogether his countenance mild, and even, sometimes playful . . . his name was Saukamappee (Young Man).
>
> *Narrative*

Saukamappee was by birth a Cree, a large tribe ranging all the way from Hudson Bay through the eastern woodlands and west along the Saskatchewan. Thompson had learned enough of the Cree language the previous winter at South Branch House to be able to converse with the old man and to understand the stories that he spun out during the long winter evenings. In his *Narrative*, Thompson recounted many of Saukamappee's stories, tales that outlined the history of the northern plains through a native's eyes. Saukamappee said that he had grown up in a Cree band that lived along the eastern fringe of the prairies. During his youth, his people were allies of the western Blackfeet Nation against their mutual enemies the Snakes, or Shoshones, who lived farther to the south and west. He was still a young man (from what Saukamappee told him, Thompson estimated that this was sometime around 1730) when Piegan Blackfeet messengers came to his band with reports of a skirmish in which several Snakes had appeared atop strange, four-legged animals, "swift as a deer." The Crees could not imagine what this meant, for-dogs were the only domesticated animals they knew. Saukamappee had recently married, and hoping to bring back an enemy scalp for his father-in-law's medicine bag, he set off with two other young men to help the Blackfeet fight the Snakes. By this time many of the Crees had acquired guns, and there were enough firearms in Saukamappee's camp for him and each of his friends to carry one.

At the war camp they met bands of Blackfeet and Piegans armed with stone-pointed lances and bows and arrows, plus seven Assiniboine men with seven more guns. The war chief positioned the ten guns on the front line; this would be their first test in battle, for until then they had been used only for hunting. Saukamappee remembered that it was with great nervousness that he lay behind a big buffalo-hide shield, clutching his single-shot musket, two extra balls in his mouth and a load of powder in his left hand. As he watched the ritual display of weapons that always preceded a pitched battle, he saw no way to win, for the Snakes filing into position opposite him far outnumbered the Blackfeet, and many of them carried *pukamoggans*, the short stone clubs that were so dangerous in close combat. But when he and his companions opened fire with their muskets a few minutes later, there was "consternation and dismay" among the Snakes, followed by a confused retreat. The delighted Blackfeet and Piegans begged the Cree gunners to stay and live with them, promising handsome young wives as incentives. There were no takers, but Saukamappee and his friends did stay on for a few days of hunting before returning east.

None of the Snakes' mysterious four-legged beasts had been present at this battle, and when the hunting party chanced upon a dead stallion, they gathered around it in awe. "We all admired him," Saukamappee told Thompson, "he put-us in mind of a Stag that had lost his horns, and we did not know what name to give him. But as he was a slave to Man, like the dog, which carried our things; he was named the Big Dog."

Soon afterward the Crees started their long walk home, each carrying a Snake scalp carefully stretched on a round willow hoop. As they approached one of their tribe's camps, the travelers stopped to paint their faces in anticipation of the night of singing, dancing, and feasting that would greet their return. Saukamappee imagined the grand appearance he would make before his wife and in-laws, but they were not at the camp. The three warriors had been gone for several months by now, and Saukamappee soon learned that his bride had run away with another man. The next morning he gave his prized scalp to a friend and left his people. He retraced his steps to one of the Piegan Blackfeet camps, where the chief made good his promise and gave his eldest daughter to Saukamappee as his new wife.

Saukamappee came to live among the Piegan Blackfeet as two dramatic waves of change converged on the northwestern plains. From the south came Spanish horses, their natural dispersal accelerated by trading and thievery. The animals thrived in the open grasslands, and the pedestrians of the plains took enthusiastically to horsemanship. Aside from their obvious utilitarian uses for hunting and transport, "Big Dogs" became new symbols of prestige and favored war prizes. From the east, emanating from Montreal and Hudson Bay, came the manufactured goods imported by the fur companies. These items, which had been embraced so wholeheartedly by the eastern tribes, met with a more mixed reaction out on the-prairies. When an early envoy from the Hudson's Bay Company visited some of the plains tribes in the mid-1700s and encouraged them to bring their furs to York Factory to trade, the chiefs listened with interest. But when they learned that they would have to ride in canoes and eat fish along the way, they declined the invitation. Still, guns and iron arrowheads were greatly desired. Although white traders made only occasional forays onto the plains at this time, the Blackfeet were able to get some firearms from Cree and Assiniboine middlemen, but at a considerable markup. The Crees charged the Blackfeet fifty beaver or wolf pelts for one musket; back on Hudson Bay the going rate was fourteen pelts per gun.

The Blackfeet tribes were the first in their part of the country to own both horses and guns, and with their new-found mobility and firepower, they soon forced their rivals off the choicest buffalo grounds and made them their own. The Piegans chased the Snakes, who had horses but no guns, away from the rich Bow River country and south into the mountains, and for many years afterward the Blackfeet bands maintained their freewheeling dominance of the northern plains. Then one day Piegan scouts brought word of a peculiar Snake encampment within their territory, and Saukamappee related how he and the other warriors in his band determined to raid it. "Next morning at dawn of day, we attacked the Tents, and with our sharp flat daggers and knives, cut through the tents and entered for the fight; but our war whoop instantly stopt, our eyes were appalled with terror; there was no one to fight but the dead and the dying, each a mass of corruption." Saukamappee was describing the devastating smallpox epidemic that swept across the continent in the early 1780s. Because the Piegans had no concept of contagious disease, they did not hesitate to loot the infected camp, carrying home blankets and tents with their plunder. "The second day after this dreadful disease broke out in our camp, and spread from one tent to another as if the Bad Spirit carried it. We had no belief that one Man could give it to another, any more than a wounded Man could give his wound to another." Saukamappee said that many people drowned when they rushed into the river to relieve the unbearable itching. One-third of his own band was wiped out, while in other camps everyone died, he said. "When at length it left us, and we moved about to find our people, it was no longer with the song and the dance; but with tears, shrieks, and howlings of despair . . . Our hearts were low and dejected, and we shall never be again the same people."

It was about seven years after the smallpox plague when

Thompson met the Piegans, and scars were still visible on many of their faces. Those who had survived carried on the lifestyle and customs of their ancestors, and the winter that Thompson spent among them gave him an inside look at a traditional plains culture relatively untouched by contact with white men. Despite the introduction of guns and horses into their territory, many of the warriors still had only bows and arrows, and Saukamappee still walked wherever he went, carrying his pipestems and medicine bag over his shoulder. Whenever the Piegans struck camp, one of the old men would scoop burning embers from a campfire into a rough wooden bowl filled with dirt, then carefully tend the hot coals all the way to the next camp, where a new fire was stoked from the bowl.

The Piegans hospitably accepted the young white visitor into their daily lives. When scouts reported buffalo nearby, he sometimes rode out with the hunters to shoot a few days' provisions. As cold weather came on and the bison moved toward the foothills for food and shelter from the wind, the people herded small groups of them into rough impoundments and butchered them. The women sliced and smoked strips of jerky, then pounded some of the dried meat into a coarse meal called beat meat. This they mixed with dried berries and buffalo grease to make pemmican. Shaped into croquettes and packed into skin bags, these dense cakes provided a staple food that kept for months without spoiling. In Thompson's opinion, the women at his camp were too heavy-handed with the bitter chokecherries, and the result "required the powers of an Ostrich to digest."

Whatever he thought of their pemmican recipe, he did have the sensibility to see that the endless chores of the Piegan women—gathering firewood, cooking, curing and drying meat, preparing animal skins and sewing clothes, setting up the tipi and breaking it down—amounted to a crushing burden, and that for them the value of European trade goods went beyond bright beads and baubles: "See the wife of an Indian sewing their leather clothing with a pointed brittle bone or a sharp thorn and the time and trouble it takes. Show them an awl or strong needle and they will gladly give the finest Beaver or Wolf skin they have to purchase it."

Thompson took a great interest in the routines and everyday doings of the camp. He watched young bachelors painstakingly paint their faces in the little mirrors the traders had brought, then plant themselves in a conspicuous spot to be admired. He listened to the camp's civil chief deliver his evening bulletins of news from other bands and daily instructions for hunting. He turned a curious eye on the gambling games that dominated the leisure time of the men, and decided that the need for extra help around the tent might justify polygamy. His musings about Blackfeet theology and morals, though filtered through his devout Christian eyes, still show a real fascination for a different world view. Thompson was at the time only seventeen years old, and his-winter among the Piegans instilled in him a romantic admiration.

> Their walk is erect, light and easy, and may be said to be graceful. When on the plains in company with white men, the erect walk of the Indian is shown to great advantage. The Indian with his arms folded in his robe seems to glide over the ground; and the white people seldom in an erect posture, their bodies swayed from right to left, and some with their arms, as if to saw a passage through the air. I have often been vexed at the comparison.
>
> *Narrative*

During his stay Thompson also learned something of the differences that horses had made in the lives of the Piegans. One afternoon in early January, a group of young men arrived in camp singing victory songs. More than two moons earlier, Saukamappee explained, a large war party of about 250 warriors under the leadership of the war chief Kootanae Appee had departed on horseback on a mission of revenge against the Snakes, who had murdered a small group of Piegans hunting bighorn sheep in the mountains the previous fall. When days of travel failed to turn up any sign of their foes, Kootanae Appee had pressed on, riding farther and farther south until he and his men came upon a silver caravan led by Spaniards in what must have been southern Colorado. After routing the pack train, the Piegans had discarded saddlebags full of the "white stone" as nuisances, then ridden back north with a herd of horses and mules, some of them still wearing saddles of "thick well tanned leather of a chocolate color with figures of flowers as if done by a hot iron."

A few days after the arrival of the warriors, Kootanae Appee himself paid a visit to the camp, leading a dark brown Spanish mule as a gift for Saukamappee so that the old man would no longer have to walk from camp to camp. Thompson, who was in the tent with his mentor, had heard many stories about the great war chief, but this was their first meeting. "He was apparently forty years of age and his height between six feet two to four inches, more formed for activity than strength yet well formed for either; his face a full oval, high forehead and nose somewhat aquiline; his large black eyes, and countenance, were open, frank but somewhat stern; he was a noble specimen of the Indian warrior of the great plains." When Kootanae Appee turned to greet Thompson, the awed teenager unwittingly committed a Piegan faux pas. "On entering the tent he gave me his left hand, and I gave him my right hand, upon which he looked at me and smiled as much as to say a contest would not be equal; at his going away the same took place." Saukamappee later cautioned his-young guest that to the Blackfeet, the left hand was the hand of greeting, whereas offering the right—the hand that threw spears and pulled triggers—was an insult, and a challenge to fight: "If one of our people offers you his left hand, give him your left hand, for the right hand is no mark of friendship."

I HAD BEEN driving through Saukamappee's old territory all day, across the prairies of western Alberta, and I was tired. Evening seems to linger forever here in the summer, making it hard to know when to stop. As I drove numbly along, the grassland and wheat fields began to undulate like ocean swells; the only turnoffs were wide tractor entrances to the grain fields, and I passed by each one slower and slower, wondering if I should drag out my sleeping bag and nestle in between the furrows. I finally did pull off, to stumble through a forest of stiff barley, but there were too many clods for comfort. To the west a line of thick, dark clouds strung out along the horizon. That would be the Rockies, and there would be trees growing out of the hills at their feet. A canopy to sleep under, and a carpet of soft, dry needles. I wondered how long it might take to reach that haven, and how hard it might be raining when I got there.

I supposed that Saukamappee would have made this trip from flatlands to foothills many times, after berries or late buffalo, or to escape the summer's heat, or to catch the same whiff of trees that I was after now. He would have made his trips on foot, though, season after season, from the time he came to live with the Piegans until the day Kootanae Appee brought home that dark brown Spanish mule. Their ancestors would have made the same trek, and every one of them, from the time they wandered in behind the melting ice, would have walked to get there.

I wheeled into a farm-town grocery store and bought three sticks of venison jerky, then almost lost my snack to a couple of mutts in the parking lot. They were a mismatched pair, one yellow, one a piebald blue, sharing a lean, sinewy build and wary reserve. They sniffed around my heels on the way to the car, but the moment I turned to offer a pet they cowered back toward a dumpster. When I pulled out of the parking lot a few minutes later, they were laying for me beside the road, and I left town in a flurry of tire-biting yips and snarls. They soon lost interest and dropped back, and in my rearview mirror I watched them tussle over a potato chip bag beside the road.

I finished my last bite of jerky, and the miles began to unroll again. A few last rays of sun shot out beneath the low clouds, and the grasslands came alive. An upland sandpiper landed on a fence post just ahead of the car to arch its wings in a relaxing stretch. Sky, birds, and landscape all assumed the colors of ripening wheat. A huge splotch of yellow-black thunderhead hung over the road far, far ahead. I wondered how close Saukamappee had let the thunderheads move in before he stopped to camp, and how often his tipi smelled of wet dog fur. Because dogs would have been along, too, walking at the heels of his people: generation after generation of companions and load-bearers and mischief makers. Before the Big Dogs arrived, little dogs were the beasts of burden. They were the ones strapped into harness winter and summer, pulling travois and sleds.

I thought of all the little dogs whose pace had ever matched mine. I never knew any to follow a straight line for very long, and I tried to imagine how I would keep them on course from here to the mountains. Probably I wouldn't. David Thompson once watched a group of plains women on the way from one camp to another on a hot summer day. (The men always had urgent hunting to do on moving day, he said.) The dogs were all carrying saddlebags or pulling loaded travois, and the women were mushing them down the trail when a fair-sized pond appeared in the distance. In an instant the dogs made straight for the lake; once there they lay down and wallowed in the cool water, baggage and all. While the old men cheered, the women threw off their own packs and ran into the pond, swinging big sticks to chase the mongrels back onto the trail. Some of the dogs swam for deep water to avoid a beating and surely would have drowned if the women hadn't hauled them out.

I could picture that bolt toward the pond, bright tongues lapping at muddy water. My own tongue flapped out with a deep yawn, and I wheeled the radio dial in search of entertainment. Beyond country music and the CBC, I chanced on a live boxing card being broadcast from the Agricultural Pavilion in Edmonton. The first match was just under way, and no one had even thrown a punch when my path intersected with the blooming thunderheads. Raindrops came large and hard, and I crept along in the deluge, listening to static punctuated by an occasional lucid word. I thought I heard a knockdown, but everything else was lost in the sheets of water that swept across the road and down into the fields. By the time I drove out the other side of the storm, it was night.

A great horned owl leaped up from the path of my headlights, took five stiff beats, and glided into the trees. Trees. The highway curved for the first time in hours. A dirt road, messy with the tracks of logging trailers, angled off into the forest. I followed it over one gentle hill and down, then up onto another. It was a narrow track, with no place to pull off. I crept along, waiting for that flat spot. The pugilists up in Edmonton were still at it, and as I searched for a camping place, the radio bell rang on a late round of the last match on the card. Two boxers named David Fiddler and Danny Stonewalker seemed to be going at it pretty good, and the crowd was whooping it up.

I came to a crossroads at the end of the round and left the radio on while I circled the car to test the ground, clasping and unclasping my cramped fists. The earth felt spongy and extremely inviting. Then, just as Fiddler walked into a solid right hand, the mosquitoes arrived. I slapped at my ankles and neck for a couple of minutes, trying to gauge their density, while Stonewalker dispatched his opponent. I stepped around to the back of my car and dug into the trunk for tarp and sleeping bag.

The sky above the hilltop was impossibly deep. Moonlight revealed the landscape around me as a shadowy ruin of skidder tracks and small, splintered trees. I thought I could smell moose. I cleared a couple of springy limbs out of the way and curled up in my bag, already asleep. The bugs weren't bad at all, and the small dogs of Saukamappee scampered through my dreams.

CHAPTER TWO

A WELL-REGULATED WATCH

1788–1799

WITH THE COMING of spring of 1788, Thompson and his companions left Saukamappee's camp and led a small contingent of Piegans loaded with beaver, fox, and wolf pelts back to Manchester House. House Master William Tomison was shocked at his apprentice's appearance: "He viewed me all round and muttered 'ragged, very ragged, can't be mended, must have a new jacket.'" The resident tailor made Thompson presentable again, and the routines of life at the trading post occupied the rest of the year. One of the things requiring attention was the state of the trade tobacco that the Bay Company had sent inland that fall. Tomison compared its taste to rotten turnips and had his men rub it down with sugar in hopes of improving its flavor; he was afraid the natives would refuse to trade with him when they learned that the Nor'Westers were offering an excellent crop next door. Tomison had no fondness for these neighbors, whom he called "those rogues from Canada," and argued with them throughout the winter. He didn't approve of the profligacy with which they dispensed rum among the natives, and it galled him that they had more than twice as many workers as he did.

Two days before Christmas, Tomison lost one of his valuable hands when David Thompson tumbled down a steep riverbank while hauling home a sledload of meat and broke the large bone in his right leg. The apprentice was across the river from the trade house and over a mile away when the accident happened, and his leg was extremely swollen by the time his co-workers got him home. William Tomison wrote that he set the leg and "put splinters around it with bandages in the best manner I could but such accidents would require a more skilful person than I am." Tomison's journal entries for the next few months indicate that the boy had a rough time of it.

DECEMBER 24: William Folster making a cradle Bed for David Thompson.

DECEMBER 31: David Thompson has been but indifferent for these three days past.

JANUARY 12, 1789: David Thompson so far recovered as not to want any attendance at night.

JANUARY 17: Took the bandages off David Thompson's leg and looked at it then bound it up again, he has but little pain in it, but still very weak.

MARCH 29: David Thompson was out of bed today for the first time but had not set long before his foot and ancle swelled a good deal so that he was obliged to lie down again. God only knows how it may turn out.

APRIL 13: As to David Thompson he mends but very slowly.

MAY 1: David Thompson's leg I am afraid will turn out to be a mortification as the joint of his ancle has never lowered of the swelling.

Thompson later wrote that "Mr. Tomison behaved with the tenderness of a father to me, and alleviated my sufferings all he could."

When the spring canoes left with the furs for York Factory, Tomison floated the invalid downstream as far as Cumberland House. There it was decided that young Thompson could not continue on to York Factory, because he was in so much pain that he could not bear to be moved. He was left with Cumberland House Master Malcolm Ross, who wrote that he was concerned about a wound that had opened up over the fracture, "which I am afraid will prove bad." Ross set up a bed for Thompson in the warehouse, where the boy lay "helpless" for two months. He finally sat up in a chair on August 10, but it wasn't until the end of that month that he began to hobble around on crutches. He made slow progress for the rest of the fall and, possibly as a way to keep himself occupied, began keeping a daily journal. He ruled off neat columns for temperature, wind direction, wind speed, and general remarks on the weather, then filled them in three or four times a day.

The slow healing of his leg kept Thompson pinned to Cumberland House and meant that he was on hand for the October arrival of Philip Turnor, the Hudson's Bay Company "surveyor and astronomer." Most of the interior of North America at this time remained uncharted ground, and the company governors had hired Turnor to scientifically survey and map several of the river routes in their territory. Thompson had learned the rudiments of navigation at the Grey Coat School, and under Turnor's professional tutelage he renewed his study of practical astronomy, as the trade was then known.

In 1790 this was not a straightforward skill to master. To begin with, a student needed a full knowledge of the solar system, because the relative movements of stars and planets formed the basis for all calculations. Latitude could be reckoned fairly easily by measuring the altitude of the sun or a nighttime star with a sextant, then referring to set tables and formulas. Longitude, on the other hand, was determined by comparing the exact time at one's location with the exact time on the prime meridian, which required an accurate clock set to Greenwich Mean Time. The timepieces of Thompson's day could stand up to the rolling motions of a ship, but not the hard jarring of land travel, and an astronomer had to constantly adjust his watch to the Greenwich standard. He could do this by timing the appearance and immersion of one of Jupiter's moons, if he had a good telescope, or by watching a lunar eclipse, if one happened to be on the schedule. More commonly he would use the Earth's moon as one hand of a giant celestial clock, then perform three or four hours of trigonometry to interpolate the angle between its location and that of certain stars. For this purpose all navigators and surveyors were issued the annual *Nautical Almanac* in advance of each year. The *Almanac* and its companion, *Tables Requisite*, laid out the positions of specific stars and planets at set times for every day of the year. Thus an astronomer in the field needed a steady hand and eye, a firm grasp of mathematics, and the stamina to stay up through the night, waiting for a favorable turn in the weather or the right configuration of heavenly bodies. Because so many parts of the process were subject to error, a surveyor would take two or more observations at the same location whenever possible, then average his results to obtain the mean longitude or latitude.

David Thompson showed a knack for the meticulous points of celestial observation. Throughout the winter and spring of 1790, using a small sextant that Turnor loaned him, the apprentice tested his progress by taking readings on Cumberland House over and over again, doggedly reshooting the points and refactoring the tedious equations. After compiling two and a half pages of minutely numbered shots, neatly stacked up in his notebook, Thompson was satisfied that he had the trading depot firmly located on the globe:

> The mean of the foregoing observations places Cumberland House in Latitude 53° 56' 44" N Longitude 102° 13' West of Greenwich and the

Variation by the Transits of the Sun and a well regulated Watch is 11° 30' East.

(sgn) David Thompson

Thompson's work so impressed Philip Turnor that the astronomer sent his student's coordinates for Cumberland House back to the Bay Company in London, along with a note:

> I have inserted some Observations which were made and worked by Your Honors' unfortunate apprentice, David Thompson. I am fully convinced they are genuine, and should he ever recover his strength far enough to be capable of undertaking expeditions I think Your Honors may rely on his reports of the situation of any place he may visit.

Turnor and Malcolm Ross were planning a surveying expedition north into the Athabasca region the next fall, and Turnor needed an assistant. Thompson wanted the position, but his leg was still very weak and, in addition, "by much attention to my calculations in the night, with no other light than a small candle my right eye became so much inflamed that I lost its sight, and in the early part of May when the rivers and lakes became navigable, my health and strength were thought too weak to accompany Mr. Turnor as his assistant." There was a bright young clerk named Peter Fidler on hand, and when Thompson's health proved too unstable, Turnor quickly trained Fidler for the trip to Athabasca instead.

Thompson might have been disappointed, but he had found his focus, and relying on his one good eye, he soon began taking observations again. From then on, no matter how bizarre or troubled the conditions, he doggedly practiced his craft, which remained an arcane, incomprehensible occupation to most of his companions.

Both Canadians and Indians often inquired of me why I observed the Sun, and sometimes the Moon, in the day time, and passed whole nights with my instruments looking at the Moon and Stars. I told them it was to determine the distance and direction from the place I observed to other places; neither the Canadians nor the Indians believed me for both argued that if what I said was truth, I ought to look to the ground, and over it; and not to the Stars.

Narrative

Thompson *did* look to the ground a good deal, in fact, for it was necessary for an astronomer to supplement his celestial observations with detailed land surveys. In the summer of 1790, the budding geographer put his surveying skills to work by charting the 750-mile route from Cumberland House to York Factory. With a notebook in his lap and a compass in hand, he jotted down each twist and turn in the river's course: "S40E ¼ M[ile] S20E ½ M strong rapid on the right S8W 1-M S55E ¹⁄₁₀ M" and on and on and on. Later he sent these lists of distances and directions, along with any coordinates of latitude and longitude that he had been able to obtain, to the Bay Company headquarters in London, where they were passed on to professional cartographers and plotted onto the official maps of the region.

Thompson was twenty years old upon his arrival at York Factory, with his apprenticeship due to expire the next May. The customary reward for a young clerk who completed the program was a new suit of clothes. But in a letter to London, Thompson asked the governors to apply the price of his suit toward a set of surveying instruments, with any outstanding balance to be charged against his future wages. The company governors obviously decided his talents were worth encouraging, for in the summer of 1791, the supply ship brought him not only new clothes but also the gift of a ten-inch brass sextant made by Dollond—the standard navigational instrument of that era. They also sent a standard contract for three years' service at fifteen pounds per year.

The next summer Thompson received a brass compass, a Fahrenheit thermometer, and a case of instruments, along with a letter from the governors stating that these were "a reward for your assiduity." In a supply order to London that same year, he requested astronomical almanacs to go along with his instruments, plus two dozen coat buttons, a quire of tracing paper, and ten books, including a spelling dictionary, a pocket-sized New Testament, four volumes of Dr. Johnson's *Rambler*, and Milton's *Paradise Lost*. On the same supply list, Malcolm Ross and Peter Fidler both asked for an array of surveying implements, but not all of their co-workers displayed such a serious bent: one man ordered a magic lantern, an umbrella, and fiddle strings, as well as "12 skyrockets and other curious fireworks."

Two years later, when it was time to renew his contract, Thompson was bold enough to ask for a raise. The governors awarded him the substantial sum of sixty pounds per year—quadruple his previous salary and more than his superior, twenty-year company veteran Malcolm Ross, was making at the time. They also sent him another gift crucial to his surveying work: a fine watch made by London clockmaker Joseph Jolly, worth more than twelve pounds in itself. During these years between 1791 and 1796, Thompson worked all over the Bay Company's territory, spending another winter with William Tomison at a new post on the Saskatchewan and helping build several trade houses in what the furmen called the Muskrat Country north of Lake Winnipeg. All the while he made observations with his new instruments and surveyed every route he traveled. He also became well acquainted with the Cree and Chipewyan peoples who lived in the area.

I had always admired the tact of the Indian in being able to guide himself through the darkest pine forests to exactly the place he intended to go, his keen, constant

HUDSON BAY

CHIPEWYAN

Lake Athabasca

Churchill Factory

Reindeer Lake

Nelson R.

York Factory

1.

Churchill R.

CREE

N. Saskatchewan R.

4.

2.

3.

Lake Winnipeg

S. Saskatchewan R.

Assiniboine R.

Lake of the Woods

Rainy L.

6.

5.

Turtle Lake

Missouri R.

Red R.

Mandan & Hidatsa Villages

Mississippi R.

Yellowstone R.

SPANISH

LOUISIANA

Legend

1. Île á la Crosse
2. Cumberland House
3. Manchester House
4. Fort George
5. Assiniboine Post
6. Grand Portage

0   200   400 k
0   200   400 mi

THOMPSON'S FIRST SURVEYS

attention on every thing; the removal of the small-
est stone, the bent or broken twig; a slight mark on the
ground, all spoke plain language to him. I was anxious
to acquire this knowledge, and often being in company
with them, sometimes for several months, I paid attention to what they pointed out to me, and became almost
equal to some of them; which became of great use to me.

Narrative

However instructive Thompson's relations with the local
tribes, these five years were not without their frustrations.
For much of this time, he and Malcolm Ross were supposed
to be looking for a more direct way from York Factory to
Lake Athabasca, but they were repeatedly thwarted by manpower shortages and contradictory orders from the governors
in London, the head of York Factory, and William Tomison,
who was in charge of the inland trade. In the summer of
1796, after many delays, Thompson set off to scout a new
route with two Chipewyans. It was a rugged venture, and in
a canoe accident he lost everything he had with him, including his shoes. He located his precious cork-lined box of instruments some distance downstream, repaired the canoe,
and made it back to his appointed meeting place with Ross.
Certain that he had been on the right track, Thompson convinced his boss to try again with three canoes that September.
By then, however, the water level of the river he wanted to
follow had dropped too low for their boats, and the men were
forced to retreat and build an impromptu shack for the winter
on Reindeer Lake, far removed from any of the other Bay
Company houses. They spent the next six months cramped,
cold, and hungry.

Thompson's contract was up for renewal in the spring of
1797, and he had already been informed that he was slated to
succeed Malcolm Ross, who was retiring that summer, as the
person in charge of extending the trade northward to Lake
Athabasca. But on May 21, Ross entered a surprising piece of

news in his journal: "2 Geese from the Indians. This morning Mr. David Thompson acquainted Me with his time being out with your Honours and thought himself a freeborn subject and at liberty to choose any service he thought to be most to his advantage and is to quit your service and enter the Canadian company's Employ." Although this decision to cross over to the rival North West Company was a dramatic move, Thompson's own notes shed no further light on the subject. "May 22 Monday. A Cold Day put my baggage in Order, etc. etc." Ignoring the Hudson's Bay Company's policy that a year's notice of intent be given so that the London governors would have time to appoint a replacement, Thompson left Reindeer Lake on snowshoes early the next morning in a heavy snowstorm. "May 23 Tuesday. At 3½ A.M. set off . . . This day left the Service of the Hudsons Bay Co and entered that of the Company of Merchants from Canada." He then added the words "May God Almighty prosper me," and closed his journal.

In his *Narrative*, Thompson cites as his motivation for quitting a letter from York Factory that ordered him to stop exploring. But the chief of York Factory, upon hearing of Thompson's departure, noted that he had received information indicating that the surveyor had been "in treaty" with the Nor'Westers for some time. This would explain why Thompson had not sent any of his survey notes back to London for the previous two years, and it might also explain why Alexander Fraser, a partner of the North West Company, had visited Thompson and Ross in early April. One thing that is clear from both Ross's and Thompson's brief accounts is that Thompson felt certain of a job with the competition.

At any rate, it was to Fraser's trade house, eighty miles south, that Thompson went upon leaving Reindeer Lake. He helped around the post for a few days and wrote two letters to his former employers at York Factory—one berating the chief factor there and the other asking a favor of the governing council, in a rather testy tone:

Gentlemen—

As I am now in the employ of the NW Co. of Merchants from Canada you may perhaps not think it consistent with your Duty to send my Books, Mathematical Instruments etc. etc. to Cumberland House, should this be the Case you will please to reship them for England; tho' I must confess I am utterly at a loss to know how the reading of Books or observing the motions of the heavenly Bodies can be detrimental to the interest of the Honble. Hudsons Bay Company.

Your Humble Servant
David Thompson

The books and instruments he was so anxious to receive included *Nautical Almanac*s and an expensive new telescope that he had ordered from London the previous year. As it turned out, his parcel had already been sent inland before word of his resignation arrived at York. His former boss, William Tomison, upon learning of the incident, railed that any man who had forwarded a package for "so base a man as Thompson ought to have both his ears cut off which I should not have scrupled at had he been my brother."

Thompson, meanwhile, had made his way south to Grand Portage, the North West Company's field headquarters on Lake Superior. This was the site of the company's gala summer rendezvous, where traders from all over the territory convened to turn in their year's furs and pick up new trade goods and supplies that had been ferried in from Montreal. This was also the occasion for an annual meeting between the two arms of the company: the "agents," who handled the business in Montreal, and the "proprietors," or wintering partners, who oversaw the trade at the interior posts. Unlike the highly centralized bureaucracy of the Hudson's Bay Company, the Nor'Westers were more democratic, with major decisions being approved at these annual meetings at Grand Portage. They also paid better than the Bay Company.

Thompson did not record his salary that first year, but by 1799 he was listed as one of the better-paid clerks of the company, pulling down one hundred pounds a year plus twenty pounds' worth of such "equipment and necessaries" as clothing, tea, sugar, and chocolate. There was additional economic incentive as well, for it was possible for a diligent clerk to work his way up to the rank of field partner and share in the annual profits.

In the big dining hall at Grand Portage, Thompson drank fresh milk from cows the company pastured nearby and dined with the partners and other clerks. He also met head agents William McGillivray and Alexander Mackenzie, up from Montreal for the rendezvous. Both men had begun their careers as clerks in the field, and Mackenzie had become Canada's most celebrated explorer by leading expeditions to the Arctic and Pacific Oceans several years earlier. Now these men had an important expedition planned for their new employee. At the end of the American Revolution, diplomats had established the border between the United States and British Canada as a line that ran through the centers of Lake Superior, Rainy Lake, and Lake of the Woods, then west along the 49th parallel to an undetermined point north of the headwaters of the Mississippi River. There was now a movement down in the States to restrict trade south of this line, but no one was sure exactly where the boundary lay, and the partners wanted Thompson to find out. He was also to pay a goodwill visit to some Mandan villages on the Missouri River and, while he was at it, collect any large fossils he came across—new discoveries of the bones of mammoths and other big Ice Age mammals had excited great interest among collectors, including someone in the North West Company.

In early August, a little more than two weeks after he had arrived at Grand Portage, Thompson hitched a ride with a canoe brigade heading to Rainy Lake and started his survey. This was his first trip in the company of the French Canadian voyageurs that the North West Company hired from the large French population of Quebec. These men signed contracts with the company according to their paddling position in the canoe: the *gouvernail* in the stern and the *avant* in the bow were the key men, and the best paid. Thompson found the voyageurs "a fine, hardy, good humoured set of Men, fond of full feeding . . . eating full eight pounds of fresh meat per day." They were also noted for their short, stocky frames, their repertoire of paddle songs, and their fondness for a smoke—distances on rivers and lakes were measured in "pipes," for the amount of water the men could cover before putting down their paddles to fill a bowl. The patois of the voyageurs was the everyday language of the Nor'Westers, and if Thompson didn't speak French already, he started learning it now.

By late November the surveyor had made a big loop north through Lake Winnipeg and back south to a North West Company house on the Assiniboine River in what is now southern Manitoba. Even though winter had already set in, he decided to travel overland to the Mandan villages on the Missouri. He found an interpreter who knew the Mandan language and organized a trading party of French Canadians outfitted with dog teams purchased from local Assiniboine Indians. The first night out, November 30, 1797, his thermometer read twenty below zero. The next day it plummeted to thirty-seven below, and steady high winds kept smoke from their fire swirling inside the tent; the men spent most of the day out wandering in the woods for relief. "We could not proceed, but had the good fortune to kill a good bison cow, which kept us in good humor."

The Assiniboine dogs were not accustomed to hauling sleds, and the French Canadians flogged them enthusiastically to keep them in line. "When on the march the noise was intolerable, and made me keep 2 or 3 miles ahead." Over the next four weeks, they trudged through the gamut of winter weather. When a blizzard bore down across the plains, Thompson amazed his companions by using his compass to

direct them to a protective grove of trees that he had spotted before the blowing snow engulfed them. A few days later,
a howling chinook raised the temperature fifty-six degrees
in twelve hours. As they entered the hilly country near the
Missouri River, the rough terrain slowed their progress, as did
retrieving dogs who kept breaking away to chase herds of buffalo. On December 30, after thirty-three days and over two
hundred miles, they reached the frozen Missouri and walked
on the ice to a cluster of Mandan and Hidatsa villages.

Here Thompson encountered an agricultural society very
different from anything he had seen before. He took a census
of the five stockaded villages and described large, earth-
domed lodges furnished with wooden sofas covered in bison
robes. He ate the corn porridge seasoned with ashes that
the villagers offered him, and purchased a quantity of dried
corn and beans. He learned that they also raised pumpkins
and melons in the rich river bottoms, which they cultivated
with hoes fashioned from the shoulder blades of bison and
deer. In one of the villages, Thompson met a Frenchman who
had been living among the Mandans for fifteen years and had
risen to a position of prominence. While presenting him with
gifts of tobacco, soap, a bottle of peppermint, a lump of sugar,
and a dog, Thompson heard that two visitors had recently
arrived from the headwaters of the Missouri, near the Rocky
Mountains. The surveyor immediately arranged to meet the
pair and spent a day questioning them about the course of the
upper Missouri.

The Missouri River at that time was still part of the
Spanish-owned Louisiana Territory, but Canadian fur traders
frequently visited the Mandan villages, and the North West
Company was very interested in trade possibilities farther
upriver. The two men from the mountains described their
homeland, measuring distances between landmarks in days of
good walking, and Thompson drew out rough maps for them
to examine and correct. They told him about large tributaries
called the Yellow Stone and the Shell, about a high fall at the

source of the Missouri, and three high ridges of mountains. This last bit of information ran contrary to the generally accepted notion that the Rockies consisted of a single low ridge or "Height of Land" that could be crossed by a short portage, but Thompson had good reason to believe that the natives knew something the European geographers did not. "They appeared to be very intelligent, as almost all the Natives of the Mountains are – They fully comprehended with a little explanation the drift of all my Questions, and answered direct to them. When done I gave them a little Tobacco – for which they were thankful."

Thompson was staying in the lodge of one of the chiefs, and during a few days of bad weather, he conversed with the people about their traditions while making himself a pair of snowshoes. He spent one clear night observing for latitude and longitude, and on other evenings watched "their Amusements of Dancing Singing etc. which were always conducted with the highest order and Decorum after their Idea of thinking; but to me, a stranger, I could not help thinking them the most uxorious Race I have seen and one of the old Priests of Venus would quickly have got them to build a Temple." In his *Narrative*, Thompson recalled a group of handsome young women dressed in thin white deerskins, who danced to the accompaniment of drum, tambour, rattle, and flute. "When the music struck up, part of the men sang, and the women keeping a straight line and respective distance, danced with a light step and slow, graceful motion."

THE DOUBLE DOORS of the tavern swung open, and I turned to watch as a dozen men and women, singing in what sounded like raucous Norwegian, burst through and swept past me like a breaking wave. The leader of the mob balanced an anvil-sized box on the tips of his raised fingers. He swooped his arms low to reveal a miniature black coffin, its lid sparkling with lit candles and a painted inscription: THE END OF YOUTH. The wave re-formed and rolled away on a direct line toward a crowded back corner, where the casket was laid down in front of one youthful, aging man. Amid a flurry of cheers, he blew out the candles and pulled mementos from the box—a baby doll, an inkwell, and an Indian headdress decorated with brightly dyed chicken feathers.

"Hey Carl, throw me down a pack a them Camels."

The bartender, with the slightest of nods, tossed a fresh pack down the row of stools to a lean, hatchet-faced guy who had wandered in behind the parade. He made a nice catch, hung a cigarette between his lips, and patted his pockets for matches as he settled onto the stool next to mine. Flakes of sawdust drifted away from his flannel shirt.

"Got a light, friend?" he asked, with a grizzled smile. He spoke with a Dakotan's deliberate, wide-voweled accent, and although I shook my head no, his smile didn't fade a bit. He wheeled around so he could scan the crowd and hailed a passing logger for a match. He took a long drag on his Camel, then rolled his stool back to front position and turned his ear toward a conversation that was going on to our right.

It had begun when the woman sitting next to me mentioned that she had recently unearthed the remains of a steam-powered tractor from a gully on her grandmother's ranch. The stack was as thick as a tree trunk, she said, and at first she had thought it was a train locomotive. The bartender had taken an interest and started prodding the lady for more details; her description of waffle cleats on great cast-iron wheels and a rivet-dimpled boiler tank touched off a discussion about the age of the thing. Estimates ranged from the first Homestead Act to the Battle of Midway. The Dakotan listened for a minute, then tossed his head toward me with a snort.

"Aaaaah," he said. "You think that steamer's old? Don't talk to me about no *old*. I've been there. I've seen the Mandan villages."

I started to ask him which villages, but he was gazing intently at the bottles behind the bar. "I've been lucky," he growled. "I've got to go places nobody else's ever been."

The Norwegian drinking chorus was now back on its feet, snaking around in front of the bar as a human chain. My neighbor lit up another cigarette and ignored the ruckus.

"I've got to touch things that hasn't been touched," he said. "I'll tell ya what—you're looking at somebody that had free run of the whole Standing Rock Indian Reservation. Prince Maximilian? You read his diary and it's just the same now as it was then. You look off to where he saw that butte, and there it is." He looked out over the crowded bar, beyond the curl of the line dance.

"Those Mandans. The stuff they left behind—shoot, you're tripping over 'em all the time. We used to take a bucket for the arrowheads, and have to pack the rest. I got spearpoints as long as your forearm."

The Dakotan wiped at the bartop with his sleeve. "I was, out there one day, on a long mud flat, and I found this pipe, made out of soapstone. Not much bigger than this." He held out his curled left hand and stared at it, whistling in admiration.

"That sucker was beautiful, but it was only half there—split right down the middle. Some compadre must have carried off that other half, and meant to join it back together one day.

"That was right about the time they closed up the gates on the big dam. I got out there in my canoe and paddled all around. For a long time the water level didn't change that much, and I went from one island to the next. I just had a feeling like I was going to find it. That water kept coming up, and I kept on mucking around, but I never did find the other half of that pipe."

He brought his right hand slowly across to clasp his left. The glow in his eyes damped down, then rekindled.

"There was another day, across the river. There had come

a big rain, and I was trucking down this wash, slipping and sliding in the gumbo. I'd been that way one thousand times, always picking up things, and I come around a corner I knew like the back of my hand and whoooa, here's a whole crew of people. The Smithsonian boys. They're out there picking away with their little scrapers and tweezers. And they've dug up a whole, complete skeleton, TRI-CER-O-TOPS! Head bigger'n a wheelbarrow! Oh, I'll tell ya about it. Don't talk to me about no *old*. I cut my teeth in the Mandan country."

ON JANUARY 10, 1798, Thompson and his party left the Mandan villages with wolf pelts and buffalo robes, but no large fossil bones. By the end of the month, they had made their way back to the North West post on the Assiniboine River, where they had started. Here Thompson spent three weeks calculating the positions he had shot on the trip and drafting a rough map. In late February he hit the trail again, and by early spring he had used a light canoe to trace the headwaters of the Mississippi to Turtle Lake, which he decided must be the source of the river. Although later surveyors selected another pothole nearby as the Mississippi's official point of origin, Thompson did perform the first accurate survey of its upper drainages, near latitude 48° N.

Struggling downstream from Turtle Lake through the emerging shoots of wild rice, he crossed to Lake Superior and followed the lake's south shore to the site of modern Sault Ste. Marie. There he met North West agent Alexander Mackenzie, on his way to Grand Portage for the summer rendezvous. Describing their encounter in his *Narrative*, Thompson wrote, "Upon my report to him of the surveys I had made, and the number of astronomical observations for latitude, longitude, and variation of the compass, he was pleased to say I had performed more in ten months than he expected could be done in two years." Thompson continued

his work along the east and north shores of Lake Superior,
and his arrival back at Grand Portage in June 1798 completed
a circuit of four thousand miles. He had discovered that several North West trading houses, as well as Grand Portage
itself, lay south of the proposed U.S. boundary, and in the
process he had filled in a large blank space on the map of
North America. When Alexander Mackenzie published an account of his own explorations three years later, he included,
with a small credit, Thompson's map work of points from
Lake Winnipeg down into the headwaters of the Mississippi.

The North West partners next sent Thompson off to the
opposite corner of their domain, the Athabasca region, where
he built a new trade house and explored along the Athabasca
River. In the spring, returning south with a load of furs, he
stopped at Île à la Crosse on the Churchill River, and there,
on June 10, 1799, he married Charlotte Small. Charlotte was
the daughter of Patrick Small, one of the original North West
Company partners. After living and trading at Île à la Crosse
for several years, Small had retired to England with his fur
profits, leaving his native wife and half-breed children behind.
Charlotte's mother was a Cree, a tribe that Thompson knew
well. In one draft of his *Narrative,* he wrote: "My lovely wife
is of the blood of these people, speaking their language, and
well educated in the English language, which gives me a
great advantage." According to an entry in the Thompson
family Bible, Charlotte was born on September 1, 1785,
which would have made her not quite fourteen years old in
the spring of 1799; Thompson had just turned twenty-nine. It
was accepted practice for a winterer to take a young teenage
wife of native or mixed blood, "after the fashion of the country," as official company documents phrased it. This was also
in keeping with the nuptial customs of the Crees, as recorded
by Thompson: "Their marriages are without noise or ceremony; nothing is requisite but the consent of the parties and
the parents . . . when contrariety of disposition prevails, so
that they cannot live peaceably together, they separate with as

little ceremony as they came together, and both parties are free to attach themselves to whom they will, without any stain on their characters."

The newlyweds spent the winter at Fort George on the upper Saskatchewan, where Thompson laid out big sheets of drawing paper that had been sent from Montreal and began transforming the columns of figures from his notebooks into points on a map. He also took his first tentative stab at writing up his adventures in narrative form. During the winter, he was visited by John McDonald of Garth. (There were so many McDonalds in the North West Company that this one identified himself by the name of his ancestral estate in Scotland.) McDonald of Garth was Thompson's new brother-in-law, having married another of Patrick Small's daughters, and he also worked in the western Saskatchewan district, known as "Fort des Prairies."

For several years, McDonald of Garth and other traders along the Saskatchewan had been hearing about a tribe that lived on the west side of the Rocky Mountains. The name of these people is variously spelled in the early records as the "Cotta na haos," "Cuttenchas," "Cottonahaws," and "Coutonees"; Thompson called them the Kootanaes. (Today they are known as the Kutenais or Kootenays in Canada and the Kootenais in the United States.) Their country was reputed to abound in fur-bearing animals of all types, which they were anxious to trade; but the east-side posts were far away. This untapped source of furs was of great interest to everyone in the Fort des Prairies Department, for as that district filled with trade houses, the number of pelts taken in steadily dwindled. In order to give the Kootenais a convenient place to trade, McDonald of Garth had spent of the fall of 1799 building a new post far up the Saskatchewan at the base of the mountains. In the spring of 1800, Thompson rode up on horseback for a quick reconnaissance, and that fall he and Charlotte took up residence at the company's westernmost establishment, the new Rocky Mountain House.

CHAPTER THREE

SMOKING
WITH EAGLES

1800–1806

ALL THE WHILE I read Thompson, I had pictured Rocky Mountain House as being in the foothills, but as I approached the provincial park that preserves its site, the flatness of the surrounding countryside was what impressed me most. A pasture of tall grasses could have been a rug unrolled; its only relief was a small group of buffalo, their round backs bunched up black and shiny within a stout wire fence. Beyond the animals the white cone of a tipi stuck up from the grassland, and a line of stubby spruce trees stretched along the Saskatchewan River. I knew that a wall of mountains rose up fifty miles or so behind me, but today the whole horizon had sunk into a yellow haze.

I walked toward the river and the tipi, which stands near the site of the first rough fort that McDonald of Garth built for the North West Company in the fall of 1799. The Hudson's Bay Company built its Acton House that same fall less than a mile away, and during the next eight decades edifices were raised, added on to, burned, rebuilt in different spots, and neglected for seasons at a time. A sign notes that one carefully preserved rotted timber might have belonged to that first trading post, but it's hard to tell for sure. Later incarnations are better documented, with foundation outlines and a reconstructed bastion. Down by the landing beach is a replica of one of the flat-bottomed bateaux that sometimes hauled cargo on the river, and when I punched a button on the kiosk nearby I heard the slap of fat oars against the water, followed by the grunts and hissing *Sacré bleu*s of paddlers as they worked themselves silly for the Englishmen.

Remnants from the various sites are displayed inside an interpretive center on the grounds, and as I stepped inside, a silver-haired man was questioning a young guide. "I'll tell you what I want to know," the man said. "What I want to know is, if this place is called Rocky Mountain House, then where the hell are the mountains?"

I noticed that several people around the lobby leaned in to catch the answer. The guide explained that usually you could see the Rockies off to the west, but that smoke from a big forest fire up in the Northwest Territories was obscuring the view today. The man still looked vaguely dissatisfied, as if the ranger were somehow responsible for the lack of visibility. I was about to step up and tell him that there had often been prairie fires even back in David Thompson's time, when a woman with a troubled expression entered the foyer and walked directly up to the guide. "Excuse me," she said, "but I thought there were supposed to be mountains around here . . ."

I moved on into the adjacent exhibit hall, which was momentarily empty of visitors. The first display I came upon was a collection of antique surveying instruments. Here was a ten-inch brass Dollond sextant, exactly like the one Thompson had carried, and a smaller box full of drawing equipment: pens and nibs, protractors, compasses, dividers, and rules. There was even a copy of a *Nautical Almanac*, and a Jolly watch that looked as if it would still keep pretty good time.

Across the corridor I stopped at an array of trade items, several of which I had wondered about when I came across them in Thompson's journals. A "dag" turned out to be a wide, heavy knife, shipped without a handle to save space and weight in the canoes. "Hawks bells" were the same little jingle bells that falconers hang from the jesses of captive hawks; farther along I saw them used as decorations on buckskin jackets and bags. A small copper pot, plain metal rings, glass beads of different colors, a sewing awl, a thick twist of tobacco—every one of these items had gone through an epic of packing and repacking, wetting and drying, loading and unloading, inventorying and pricing, on its journey to this spot.

In the next hallway I almost bumped my head on the vessel that had ferried all this stuff across the continent: a genuine birchbark canoe. It looked to be about fourteen feet long, which would have made it a "light" canoe, used for running messages and carrying small loads. I reached one hand up and touched the birch rind. It was paper, yet wood, calked solid at each seam, sewn neatly to the wooden gunwales. The tribes of the eastern woodlands had developed these craft, and the early French traders had been quick to see their value. Light enough for two men to carry, yet strong enough to hold many times their own weight, they could be built in different sizes depending on where and how they were to be used. Twenty-five feet was the standard length for the *canots du nord* (Northern canoes) that Thompson used for hauling cargo; he estimated that one of these boats, fully loaded, could carry twenty-nine hundred pounds of supplies. During his years with the woodland tribes, he became skilled in their construction and repair. The first requirement for a good canoe was quality bark, or rind, and it took an experienced eye to spot the right tree. Cree canoe builders taught Thompson to pay special attention to the dark horizontal nicks, or "cores," that mark every birch trunk. They told him that these nicks were scars left from floggings by Weesaukajauk, the Flatterer, an impish deity whom the birch species once disobeyed. Some trees had been whipped so severely that the nicks penetrated all the way through the rind, and this made for a leaky boat. After the bark was carefully peeled from the trees, thin tendrils of coniferous roots, called *watap*, were stripped out of the ground and used to sew the canoe together. Then the seams were calked with the rendered sap of fir, spruce, or pine. A bundle of watap and a bucket of gum rode along as necessities on every voyage to repair rips in the bark or leaks around the nicks of Weesaukajauk.

Other exhibits along the hallways showed off native costumes and accoutrements, and weapons of hunting and war. One small case held miscellaneous relics that had been found in the immediate vicinity of the old trade houses, and it was this random collection of everyday objects that evoked most strongly the meeting of disparate cultures that had taken place around those rotting timbers out in the yard. There were stone arrowheads, buttons, a small bottle, a child's whizzer toy, and a delicate whistle sectioned from a bird's hollow wing bone.

Back outside, there was plenty of light left in the day, and I thought I would climb across a fence and take a shortcut over to a nature trail marked on the map. The park is nestled in a pocket between prairie and muskeg, where the effects of the last glacial ice sheet linger like a slow-drying sponge, and when I hopped down I landed in ankle-deep ooze. After five squishy steps I retreated to a gravel road that led through the grassland and ended at a walking-beam oil pump. The blue steel grasshopper bobbed slowly up and down, surrounded by a knobby, unnavigable bog of spruce. A heavy petroleum smell hung in the air, and as I drove away from the park I passed the twin flames of a small natural gas plant. The odor hung with me until I reached the bridge over the Saskatchewan River and climbed a hill toward town.

The settlement of Rocky Mountain House sits in open country set back from the river. The main street is laid out wide enough for a cattle drive, and the evening traffic suggested that the trading-post culture of the last century had

moved only a few miles up to the crossroads. At the bottom of
the main drag, I spotted the David Thompson Hotel, a two-
story concrete-block affair, blue with a bright red false front.
A Conestoga wagon rides across its roof, above a cowboy
mural touting "Rocky's Largest Country Party Bar." When I
tried to jaywalk across to the saloon, I found myself dodging
a series of big-tired pickups that rumbled along the rolling
streets. Back at my car a note on the windshield informed me
that although I had parked a little crooked, the city fathers
were going to let me off this time, and they hoped that I enjoyed my visit.

Later that evening I wandered back down to the
Saskatchewan. Fresh out of the mountains, the river ran fast
and milky under the bridge. I followed a trail that led upstream to a point opposite the cluster of old trade houses and
sat down beside a clump of wolf willows to watch it get dark.
Along the flat, big cottonwoods rose above the dark green
of alder and serviceberry bushes. Pearly wolf willow berries,
beads for Blackfeet children, mirrored the ice-green color of
the Saskatchewan. A muted laugh rang across the water, followed by the dips and drips of smooth paddle strokes. By the
light reflected off the river, I could make out bright orange
flags and life jackets suspended over a loose formation of
canoes. As they came closer, the laughter increased. Then
three dark fiberglass hulls coasted quietly into the big eddy,
and the paddlers drew them in, one by one, to scuff up on to
the gravel bar for their final stop of the day.

AS DAVID THOMPSON approached that same landing
spot in the fall of 1800, he was paddling through territory frequented by several tribes. His old Piegan friends, along with
their Blood and Blackfeet kin, still ranged freely between the
Saskatchewan and Missouri Rivers. Several Cree and Stoney
Assiniboine bands had moved into the vicinity, and some of

RIVERS OF THE EAST SLOPE

them worked as hunters for the fur companies. Then there were the Kootenais across the Divide, whom the traders were counting on to bring in the next great bounty of beaver.

Thompson had not been at Rocky Mountain House very long when he heard that a group of Kootenais was heading over the mountains with a load of pelts. He quickly hired two guides—a Cree named He Dog and a Piegan named Old Bear—and gathered five men and eleven horses to go and meet the new customers and guide them to the trade house. The Nor'Westers set out on October 5 and were a few hours down the trail before someone realized that they had forgotten to bring a cooking pot. The voyageur La Gasse hurried back to the post and caught up with the party that evening, two kettles in hand. On the second day out, they stopped for a brief smoke with five tents of Piegans, then continued south until they struck the Red Deer River, which they followed upstream to an open plain. "Here we had a grand view of the Rocky Mountains, forming a concave Segment of a Circle . . . all its snowy cliffs to the Southward ever bright in the Beams of the Sun, while the most northern were darkened by a Tempest & by the Storm, which spent its Force only on the summits." As they climbed higher into the foothills, Thompson studied the huge piles of driftwood far up on the riverbanks, untouched by high-water marks for several years. Had so much of the mountain been eroded away that it no longer attracted storm clouds, he wondered, or had there been a change in local weather patterns?

Late on the third afternoon, Old Bear brought them to his own small camp, and here they put up for a few days. Thompson hunted and took observations for latitude and longitude while he waited for another guide who had promised to come and lead them farther into the mountains. When the new guide did show up, he immediately made clear that his primary interest was tobacco. As for the other Piegans in camp, "They are so jealous of the Kootanaes coming in to Trade that they do all they can to persuade me

to return, assuring me that it is impossible for me to find
them and that in endeavoring to search them out, our Horses
will fall by Fatigue and Hunger, and perhaps also ourselves."

The Piegans seemed to have an on-again, off-again relationship with the Kootenais. Both tribes had long traditions of travel back and forth across the Divide for hunting
and trade; sometimes they were in a state of war, at other
times they would declare a truce and meet amiably. In 1792
Hudson's Bay Company surveyor Peter Fidler had traveled with a group of Piegans up into the foothills to meet a
Kootenai band that had come across the mountains to trade.
He was the first white man to meet the Kootenais, and he
watched as they chopped firewood with hatchets crafted from
sharpened elk antlers, then swapped their good horses and
furs for the old kettles and broken iron tools that the Piegans
had brought along. Fidler figured that any trade house would
have given the Kootenais as much for one pelt as the Piegans
gave them for ten, but the Kootenais walked home happy with
their trifles, and wanted more. What they wanted most was
guns. In the years that followed, however, the Piegans would
trade them only a few, jealously preserving their own arms
superiority as well as the healthy profit margin they gained
as middlemen. The Kootenais repeatedly tried to elude the
Piegans and other Blackfeet tribes and go directly to the trade
houses, but they were rarely successful.

Now traders had come in search of the Kootenais, and
the Piegans were trying to scare them off by feigning concern
for their safety. The new guide told the Nor'Westers to
ignore these dissuasions, and led them upriver. The first afternoon out, Thompson shot a bighorn sheep whose horns
measured thirty-five inches along the curl. The next day he
had a chance to climb a high knoll, where he had a good view
of range after range of wooded hills rippling toward a distinctive peak. He killed a fisher, another example of the plentiful
variety of game they were finding—so far they had seen wolverine, elk, moose, mule deer, and "Grisled Bears but too

many." They stopped to camp that night with two tents of Piegans who had spent the day eagle hunting, a sport Thompson had observed closely during his first winter on the plains:

> The natives made shallow pits which they covered with slender willows and grass under which they lay, with a large piece of fresh meat opposite their breasts; thus arranged they patiently await the flight of the eagle, which is first seen very high, scaling in rude circles, but gradually lowering, till at length he seems determined to pounce upon the meat, his descent is then very swift with his claws extended, the moment he touches the meat the Indians grasp his two legs in his hands, and dashes him, through the slender willows to the bottom of the pit and strikes his head till he is dead . . . Lying in this position, and frequently somewhat benumbed, it requires an active man to pull down an Eagle with his wings expanded, and dash him to the ground . . . As the Eagle never loses his courage, the whole must be quickly done, or the Eagle will dart his beak in the mans face, and thus get away.
>
> *Narrative*

Eight birds had been captured on this hunt, and that evening the Piegans cleared a spot in the back of their tent and laid the eagles on a patch of clean grass with their heads pointing toward the fire. During the next three hours, the Piegans sang and shook a rattle while a medicine pipe was passed; each man in turn smoked the pipe and then presented it to each of the eagles. These birds' feathers would adorn war bonnets and shields, and the claws, beaks, and other parts would be preserved for ceremonial uses. After the consecration, Thompson went out for some stellar observations, and noted the latitude of the camp (51° 41' 41" N) in his journal the next morning.

They all stayed put for a day of bad weather and fruitless

hunting. That evening two young Piegans showed up with a pair of mares and reported that the Kootenais, from whom they had stolen the horses, "would be on the Heights of the Mountain the Morrow." The morrow was October 14, a Tuesday, and their guide led the Nor'Westers high up the headwaters of the Red Deer River in what is now Banff National Park. In midafternoon, at the base of some high cliffs, they met a Kootenai chief with twenty-six men and seven women. The chief presented Thompson with a bow and a quiver of arrows, a red foxskin cap, and a fine yellow horse loaded with fifty beaver pelts. Thompson told him to hold on to the horse and furs until they could trade properly at Rocky Mountain House and pulled out a fathom of his good tobacco for an introductory smoke. The Kootenais were poorly clothed for the cold weather and had only eleven horses among them—they said they had started out with more, but several had been stolen by Piegans who met them on the way over. Despite such discouragements, the travelers assured the surveyor that they were ready to make for the trading post, and together they camped for the night.

They headed down the mountain on Wednesday, and by the time they made camp, the sun had already set. It was not too dark, however, for one of the men from a nearby Piegan camp to notice a handsome black horse and boldly snatch it on the spot. The Kootenais grabbed their weapons, the thief let go his prize, and the commotion brought out a Piegan chief who lectured his men on their rude behavior, "that it was an Act neither brave nor manly to rob a few Strangers, their allies, of their poor starved horses." The Kootenais decided they had seen enough and prepared to head home that night. Thompson enlisted the help of a voyageur named Michel Boulard, who was good with native languages; together the two men reasoned with the travelers until midnight and finally convinced them to continue.

The next morning they discovered that the incorrigible Piegans had stolen five more horses during the night, including the yellow one given to Thompson. The Kootenais again determined to turn around, and it was only after "much ado" and the loan of a horse to carry some of their baggage that Thompson was able to get them to come with him. The thought of the guns they would be able to get at the trade house helped move them in that direction. "They complained much & bitterly to me of what had been stolen & plundered from them . . . several of the principal of them went so far as to kneel down and swear by the Sun, the Skies, and Earth, that they would revenge themselves."

For the next five days, Thompson refereed a running game of cat-and-mouse as several young Piegans followed along to pester the Kootenais. On Thursday an altercation seemed certain to end in bloodshed until Thompson and Boulard rushed up and chased away three young rowdies who were trying to stop the caravan. They camped Friday night near a friendly Piegan chief who invited them all to come and feast with him. Some of the young men at this camp challenged the Kootenais to a gambling match, then lost every game until the party broke up at midnight. On Saturday morning the Kootenais awoke to find they had only two horses left. Thompson quickly rode back to Rocky Mountain House to fetch fresh mounts so that he could keep things moving. Still hassling with young Piegans, the party arrived safely at the trading post on Monday afternoon. "Thank God," wrote Thompson, and passed out rum all around.

The next day he purchased ten bear, two wolverine, five fisher, and over a hundred beaver pelts from the Kootenais. One old man was savvy enough to take his five bear hides next door to Acton House to see if he could strike a better deal with the Hudson's Bay trader there. Throughout their ordeal, Thompson had been impressed by the Kootenais' spirit and fortitude, and by the steady demeanor of the four old men who led them. After the trading was finished, the surveyor questioned these elders about the geography of their homeland and about the mountains between. He learned that the Kootenais were a small tribe with a broad knowledge of both sides of the Divide. Two or three times a year, several of their bands would get together and cross over to hunt buffalo on the east side. Sometimes they were harassed by Blackfeet, but often they were able to dry their meat and stretch their hides in peace. They had once had many routes across the mountains, they said, but smallpox had decimated their numbers, and all but a few trails had fallen into disuse.

This was the sort of information Thompson needed, and he asked the Kootenais to come back the next spring and guide him to their country. He loaned the chief a horse to carry his baggage and fitted out two voyageurs, La Gasse and Le Blanc, to go home with them and spend the winter. In hopes of avoiding any more Piegan woes, the Kootenais decided to return home by a northerly route, through wooded country where the Blackfeet rarely ventured. On October 22 they set off along the north bank of the Saskatchewan. When it was time to depart, La Gasse and Le Blanc couldn't find their horses, but by the next morning they were ready. Thompson rode along with them until they caught up with the Kootenai party just past noon, then he bid his pioneers adieu and returned to Rocky Mountain House.

Upon his return he found that Duncan McGillivray had just arrived. The younger brother of Chief Superintendent William McGillivray, Duncan had worked in the Fort des Prairies Department for seven years and had helped build many of the posts that had leapfrogged up the Saskatchewan. Now that the trade had pushed all the way to the foot of the Rocky Mountains, Duncan was one of several prominent partners who saw no reason to stop there. As their network had stretched farther and farther north and west, the long commutes across the continent had grown increasingly inefficient. Precious time and manpower were being spent getting from the outposts back and forth to Grand Portage, and from Lake Superior back and forth to Montreal; by the time a canoe brigade reached Lake Athabasca or Rocky Mountain

House, it was actually much closer to the Pacific Ocean than to Montreal. The explorations of Captain James Cook and other mariners had failed to uncover any Northwest Passage by sea, but for years furmen had been talking about the "Great River of the West," rumored to run all the way from the Rockies to the Pacific. If such a river could be found, it would not only provide them with a transcontinental passage and a western port, but also open a lucrative trade route to China and Russia.

In the 1780s Alexander Mackenzie, working around Lake Athabasca, had become convinced that just such a river lay close at hand. In 1789 he had led a small party from Lake Athabasca to Great Slave Lake, then west along the river he assumed would quickly take him to the Pacific. But that river, later named for him, soon turned north and led him straight to the Arctic Ocean—a remarkable piece of pioneering, but the wrong ocean on which to found an economic empire. Four years later Mackenzie tried another route. This time he made his way up a tributary of the Peace River and carried his canoe 817 paces across the Continental Divide. On the other side he traced a river that he called the Tacoutche Tesse to the beginnings of a wild canyon in what is now west-central British Columbia. As the river turned south, Mackenzie broke away from its tortuous course and followed native trails through dense rain forest to Bella Coola, a village on the Pacific Coast near latitude 52° N. Again his trip provided landmark information about the geography of the Northwest, but did little to further commerce.

When Mackenzie returned from his disappointing trip to Bella Coola in 1793, he learned that the previous May an American sea captain named Robert Gray had discovered the mouth of a big river on the west coast just north of the 46th parallel. Gray had claimed the river for the United States and named it after his ship, the *Columbia*. George Vancouver's British expedition had arrived at the same wide mouth five months later, and his lieutenant William Broughton had

ALEXANDER MACKENZIE'S CONJECTURE

crossed the bar and rowed a dory a hundred miles upstream before reaching impassable cascades. Broughton decided that the Americans had never made it into the river proper; he drew a chart of his discoveries, named the prominent landmarks he passed, and with Vancouver claimed the Columbia for Great Britain. Such a large river, lying to the south of his own route, rekindled Mackenzie's hope for a trade artery to the Pacific. He was convinced that the Tacoutche Tesse and the Columbia were the same river, and dotted in its projected course on a map that appeared in his book about his two great adventures.

For the next several years, Mackenzie lobbied for an expedition to follow this dotted line and find out how much of it was navigable, both to extend the fur trade across the continent and to secure for Great Britain that wedge of uncharted country between the Rocky Mountains and the dark green coast. Disgruntled with his partners, Mackenzie resigned from the North West Company in 1799, but William and Duncan McGillivray remained enthusiastic supporters of his vision of transcontinental trade. Now Duncan had come to Rocky Mountain House to lead an expedition across the mountains to the Pacific Ocean the next spring, and David Thompson was to go along as his astronomer.

In mid-November, Thompson took McGillivray on a scouting expedition southward to look for an eligible pass over the Continental Divide. Along the way they stopped to visit a Piegan band on the Bow River, in the same area as Saukamappee's old winter camp. In the twelve years since Thompson had wintered there, the Piegans and other Blackfeet tribes had continued to fight with the Snakes and to live out their seasonal chase for the buffalo. Though the bison herds remained the most important commodity in their lives, it was inevitable that the proximity of the Saskatchewan trade houses would undermine the tribes' self-sufficiency. The Blackfeet now had large numbers of muskets, but they always needed more powder and lead balls. They had stopped growing their own varieties of tobacco because they preferred the smooth Brazilian and Virginia strains offered by the traders. Some of them had developed an unfortunate taste for the whiskey that both companies used to gain a competitive edge. None of the Blackfeet tribes, however, had entered the beaver-trapping culture with much enthusiasm, preferring to offer wolf pelts and buffalo meat for trade.

McGillivray and Thompson had not been in the Piegan camp long when Sac o tow wow, the principal chief, paid them a visit. Sac o tow wow had guns on his mind, complaining that the Nor'Westers had traded arms to the Kootenais and that the Flatheads would soon have guns, too, and would use them to attack his people. The Flatheads, a populous tribe who lived south of the Kootenais, were steadfast enemies of the Blackfeet. Thompson reminded Sac o tow wow

that it was the Blackfeet themselves who had introduced firearms to the west-side tribes, by trading the Kootenais guns
for horses.

The furmen had another agenda for their visit. Many of
the beaver grounds in eastern Canada were now completely
trapped out, and some of the Iroquois who lived there wanted
to move west. Since the Blackfeet had not shown much interest in hunting beaver, the North West Company thought it
might be a good idea to resettle some experienced Iroquois
trappers nearby: "Those Indians would behave quietly, would
reside in the woody Hills at the foot of the Mountain and
serve as a Barrier between them and their Enemies – upon
these Terms they gave us Permission to bring them up as soon
as we pleased. Cut a Pipe of Tobacco to each Man & gave
them a few pints of Mixed Rum to drink." ("Mixed rum" was
rum mixed with water; the traders varied the strength of the
mixture according to the occasion and the tribe.)

As McGillivray and Thompson pushed on up the Bow
River, they amused themselves by dogging buffalo that grazed
in the foothills. They came upon a second Piegan camp,
of about forty tents, and made another pitch for relocating
Iroquois. These Piegans responded quite favorably to the
idea, but when they learned that the white men were planning
to go up into the mountains, they warned them to beware of
the Flatheads, who were "constantly hovering about there to
steal horses or to dispatch any small weak party they might
chance to fall in with." The two explorers kept a sharp watch
but encountered only buffalo, moose, bighorn sheep, and expansive views of the snowcapped Rockies: "Never before did
I behold so just, so perfect a resemblance to the waves of the
ocean in the wintry storm," wrote Thompson. Here he and
McGillivray could see the daunting breadth of these mountains: this was no single ridge, and it would take more than
Mackenzie's 817-step portage to make it across the "Height
of Land" in these latitudes. They would need a guide who
knew the country, and horses to pack the goods.

The two explorers were back at Rocky Mountain House by early December, and Thompson remained there while Duncan McGillivray rode north to examine a possible crossing up the Brazeau River. McGillivray returned after two weeks, having found the river's course too rugged for horses, and apparently having pushed himself beyond his physical limits. According to Thompson, McGillivray "took no precautions against the effect of exposure to the weather, wet feet, etc. The consequence was that early in February he began to feel attacks of acute rheumatism, which became so violent as to oblige him to keep his bed." Though still a young man, McGillivray had suffered for at least five years from what he called "rheumatism or some other vile disorder of that nature."

McGillivray had spent the previous year in Montreal and had apparently brought west with him extracts from George Vancouver's recently published *Voyage of Discovery to the North Pacific Ocean*. Over the winter Thompson copied the parts pertaining to the Columbia River and the Northwest coast into a separate notebook, presumably so that he and McGillivray would be able to use the information when they arrived at the Pacific. What these men were planning was a historic transcontinental crossing, only the second north of Mexico. By the time they returned, they hoped to be the first to have pioneered a practical trade route to the sea.

Of what lay between Rocky Mountain House and the Pacific Ocean, they knew nothing except for what the Kootenais had told Thompson the previous fall. Before they left, the Kootenai chiefs had promised to send someone to guide the Nor'Westers as far west as their country in the spring. At the end of May, La Gasse and Le Blanc, the two voyageurs who had gone to winter with the Kootenais, did return to Rocky Mountain House. They brought with them a load of beaver pelts and valuable information about the country across the mountains, but not the native guide that McGillivray and Thompson were waiting for—a young

Kootenai had accompanied the two voyageurs east, as agreed, but he had been killed by a group of Stoney Assiniboines along the way. Despite this setback, McGillivray remained determined to launch his expedition. For some reason, neither La Gasse nor Le Blanc was mentioned as a possible guide, and McGillivray hired a Cree named the Rook who said he knew a good horse trail up a tributary of the Saskatchewan and across the Divide. Thompson thought the Rook "a Man so timourous by Nature, of so wavering a Disposition, & withal so addicted to flattering & lying, as to make every Thing he said or did, equivocal and doubtful." McGillivray, who also had reservations about the man's character, promised him a large reward if he performed well. As an extra precaution, he made the Rook swear an oath to the Great Spirit over his medicine pipe.

When it was time to leave, McGillivray's poor health prevented him from making the journey, and in his place he appointed James Hughes, the proprietor in charge of Rocky Mountain House, to head the party. Thompson's journals for this part of 1801 have never been found, and the only description of this trip comes from a report he wrote for Duncan and William McGillivray. The account begins on June 6, 1801, with Thompson and Hughes starting west "in order to penetrate to the Pacific Ocean." They had with them the Rook, his wife, and an old Kootenai woman who had been captured by the Blackfeet years before and wanted to return to her people. Nine voyageurs led thirteen horses loaded with trade goods, necessities, and enough birch rind to build a canoe once they reached the west side of the mountains. They made slow but steady headway through the woods on the north shore of the Saskatchewan until the second afternoon, when a deep ravine blocked their path. They were traveling along a bench high above the river, and as they prepared to descend the steep bank, one of the horses stumbled and began rolling toward the lip of the sheer cliff. A pine tree stopped the animal just short of the edge, but partway down the bank another horse lost its footing and plunged into the river. The voyageur who volunteered to rescue it from the opposite shore was swamped by a wave in the middle of the river and bucked off *his* horse, leaving a man, two horses, and 120 pounds of valuables on the wrong side of the river.

Mishaps of this sort happened several times during the next few days, as the explorers continually found themselves pinned between steep slopes and fast water. The horses "rolled down so often, & received such violent Shocks from the Trees against which they brought up, as to deprive them for a Time of Motion." When they did reach a flat bench, the ground was so boggy that the animals sometimes sank up to their bellies in the mud. Part of their troubles could be put down to inexperience, because none of these men had ever tried to cross mountains with packhorses before. Learning on the job, the Nor'Westers slogged on through steady rain into the front range of mountains, and this time Thompson did not rhapsodize about the rugged landscape as he had back on the Red Deer: "The Scene around us has nothing of the agreeable in it, All Nature seems to frown, the Mountains are dreary, rude & wild, beyond the power of the Pencil."

The Rook led them along animal trails over the first ridge of the Rockies and then turned up the north branch of the Ram River. Fresh buffalo for dinner and the sight of greening hills to the west improved Thompson's spirits. But now the Rook was visibly discouraged, and when a violent thunderstorm forced them to make camp early, Hughes thought some rum might perk him up. While thunder and lightning crashed across the hills, the guide proceeded to get drunk with his wife. The next morning, feeling rough, he asked for "a little Medicine." Hughes obliged, but whatever he administered did not help. Sitting around the campfire with the rest of the men, the Rook called his wife to him. He took a sharp flint and sliced open a vein in her forearm, "she assisting him with great good Will." In front of the astonished furmen, he drew a cup of her blood into a wooden bowl and drank it down.

"While I was considering from whence so savage an Action could arise, one of our Men with Indignation exclaimed to our Guide, I have eaten & smoked with thee, but henceforward thou & me shall never eat & smoke together."

The Rook assured the white men that his wife's healthy blood was an invigorating tonic, that this was an established custom among his people, and that he would certainly offer his own arm to refresh his wife if her stomach were out of order. He smoked his morning pipe "with great tranquility," and soon the party was on its way again. Their route for the day led along a steep sidehill with patches of ice that tumbled two more horses into the river and wet their supply of salt and sugar. The next day they climbed up a narrow streambed high into the mountains, where the willows had not even started to bud and there was no fresh grass for the horses. Late that evening the Rook came to Thompson and Hughes "with a woful countenance"; he had dreamed about "bad Indians" and asked permission to go home lest he die without seeing his children again. When Hughes kidded him that there was nothing to fear besides mountain goats, and that he himself would personally defend him from these, the Rook whined, "That is the way of all you white Men, you joke at every Thing 'till you are fairly Killed."

The next day, floundering through two to three feet of snow, they reached the headwaters of the Ram—a narrow lake hemmed in by a sheer mountain on one side and steep talus all the way down to the waterline on the other. When the leaders asked their guide how he had gotten his horses around this obstacle on his previous trip, the Rook replied that he had forgotten about this part of the mountain. Furious, Hughes and Thompson set out to see if they could find a way out of the cul-de-sac. After crawling on all fours across the talus to the opposite end of the lake, they calculated that their route up the Ram had paralleled the Saskatchewan, which they guessed to be only ten or twelve miles away. They decided to salvage their expedition by sending the Rook home with the horses and most of their baggage. Then they would quickly make a skin boat, float their men and a minimum of gear across the lake, descend the precipitous slope into the next valley, and bushwhack a few miles cross-country to the Saskatchewan. Once there, they would build a canoe and explore the headwaters of the larger river for a pass. But when the rest of the men heard this plan, they balked; they were used to portages that lasted for hours, not weeks, and protested that their contracts did not include undertakings such as this. Hughes and Thompson even offered to carry their shares of the load, but the voyageurs could not be persuaded. Thompson noted that the men had been reluctant to come on this trip in the first place, "however we must do them the Justice to say, that it was improbable that they could have got down the Mountain with the Baggage, without at least one half of them being crippled." The leaders had no choice but to turn around and retrace their steps.

Three days later they had followed the Ram back to its junction with the Saskatchewan. It took more than a week to find wood and split out enough boards to construct a frame for their birchbark shell, and all that time the river was rising with spring runoff and torrential rain. Hughes needed to get back to Rocky Mountain House, so he took the Rook and the horses home, leaving Thompson to launch the boat. For three days the surveyor and eight voyageurs fought their way upriver, using every trick they knew. On the afternoon of the fourth day, as they pulled themselves along by trees protruding from the riverbank, they were brought up short by a set of whirlpool rapids running through a tight canyon. There was no shore for tracking, and no way to stem the volume of water pouring down at them. Thompson climbed up the bank and walked upstream far enough to conclude that during lower water the river should be quite passable, and he resolved to start his next trip before spring runoff reached its peak. After measuring the current at twelve to fifteen knots within the canyon, he and his men turned around and shot the seventy-four miles down to Rocky Mountain House in five hours and fifty minutes.

Back at the trade house on June 30, Thompson learned that while he was gone Charlotte had given birth to their first child, a daughter they named Fanny. He stayed close to home for the rest of the summer, trading for furs and watching swarms of locusts engulf the local vegetation. In his report to the McGillivrays analyzing the pitfalls of the trip, he briefly referred to what was probably the chief cause for its failure: "How unfortunate has this Journey been from the beginning, when we had got all ready & waited a long Time! At length a Kootanae came to guide us, & he when within a few miles of the fort was murdered." But Thompson did not explain why the two voyageurs La Gasse and Le Blanc, who had just returned from the Kootenai country, had not gone along to show him and Hughes the way west.

THE CITY OF Calgary rolled up like a great ship from the trough of a wave. It was just past dawn, difficult to discern any exact features among the lights, but easy to feel the daily surge of human energy already kicking off. The Quebecois hitchhiker I had picked up in the mountains stirred around in his woolly blanket as we sailed in on the Trans-Canada Highway. He had been quiet, almost sullen, since I had picked him up an hour before. My French was as bad as his English, but he had made me understand that he was headed east and was looking for a bus. As we passed the specter of an Olympic ski ramp beside the road, he began to communicate in the language of food.

"So big mountains," he said, eyeing the grocery bag in my back seat. I signaled with a wave of my hand that he could help himself, and he gobbled down a sizable wedge of hoop cheese and half a loaf of sourdough bread from my bag. Then he fished a tin of chocolate pudding out of his rucksack and slathered it across the last portion of bread. With a river otter's smile, he raised his creation in a toast, and when I pointed at an exit sign for the Blackfoot Trail, he nodded heartily. I turned off and let the flow of morning traffic funnel us toward the angular skyline that has been laid down upon the curves of the Bow River bottoms.

We ground to a halt among the morning commuters, right beside the stately facade of a Bay Company retail store. There in the window, above the company's ironclad guarantee, hung a striped blanket very much like the one wrapped around my hitchhiker. Beneath the building's polished granite windowsills, a handful of natives napped on the promenade. The Quebecois pointed down a side street at the bus station, and I dropped him under the Greyhound sign, hard by the Bow River and the old winter camps of the Piegan Blackfeet.

Ten minutes later I arrived at the library of the Glenbow Museum. The records kept here cover all aspects of Alberta history, and as I flipped through the card catalogue, the familiar names of La Gasse and Le Blanc appeared at the top of one of the cards, in the title of a paper written by an anthropologist named Claude Schaeffer. Schaeffer studied the Blackfeet and Kootenai people for over thirty years beginning in the 1930s, and recorded many of their oral traditions. He had several contacts among the Tobacco Plains band of Kootenais, which was most likely the same band that Thompson sent La Gasse and Le Blanc home with in October 1800. In a 1965 interview, two Tobacco Plains elders began telling Schaeffer about the first white men in the memory of their tribe. As the chief and another elder recounted their story, Schaeffer saw enough parallels with what he knew of La Gasse and Le Blanc to make a connection.

There was a pair of French Canadians, the elders said, who came one year to winter with the band at Tobacco Plains. The Kootenais called the one who liked a big, roaring blaze K!isuk-ing!uku (Good Fire) and the one who let his embers burn small and quiet Sahaning!uku (Poor Fire). The Frenchmen trapped some animals that winter and spent part of their time teaching the Kootenais more efficient ways to kill beaver and how to prepare skins without damaging the pelage. In the spring they took the furs they had accumulated over the mountains to a trade house.

The two white men returned to the Tobacco Plains either in the summer or the fall, and one of them married the daughter of Kulsmayuk, the Tobacco Plains chief. After their second winter with the tribe, the trappers made another delivery east. Sometime during the next year, Kulsmayuk's daughter had a baby, and the following spring the mother and child went along with the white men to the trading post. Schaeffer's storytellers at first thought that the men had taken their furs east for three years, then upped it to five. They did agree that Chief Kulsmayuk had often warned Good Fire and Poor Fire not to take a certain route over the mountains that was frequented by the Stoney Assiniboine. In either the third spring or the fifth spring, Kulsmayuk suggested that they take a southerly trail, and sent his son along to guide them. On the east side the three men ran into a party of Stoney Assiniboine. Using sign language, the Stoneys asked where they were from and who the guide was. The Frenchmen replied that the chief's son was from an eastern tribe and continued on their way, hoping their deception worked. But the Stoneys suspected the truth and followed the voyageurs' tracks back down to the camp of the Tobacco Plains band. The Kootenai men were out hunting, and the Stoneys attacked, killing a number of women and children.

When Kulsmayuk and his hunters returned home and discovered the massacre, they believed that their white guests had knowingly betrayed them by revealing the location of the camp. When Good Fire and Poor Fire returned that fall, the chief killed them both. He was about to kill his own grand-child, the infant child of the Frenchman, but his daughter prevented him. Eventually, Kulsmayuk's son convinced his father that the two white men had been blameless, and the story of the ill-fated fire-builders passed into the pool of Kootenai tribal lore.

IN HIS ACCOUNT to the McGillivrays describing the failed trip to the Pacific in the summer of 1801, Thompson made no mention of La Gasse and Le Blanc, their firebuilding abilities, or whether they had gone back to winter with the Kootenais again. He did note that in the future he would be certain to find a guide who knew where he was going, and he included other insights that would ensure the success of a second expedition. But by the spring of 1802, North West Company plans for expansion had been replaced by worries about the company's survival. After his resignation from the North West Company in 1799, Alexander Mackenzie had joined forces with another group of traders from Quebec known as the XY Fur Company. Over the next several years the XY rivalry commanded the full attention of the North West partners. They shut down Rocky Mountain House in 1802 and assigned Thompson to a post in the Peace River country near Lake Athabasca, where the XY Company was trying to establish itself.

Thompson spent two winters in the Peace River region, trading and surveying during the good weather months, inking in maps when shut in by cold. He wrote up reports and corresponded with a variety of fur agents, including Peter Fidler, his surveying counterpart with the Bay Company. He read a popular French novel that was making the rounds of the trade houses and lent his XY competitors some food when they were in a pinch. In the summer of 1804, he traveled to the North West Company's annual rendezvous, but this year it was not held at Grand Portage—in order to be clear of the American border, the company had moved its depot farther north on Lake Superior. At the expansive new compound that was soon to be named Fort William, David Thompson was elected a field partner and given two shares in the company, valued at more than four thousand pounds sterling.

Later that fall Alexander Mackenzie capitulated in his attempt to build a third major fur-trading concern. Although the destructive rivalry ended, it took accountants in Montreal another year to work out a merger between the XY and-North West Companies. During this period, David Thompson worked around the Muskrat Country west of Hudson Bay, the same region where he had once surveyed for the Hudson's Bay Company.

Meanwhile, down in the United States, Thomas Jefferson had made the fortuitous purchase of the vast Louisiana Territory, stretching from the Mississippi River to the Rocky Mountains, and had obtained full funding from the U.S. Congress for a military expedition to assess his new acquisition. When Meriwether Lewis and William Clark started up the Missouri River in 1804, they carried a copy of the chart that David Thompson had made on his trip to the Mandans seven years earlier. They also carried the most up-to-date map of North America available at that time. Drawn by the London cartographer Aaron Arrowsmith, it contained a great deal of information gathered by Thompson, Alexander Mackenzie, and Peter Fidler. The area west of the Rocky Mountains was almost completely blank, except for Mackenzie's travels and a conjectural river called the "Great Lake River," which flowed from the Rockies straight toward the dotted line of Mackenzie's Tacoutche Tesse and the mouth of the Columbia. A legend noted that "the Indians say they sleep 8 Nights in descending this River to the Sea." Lewis and Clark hoped to descend just such a river, for they did not intend to stop at the edge of the Louisiana Territory, but to proceed on to the Pacific. With transcontinental expansion clearly in mind, Thomas Jefferson had given his men instructions to find the "most direct and practicable water communication across this continent for the purposes of commerce."

William and Duncan McGillivray and some of the other North West partners understood the implications of Lewis and Clark's trip, and with the XY situation in hand, they again turned their attention west. In the summer of 1805 they sent Simon Fraser to Lake Athabasca, where he was to cross the

Continental Divide by Mackenzie's northern route and build a post in the area they called New Caledonia. From there he was to follow the Tacoutche Tesse south to its supposed junction with the Columbia and find out if it was navigable to the sea. The partners also resolved to make a new attempt to reach the still untapped source of furs in the Kootenai country. John McDonald of Garth was now in charge of the Fort des Prairies Department, and in the summer of 1806 he recruited David Thompson to return to Rocky Mountain House and put his previous experience to use.

IN EARLY JULY of that same year, on the way home from their long swing to the Pacific, Lewis and Clark decided to split their expedition and further explore the northern tributaries of the Missouri River. Within three weeks Meriwether Lewis and three men on horseback had worked their way up into the headwaters of the Two Medicine River, in present-day Montana, but poor weather and the formidable east front of the Rockies turned them around. As the men rode down the grassy breaks of the Two Medicine, they surprised a party of eight Piegans with thirty horses. Lewis was not certain of the identity of the horsemen, but he had heard unpleasant stories about the tribes of the northern plains and had hoped to avoid them. He considered his situation—it was late afternoon, and his interpreter was hunting separately downriver—and decided to approach in a friendly manner. He was relieved to see that only two of the Piegans carried muskets; the rest were armed with bows and arrows. During the drawn-out rituals of greeting, Lewis dutifully presented a flag,-a handkerchief, and a medal to all three Piegans who identified themselves as chiefs. Then the two parties pitched camp together on a wide flat beside the river.

Lewis found the Piegans "extreemly fond of smoking and plyed them with the pipe untill late at night." The explorer told the band about his long trip and about his hopes for friendly trade among all tribes at a post he planned to build on the Missouri. The Piegans in turn described a British house on the Saskatchewan River, about six days' easy march north, to which they traveled to trade wolf and beaver skins for "arms amunition speritous liquor blankets &c."

Other tribes had told the explorers that the Piegans had a penchant for thievery, and Lewis stood the first watch himself that night. Around midnight he warned his replacement to keep a sharp eye out, then retired inside a buffalo-skin shelter set up by the Piegans. There he fell into a "profound sleep," from which he did not stir until after dawn, when he was awakened by his tentmate shouting, "Damn you let go my gun." The Piegans had gotten up early and stoked the fire, then taken advantage of a lapse in the watchman's attention to grab guns and powder pouches. By the time the groggy Americans chased down the thieves and recovered their firearms, one Piegan had been stabbed through the heart, and Lewis had shot another in the stomach.

Back at the deserted campsite, Lewis took a moment to burn two bows and quivers of arrows that the Piegans had left behind. He retrieved the flag he had presented the previous afternoon, but left an inscribed peace medal around the neck of the stabbed man, "that they might be informed who we were." Quickly choosing the best of the remaining horses, the four white men struck a cross-country course for the Missouri River, riding hard all day and deep into the night. When they finally stretched out on the plains at two the next morning, Lewis wrote that "my Indian horse carried me very well in short much better than my own would have done and leaves me with but little reason to complain of the robery."

The Piegans felt otherwise. They still remember the name of Side Hill Calf, the man stabbed to death that morning in 1806. Thereafter, all the Blackfeet tribes made a sharp distinction between the Canadian traders, dubbed "Northern White Men," and the American white men, whom they called "Big Knives."

CHAPTER FOUR

NEUTRAL GROUND

FALL 1806–WINTER 1807

WHILE MERIWETHER LEWIS was scuffling with the Piegan Blackfeet on the Two Medicine River, David Thompson was attending the North West Company's summer rendezvous at Fort William, where it was decided that he would lead the expedition across the Rocky Mountains to the Kootenai country. Up the Saskatchewan River he went, stopping to visit his friend James Hughes at Fort Augustus, the headquarters for the Fort des Prairies Department. He continued on upriver another 120 miles and arrived at Rocky Mountain House in late October. John McDonald of Garth had recently come up from Fort Augustus to check on the post, and the two men spent a couple of days inventorying the warehouse and presumably discussing logistics for Thompson's upcoming trip. Earlier that summer McDonald had set plans in motion by sending four men to cut a pack trail along an old Kootenai route through the mountains near the headwaters of the Saskatchewan. The leader of this team was Jacques Raphael Finlay, the son of an early Nor'Wester and a Chipewyan woman. Jaco, as he was known, had already worked for several years on the Saskatchewan as a clerk and interpreter and seemed a good choice for a scout. Thompson had been at Rocky Mountain House only a couple of days when two of Jaco's crew arrived back at the post. They had left Jaco building canoes across the mountains and reported that the Kootenais they had met, delighted at the news of the furmen's coming, had set off to work beaver. After a general holiday for All Saints' Day, McDonald of Garth returned to Fort Augustus and Thompson took charge of Rocky Mountain House. From then on through the turn of the year, he was taking care of post business and keeping an eye on the Hudson's Bay Company "blockheads" next door at Acton House, who, he complained, were passing out too much rum.

November 19 began as a typical day. Thompson sent two of his men out to get meat from the native hunters and traded with some Piegans. He sent off another man with presents for a band of Blood Indians, who had been fighting with the Crees, to encourage them to make peace. At some point during the activities of the day, he must have left his pen unattended, for this page of his journal is covered with the enthusiastic scribbles of a small child. In the afternoon Jaco Finlay arrived back at the post, having finished his work across the Divide. Thompson would certainly have been anxious to hear details about the unknown country, and it may have been during this visit that Jaco drew a map that later turned up among Peter Fidler's papers with the note "drawn by Jean Findley 1806." The rough sketch outlined a trail up the north branch of the Saskatchewan, across two rows of bumps labeled Stony Mountains, and down to a river running through "a fine valley between more mountains."

As the year 1806 drew to a close, Thompson made snowshoes and a sled and shared Christmas dinner with his rivals at Acton House. On New Year's Day of 1807, he received word that Kootanae Appee and eighteen of his relatives were on their way to the post. Thompson sent tobacco ahead to welcome the storied war chief he had met in Saukamappee's tent as a teenager, and delayed his own New Year's celebrations until the Piegans had finished trading and drinking the rum he gave them. When the Nor'Westers did get around to calling the holiday on January 3, the Bay men came over to help, and Thompson calculated that the party cost him five gallons of French rum.

At the end of January, Thompson turned his attention to his spring expedition. He had not forgotten the obstacles that had turned him and James Hughes around in 1801. Aside from following the Rook up the wrong trail, one of their biggest problems had been the horses, which had proved so unwieldy in the mountainous terrain. There was no way to get across the pass without pack animals, but this time Thompson intended to supplement them with canoes as far as possible. Remembering what he had seen of the Saskatchewan's narrow channel on his previous trip, he planned to get moving before spring runoff swelled the river and flooded the shorelines they needed for tracking. With an early start in mind, he sent dogsleds up the frozen Saskatchewan as far as the first ridge of mountains. There the men cached over a thousand pounds of nonperishable supplies, so both canoes and horses would have lighter loads on the first leg of the trip.

In April, after another visit from Kootanae Appee, Thompson began working on a birchbark cargo canoe and making pemmican. In mid-month a dozen Kootenais came over the mountains to trade and reported that the snow on the Divide was still "equal in height to the top of a tall Pine." Thompson sent them home with gifts for their chiefs and word that he was on his way. On April 26 he heard the first frogs of spring croaking. On the 27th he saw cranes, then a small plover on the 29th. On May 4 the ice broke up on the river, and the explorer started packing.

"May 10th Sunday A very fine Day. At 9½ A.M. sent off Mr. Finan McDonald & 5 Men in a Canoe with Goods &

CROSSING THE ROCKY MOUNTAINS

Necessaries to the expedition across the Mountains." Finan McDonald, a tall, red-headed young Scot, was Thompson's clerk and deputy. He and five voyageurs—Boisverd, Lussier, Le Camble, Beaulieu, and Buché—began paddling and line-hauling their way up the Saskatchewan. Since the snow hadn't yet started to melt in the Rockies, the level of the river remained low, but its current still ran so fast that it frequently snapped the two new tracking lines Thompson had brought from Fort William. At intervals, steep canyons closed in, and the voyageurs had to track right up the riverbed. In a report to the partners, Thompson detailed the men's troubles: "The greatest Hardship of the People lay in being continually wet up to the Waist, exposed to cold high winds, & the water, coming direct from the Snows on the Mountains, was always so excessively cold as to deprive them of all feeling in their Limbs."

While Finan McDonald and the voyageurs towed the canoe upriver, Thompson paralleled their course overland with a string of horses, several dogs, and the women and children who were going along. These included Charlotte and three Thompson children, plus Lussier's family and one other woman. He also had with him three men: Clement, Bercier, and Boulard (Thompson seemed to prefer voyageurs whose names began with the letter B). Both Boulard and Bercier had been across the Divide with Jaco Finlay the previous summer; this time the explorer was sure he had guides who knew where they were going. For the next two weeks, they followed a route through thick woods that was short on grass and hard on the horses. Thompson took advantage of the slow pace, climbing hills for views of the countryside and studying the layout of the mountains and the course of the river. His men had good luck hunting along the way, bringing in buffalo, bighorn sheep, elk, and several porcupines. They spent one night near an old Cree medicine lodge that served as a landmark on the trail, and on June 3 they reached their staging area at a place they called Kootenay Plains, where Finan

McDonald and his canoe party were already camped.

This was a pleasant spot, and Thompson gave the people and horses a couple of days to rest. He reset his watch (it had lost time), observed for latitude (52° 2' N), and hired two men from the eastern Ojibway tribe who were trapping in the area to hunt for him. On June 5 he and the voyageurs continued on upriver, leaving the women, children, and livestock with Finan McDonald at Kootenay Plains, "as this was the last & only Place, where Pasture could be found for the Horses, or animals for the People for Food."

ABOUT EIGHTY MILES upstream from Rocky Mountain House, in the midst of the first big rise of the mountains, the Saskatchewan River canyon opens out into the broad, gently undulating parklands of Kootenay Plains. It's like a piece of the prairies lifted up into the hills, and this pocket of abundant grass attracts birds and animals in large numbers. Humans have followed game to this spot for at least ten thousand years; in more recent times, it was known as a camping ground to Kootenai hunters from across the mountains, a safe place on the edge of the dangerous Piegan Blackfeet lands. Bands of Cree, Sarcee, and Stoney Assiniboine also have traditions of using Kootenay Plains in one way or another. Jaco Finlay and his family lived there for a time, as did other hunters and horsekeepers of Thompson's era. North West Company agent Alexander Henry camped on these plains in the winter of 1811:

> I observed near the foot of the rocks behind the plain the remains of an old Kootenay camp, where the wood of the tents was still standing . . . the greater part were built to be covered with pine branches and grass, and some were made of split wood thatched with grass. Formerly that nation frequented this place to make dried provisions, for which purpose it must have been

very convenient, as buffalo and sheep are always more numerous than in any other place. Moose and red deer are also plenty; jumping deer, grizzly bear, and other animals peculiar to this country are also found here.

On the morning after my own camp-out on Kootenay Plains, I found myself drawn to the benchlands west of the river. Long ridges of stone stepped up from the flats, thickening in color as they ascended from the gravelly grays of the watercourse—yellows and oranges added row by row up to a final band of deep rust that glowed at the snowline. My route pulled me into a thicket of lodgepole pine that closed off the daylight like a dark house. Under the trees, elk leg joints and knobby tire tracks, leftovers from last fall's hunting season, littered the ground beside fresh droppings. Someone had tied bits of white, red, and green sheet around in the pines, flags that surprised me every time I came upon one. Only when I reached a steep cut that broached the terrace did it occur to me that the rags might mark a trail.

It was a rough climb, over car-sized boulders and spindly deadfall pines. The line of rags disappeared at the cliff top, a couple of hundred feet above the flats, and for a while I followed an indistinct path along the brink of the precipice. Below me Kootenay Plains opened out into meadows quilted with the trembling greens of aspen. Many of the chalky white aspen trunks were scarred black up to the height of an elk's reach, rubbed raw by shovel teeth.

When the trail petered out, I veered into the open woods along the bench. The colored rags soon reappeared, all tied the same way, but now pointing in an obvious direction. They ended at a simple fire circle, placed so that anyone tending a blaze would have a view out over the cliffs. In a small clearing below, a freshly built shelter stood in plain sight: a lodge woven from standing aspen boughs, leaves still attached, perhaps head high. The boughs were bent in at the top and joined so as to form an open circle in the hut's roof. From my high vantage, the opening looked too wide to keep the rain out, but now I wasn't certain it was meant to be a shelter at all. Three much longer poles rose up out of the hole and were tied together with strips of cloth. As with the fire circle, the impression they left was formal, symbolic.

When I scanned the border between flats and pine forest again, other wickiups emerged one by one from the terrain. All except the first had lost their foliage. Some still showed off a neat lattice framework of saplings. More leaned in on teetering sticks, spiky abstract creations on the verge of collapse. All that remained of others was a charred fire ring at their center. I stared down at the angled lodge poles, wondering what kind of ceremonies had gone on at this place over the years. I thought of those old Kootenai lodges that Alexander Henry had described, and the Cree medicine lodge that David Thompson passed on his way to this spot. I thought about pictures I had seen of sun dance lodges, with those same hooped circles in the roof, and remembered the shirtless young man who had pumped gas across from me at a service station a few days before. He had two fresh scars high on his pectorals, and must have just taken part in the initiation rite; he had touched the wounds over and over with his free hand, gingerly tracing the puffy scabs.

A breeze stirred down on the flat, rattling the aspen leaves. Uneasy, I stepped back into the shelter of the woods; a spruce grouse thumped up from beneath my feet, and I froze in my tracks. The bird circled me in a slow crouch, puffing out a velvety black belly. Its bright display sacs and fleshy eyebrows pulsed with the colors of blood.

AFTER LEAVING Kootenay Plains, Thompson and his party traveled upriver for a day and a half until they reached a fork. Here they left the main branch of the Saskatchewan and turned up a smaller river (now called the Howse) that flows in from the southwest. After four miles the braided channels became too shallow for the canoe. This was where the horse trail began, but the snow was still too deep for them to follow it. Thompson sent everyone except Bercier and two other men back to Kootenay Plains to wait for some snow to melt, then pitched his tent on a knoll beside the river. They were camped right in the lap of the Rockies, in a broad bowl ringed with craggy peaks and glacial headwalls. The weather immediately turned nasty. Thompson occupied himself stalking the moose whose footprints he kept seeing in the thick woods, while three days of mixed rain and snow created perfect conditions for a rash of spring avalanches.

> June 15 Monday A fine Day, stormy Afternoon, flying clouds. Went across the Rivulet and split out 130 small Boards for Boxes for the Goods. The Snows that have fallen in the Mountains these 3 days past are in many places rushing down with such a Noise, that we can hardly persuade ourselves it is not Thunder – we hear them every Hour, sometimes oftener.

During the next week the surveyor and his men listened to more avalanches and sewed the thin fir boards together to make boxes twenty-three inches square and eight inches deep. Into these they packed most of their goods, and then they waited for the latest snow to melt. By the third week in June, Thompson could stand the delay no longer and convinced Bercier to try a scouting trip up the trail. They started out early on June 22 on two good horses, following Jaco Finlay's route of the previous summer, and by midmorning they had reached the pass (later known as Howse Pass) and crossed the Continental Divide, "where the Springs send their Rills to the Pacific Ocean; this Sight overjoyed me." Grass was springing up on the other side, and trees were beginning to leaf out. It was time to fetch the people and horses from Kootenay Plains.

Two days later the entire party gathered at Thompson's

campsite on the banks of the river and finished packing. There was quite a bit of gear left over, and Finan McDonald stayed behind to tend to the extra baggage until the men could come back for it. At 3:30 the next morning, the surveyor "started the men"; by 6:00 they had the fir boxes, the kegs of gunpowder and wine, and the rolls of tobacco loaded onto the pack animals and were climbing toward the pass. They stopped at midmorning to refresh the horses near the Kootanae Pound, a narrow strip of grassland that led up to a sheer precipice. Kootenai hunters had long used this place as a buffalo jump, herding animals up the slope and then driving them over the edge of the cliff.

While everyone else was resting, Thompson spotted five white mountain goats up on the cliffs of the pound and went off after them. The goats took a high, craggy route of escape, and in hot pursuit Thompson loosened a large boulder, which in turn unleashed a landslide that passed so close to him that he "was obliged to keep hold with my nails and feet to prevent myself sliding down." It was almost noon by the time he recovered his breath and rejoined his waiting party. Even so, they easily made it to the Divide, which Thompson called the "Height of Land," by early afternoon and stopped to camp in a marshy meadow beside Howse Pass.

The next day was not so easy, as their route down the west side of the mountains zigzagged back and forth across the Blaeberry River. Summer had arrived, and the warm weather made for increased snowmelt: "The water descending in innumerable Rills, soon swelled our Brook to a Rivulet, with a Current foaming white, the Horses with Difficulty crossed & recrossed at every 2 or 300 yards, & the Men crossed by clinging to the Tails & Manes of the Horses, & yet ran no small Danger of being swept away & drowned."

If the crossings were hair-raising for the men, they must have been doubly so for Thompson's three children, all under six years old. He described how he rode on a "capital" horse, sounding out the fords and trying to choose the safest ones, but the animals were still almost carried away at times. At the end of the day, the two Ojibway hunters Thompson had brought along hadn't killed anything, and he was beginning to worry that the 220 pounds of pemmican he had packed would not be enough to keep everyone fed. "Gave the men a large Dog for supper for want of better, of which they made a Hearty Meal."

For the next week, the party continued to cross and re-cross the heavy current. When the men weren't fighting the river, they were fighting the trees. There was seldom any semblance of a trail, and when one did appear it was often too narrow for the horses' wide pack loads. It took three days to cover two and a half miles, with most of the time spent chopping trees and clearing deadfall. The men consumed huge amounts of pemmican, and not until the fourth day did one of the hunters shoot an elk. Thompson was concerned about the scarcity of game, and with good reason, for with the arrival of warm weather, the big grazing animals had dispersed throughout the mountains in search of summer forage.

On the afternoon of June 30, the Blaeberry's unruly course ended at a large river. Here the party quickly set up camp and spread everything out to dry; Thompson lamented that water had once again gotten to his small hoard of sugar. But that was the least of his worries: his stock of pemmican was way down, his man Beaulieu lay mysteriously incapacitated, the hunters still weren't having much luck, and no fish were biting in the river. The calking gum that Jaco Finlay had left for them wasn't fit for use, and worse, the canoes he had laid up were not big enough to haul their supplies. By this time Thompson was thoroughly put out with Jaco, as he reported to the partners:

> From what has been said of the Road on the Portage, it is clearly seen that Jaco Finlay with the Men engaged last Summer to clear the Portage Road, has done a mere nothing . . . and it is the opinion of every Man with

me,-as well as mine that Jaco Finlay ought to lose at least half his wages for having so much neglected the Duty for which he was so expressly engaged at 150 £ per year,-besides a Piece of Tobacco & Sugar, & a Clerk's equipment.

Finlay's map work, on the other hand, had been quite accurate so far. The little party was camped on a big river that ran through a valley between the Rockies and another range of snow-covered mountains to the west, exactly as shown on Jaco's sketch. At this point Thompson had no idea where this big river came from, or where it went. His calculations told him that he was in latitude 50° 59' N. He knew George Vancouver's location for the mouth of the Columbia was very near the 46th parallel, far to the south and several meridians west, whereas the river he had struck was flowing almost due north, straight toward the area where Alexander Mackenzie had met the Tacoutche Tesse fifteen years before. Thompson had no way of knowing that he was actually on the long-sought Columbia River, and that it ran north for another two hundred miles before bending abruptly back for its south-westerly run to the sea.

He did know that he needed some help in coping with this utterly unfamiliar country, and on July 2 he sent off Bercier in one of the light canoes to try and find some Kootenais. He was particularly anxious to find a man he called the Old Chief, who was probably the same chief who had given him the fox-skin cap and yellow horse back in 1800 and had taken La Gasse and Le Blanc across the mountains with him. Bercier had met some of the Kootenais while he was working with Jaco the previous summer and knew that one of their bands had a camp on a lake not too far south. He paddled that way, upstream, in search of the Old Chief and sustenance.

Thompson sent Michel Boulard and three other men back across the Height of Land with the packhorses to get

WHAT THOMPSON KNEW / WHAT HE DIDN'T KNOW

Finan McDonald and the rest of the baggage. Beaulieu was
still too sick to work, so the surveyor and Augustin Boisverd
went out to search for bark and wood to build a big canoe.
Everybody was hungry, and the pemmican was all gone.
The two Ojibway hunters had not produced much, and now
Thompson sent them word that he was going to eat one of
their horses if they did not deliver some food to the campsite
soon. Half a deer and a small beaver appeared forthwith. On
July 8 Bercier returned with enough meat for a proper meal
and three Kootenai boys to help hunt. That same morning
Thompson had a chance to exercise his medical skills:

> Beaulieu has been these ten days so very ill that he could
> not help us & at length so much so, that we despaired of
> his Life – his Complaint a violent Cholic & Pain under

his ribs on the Left. This Morning, perceiving a small
Swelling close under his left Rib, mid of the side to be
enlarging – he was feeling it with attention, & by his
finger feeling something rough he sent for me. It appeared to be a small splinter – I extracted it & to our
great surprise found it was a porcurpine Quill, that had
made its appearance from the inwards, it was of the short
thick ones on the Rump & Tail of the Porcurpine. it can
be accounted for only by supposing that when he eat
part of the Dog the day we passed the Height of Land,
he had in eating the Meat swallowed the Porcurpine
Quill in the Meat, as he is a voracious eater.

West of the Divide nobody was eating voraciously. When
Finan McDonald and his helpers arrived with the rest of the
goods two days later, Thompson wrote that he "shared the
last morsel with the men." The next day, fasting, they finished the big canoe. On July 12 Thompson sent the Ojibway
hunters back east with a letter to James Hughes at Fort
Augustus, and was loading his boats when the three Kootenai
boys arrived with part of an elk. The explorer divided the
meat among his men, distributed hooks and lines so everyone
could fish along the way, and led off upstream in the small
canoe. Nobody caught any fish, but they did shoot nine swans
on July 13. On the 14th they went hunting but shot nothing;
on the 15th they found a few gooseberries for dinner; on the
16th they came upon a small Kootenai camp, whose occu-
pants could offer only a few pounds of venison. Thompson
explained that his people were starving, and gave the
Kootenais some tobacco and ammunition. "Two of them went
a hunting & killed 3 Swans, which like a Hog they devoured
without giving us a mouthful."

On July 18 the canoes reached the lake known today as
Windermere, a promising location. The woods had given way
to hilly grasslands, natural pastures for wild horses that had
escaped from the Kootenai herds. There were berries along

the shore, which the travelers soon devoured. In the afternoon, nine men from a Kootenai camp they had passed brought them half a *chevreuil*. (When Thompson said *chevreuil*, he meant deer, and from his usage it could be anything from a large mule deer to a white-tailed deer to a small pronghorn antelope. He figured that a small *chevreuil* yielded about the right amount of food for one meal for ten of his meat-hungry men.) The Nor'Westers finished off the meat the Kootenais had brought, then set out nets to catch some of the small fish they had spotted in the lake.

Michel Boulard, meanwhile, had been leading the horses upriver, and now he arrived with only three of the twenty-four mounts entrusted to him, "having left all the others behind from the badness of the Roads & his own laziness." This was a serious handicap, for the men needed horses to haul trees for buildings and to go hunting and exploring. Disturbed by these unexpected problems, Thompson had to cancel his plans to push farther south:

> From the State of the Country & the Situation of my Affairs I found myself necessitated to lay aside all Thoughts of Discovery for the present & bend my whole aim to an establishment for Trade etc.—and as our pressing necessities did not allow Time for Thought upon Thought, I set off to look out for a place where we might build, that as soon as I saw the Property in safety & a mode of living for the People I might be at liberty to seize every favourable opportunity of extending my knowledge of the country.

The next morning he and his men pulled in their nets, found them empty, and began looking for a good building site. After much searching they settled on a high bluff above the river where there was a small grove of trees. While scouting around, they came upon the body of a wild horse the Kootenais had killed the day before. Even though "a strong taint pervaded the whole carcase," they decided to cut off

some of the meat and test it. They brought a sample back
to camp, boiled it over the fire, and "shared a small piece to
every Man who joyfully eat it, in hopes of its being portable
in the Stomach. Hunger is an excellent Sauce, we found the
Taste tolerable good." Thinking they had just found a few
days' groceries, three of the men hurried back to the carcass
to "dispute with the wolves" and carried into camp a hundred
pounds of meat. But about two hours later, they all became
violently sick to their stomachs. Thompson optimistically
concluded that this had nothing to do with the innate quality
of wild horseflesh, only its advanced state of putrefaction.

That evening he called together the few Kootenai men
camped near the lake. They told him that the Old Chief and
most of their people were hunting to the southward, but that
they should be at the lake in about ten more days, along with
a large band of Flatheads, their allies and neighbors to the
south. Thompson engaged three of the Kootenais to take
some tobacco to the tribes to let them know he had arrived,
and to ask the Old Chief to hurry up. Writing to the partners
that night, he muddled through a list of worries until "Sleep
at last relieves me from a Train of anxious thoughts."

Having settled on a spot for the post he called Kootanae
House, Thompson applied his energies to the situation at
hand. He ordered men out to find birch wood to make han-
dles for their axes and other tools and sent Boulard to stay
with a nearby camp of Kootenais and encourage them to
hunt. He traded with some Kootenais for a few beaver and
four beautiful white mountain goat skins, then hafted a dart
for spearing fish in the river and sent Finan McDonald, "who
is the most clever," to try it out. The clerk returned with two
small fish that Thompson called mullet and herring—probably a bull trout and a small rainbow.

The men began felling trees, but the wood was heavy and
hard to cut, and Thompson pronounced it the worst he had
ever tried to work. "July 22nd Wednesday. A very fine Day.
Nothing in the Nets but 1 Mullet – began the Walls of the

Warehouse 16 ft. by 16 ft. – got it half way up – Men are so
weak for want of Food, that they cannot work." That evening
Boulard arrived with the meat of two *chevreuil*. A few days
later the warehouse was finished and the goods were all stored
inside. Thompson continued to worry about feeding the thirteen men and women and six children under his care, and
decided to construct a weir across the river to trap fish. About
that time two new Kootenais arrived. One of them was the
Old Chief's brother, whom the voyageurs called Capot Blanc
(White Coat). Capot Blanc told the furmen that the water
was too high for a weir, but Thompson set his men to work
anyway. They got the barrier about halfway finished before
the current washed it away.

At that point Thompson began listening to Capot Blanc,
who plainly stated that the new post was not in a very good
spot—it was too far from water and vulnerable to attack
by the Piegans, who could be counted on to come and raid
horses at least once a year. He helped Thompson find a better
place a mile downstream from the mouth of the lake, and the
surveyor drew neat plans in his journal for three buildings arranged around a yard that backed onto the river. He fiddled
with their dimensions and placement, squeezing dwellings
and storehouses together until only three-foot pathways separated them—a tight, defensible arrangement.

As the Nor'Westers busied themselves cutting more trees,
other Kootenais began to filter into their nearby camp, bringing in occasional kills of *chevreuil*, elk, and bear, but certainly
not the consistent flow of food that Thompson wanted. He
complained that they spent more time gambling than hunting, and sounded quite cross in early August when five tent-
fuls of hunters arrived and did not generously share their
supply of dried meat. Thompson was now short a hand, because Michel Boulard's contract had run out. Boulard was a
"half-engaged" or "half-free" man, which meant that he
signed an agreement to work for the company for half the
year, then spent the other six months trapping as a "free

hunter" for his own account. There was also a beverage shortage at Kootanae House: the keg of high wine (180-proof whiskey) they had brought across the pass was almost empty. In his *Narrative*, Thompson wrote that he had vowed to keep alcohol away from the west-side tribes, "and thus be clear of the sad sight of drunkenness, and its many evils." But the voyageurs expected their daily ration, and the surveyor had to admit that "a dram had often done us much good."

The men struggled to complete the living quarters and began another warehouse at their new location. Some of them went upriver and split out boards for a rough floor, then floated them down to the site. The water level in the river had begun to drop, and the Kootenais suggested that now would be a good time to build a weir. On August 13, while a couple of old men directed four of the voyageurs at that task, a message arrived at the Kootenai camp that occasioned such crying and shrieking that Thompson, certain an attack was at hand, called his men to arms. After the lamentations died down, the furmen learned that the new arrivals had come from the south, where the main band of the Kootenais had been hunting with the Flatheads. They reported that a large group of Piegans, Bloods, and Blackfeet had crossed the mountains to talk peace, and the parley had gone well until one of the Piegans stole a horse. In the ensuing fracas, the Old Chief's son had been killed, along with several Flatheads and a dozen Piegans. The Old Chief and his Kootenais were now on their way home, but most of the Flatheads, whom Thompson had been so anxious to meet, had decamped to "a military Post of the Americans." The news of Americans anywhere in the region was a surprise. There were forty-two of them, according to the Kootenai messengers, including two members of Lewis and Clark's expedition, and they were building a post somewhere to the south. It was impossible for Thompson to pinpoint the location of this unexpected competition, but wherever they were, his reaction in his-report to the partners was philosophical:

This establishment of the Americans will give a new Turn to our so long delayed settling of this Country, on which we have entered it seems too late; but in my opinion the most valuable part of the Country still remains to us & we have nothing to obstruct us, but the difficulty of getting goods from Fort des Prairies, & the still more formidable poverty of the Country in Animals. Time & Perserverance will show what we can do, & if worth our Expence & Trouble.

During the third week in August, the summer run of salmon arrived. So did twelve young Piegans, who had come across one of the passes that led from their hunting grounds to the Kootenai country. They said that their war chief Kootanae Appee had heard a rumor that the white men were building a house on the west side and had sent them "to see the Truth of the Matter." Thompson had been expecting such a visit, for he knew that the Piegans would be upset when they learned he was supplying arms to their old customers the Kootenais and their old enemies the Flatheads. The Piegans told Thompson that they were "pleased" with his new post, but he did not believe them. "What their future Intentions are Heavens knows – we hope for the best, as it is in their Power to be very troublesome to us." While Finan McDonald went out at night with a flambeau and speared salmon weighing up to twenty-six pounds ("tolerable good, but having come so far had lost all their fatness"), the Piegans hung around, worrisome to Thompson because he thought they must be the scouts for a larger party. But no more showed up, and after a week the visitors got hungry and broke camp, stealing three horses on their way out. Two Kootenais tried to chase down the horse thieves, and the ruckus put the camp into such a state of alarm that the Kootenais repitched their tents right next to the trade house and put all their valuables under the white men's protection.

The next day three new Piegans came to visit, all familiar

to Thompson from the east side and all proclaiming peaceable intentions. Not knowing how long these intentions would hold, the Nor'Westers quickly put up two heavy fences from their compound to the steep bank of the river. When thirty more Piegans arrived, led by two chiefs of Thompson's acquaintance, he went out and met them for a smoke but would not give them any rum or let them inside the yard.

Meanwhile, Bercier had gone to see what was keeping the main band of Kootenais and returned with news that they had been stricken by a "violent Distemper." One of the sick men arrived at the camp next to Kootanae House late that evening: "They sang around him all night, he says that many of them are very sick & several Children dead, it seems by the Hooping Cough." During the next week, more sick Kootenais straggled in, and Thompson administered doses of Turlington (an elixir of balsamic resin) from the supply he had brought with him. The Piegans, unalarmed by the sickness, stayed on.

At this point Thompson rehired Michel Boulard, reflecting that "he is useful in many respects more than another & many respects much less so – upon the whole he is a cheap bargain." Thompson had complained about Boulard's laziness and irresponsibility in the past, but the man was a good interpreter, and Thompson was feeling the need for someone with a knack for language. It had been twenty years since his winter with Saukamappee, and the Piegan he had learned then was not sufficient for the present situation. The tongues being spoken in his camp included English, French, Piegan Blackfeet, Kootenai, and Charlotte Thompson's Cree; the Flatheads traveling with the Kootenais spoke yet another distinct language. In a letter to the partners a few months later, Thompson described his difficulties: "What I say in French is to be spoken in Blackfoot, then in Kootanae, then in Flat Head etc. etc. so that the sense is fairly translated away before it arrives at the person spoken to."

With Boulard to help him interpret, Thompson had a talk

with the Piegans, who were finally getting hungry enough to think about leaving. As an inducement for them to decamp peacefully, he presented each chief with a foot of tobacco and five rounds of ammunition, and the other men with two inches of smoke and a paper of vermilion, the powdered red clay that the natives valued for body paint. After they were gone, Thompson heard a rumor that they were only waiting for the right occasion to plunder his post and drive him from the country. Two Piegans had stayed behind to gamble with the Kootenais, and Thompson called them in for a reckoning. They confessed that several of the young men had been looking to start trouble, but that the elders wanted to stay on good terms with the white men and had calmed things down for the time being. "I told them that we were well prepared for the worst that could happen, & that if any Trouble was given us, it was a very easy thing to build out of their Power, & where they would never get a pipe of Tobacco from us."

Three days later a more congenial group arrived—a dozen Flat Bow men and one woman, carrying small packs of furs on their backs. These people were a band of the Kootenais who lived to the south and west, and they had never seen white people before. They told Thompson that no elk or moose lived in their country, but sturgeon and berries were plentiful, and beaver abounded. They had brought beaver, bear, cat, otter, and fisher skins to trade, with a little sturgeon oil and a bushel of berries thrown in, which they exchanged for some ammunition, axes, and a kettle. Among the Flat Bows were two old men who "spoke much to the purpose on all questions I asked, & after drawing a Chart of their country & from thence to the Sea, & describing the Nations along the River, they assured me that from this House to the Sea & back again was only the Voyage of a Summer Moon; but from the number of Falls etc. it does not appear easy to go without a Guide." Thompson tried to talk the Flat Bows into taking him on a quick trip south to see whether the large river flowing through their homeland might possibly be the Columbia. But the old men told him that it was too late in the fall and that besides, he would have to wait for their chief, Ugly Head, "as he alone was capable of protecting us in distant Countries."

While Thompson was smoking and talking with the Flat Bows, dogs were also on his mind. The Kootenais had often warned the Nor'Westers not to let their dogs eat raw salmon flesh, but no one had paid any attention. For the past two weeks, however, several of the camp dogs had been very dull and lethargic, "always lying down in some lonesome place and sleeping, refusing all food, & scarcely lifting their Head even at the voice of their Master." On the evening of September 18, three of their best pups "made their exit."

On September 23 Finan McDonald and five voyageurs headed back across the mountains to drop off the summer's furs and pick up more supplies. Because of their horse shortage, Thompson was obliged to buy one from the Kootenais, who charged him a gun and a foot of tobacco for one sorry animal. These were black market prices for the explorer— back at Rocky Mountain House, he had purchased two good horses for five pints of rum—but the trip had to be made. Along with the pelts, Thompson sent off his report on the summer's adventures, a request for an extra man for the coming year, and a strange letter he had received from a Kootenai messenger. Dated July 10, 1807, at "Fort Lewis, Yellow River, Columbia" and signed "Zachery Perch, Captain and Commander, and James Roseman, Lieutenant, U.S. Army," the letter addressed itself to "Foreigners who may at present be carrying on a Traffic with the Indians within our Territories." It listed rigid mandates concerning liquor sales, flag raising, and trade practices, then ended with a sweeping American claim for the entire Northwest—including the Columbia River and all its branches, "of which we have now taken possession and on which we are now settled down to the Pacific Ocean." This epistle must have come from the same Americans whom the Kootenais had told him about earlier, and although Thompson did not record his reaction, he had learned enough about the area to deduce that the authors were either outrageous liars or had seriously misplaced the Pacific Ocean. As far as anyone knows, he did not honor the officers with a reply.

Two days after Finan McDonald departed, the long-awaited Old Chief of the Kootenais arrived, accompanied by the Flat Bow chief Ugly Head, so named for his curly hair. They told Thompson that during their peace parley with the Blackfeet tribes a few weeks earlier, they had heard that a party of Bloods and Blackfeet had pillaged Fort Augustus on the Saskatchewan during the summer. They did not know whether anyone had been killed, only that the raiding party had gotten away with guns, ammunition, tobacco, and the clothes off the traders' backs. This was alarming news to Thompson, for Fort Augustus was the residence of his colleagues James Hughes and McDonald of Garth and the destination of Finan McDonald. There had been other violent episodes with the Blackfeet tribes on the Saskatchewan, and Thompson knew just how vulnerable his little outpost would be if the trouble spread. All but three of his voyageurs had gone east with Finan McDonald, and even if they made the trip safely, it would be weeks before they returned. As it turned out, the men at Fort Augustus were safe, but the Hudson Bay Company's South Branch House had been over-run and the chief trader there killed.

When Ugly Head offered to guide Thompson to his country for a quick visit, the surveyor juggled his concern about an attack with his desire to investigate the course of the river on which the Flat Bows lived. On October 2 he made up his mind and, leaving his family and Kootanae House under the care of his three remaining men, he set off with Ugly Head and his wife, communicating by signs and a few words. With snow gathering on the mountaintops, they headed south on horseback from Windermere Lake and around a second lake, then crossed over a short portage to a large river that swept south out of the Rockies. They rode downriver on a well-used path through open woods and grassy meadows. Thompson had spent the summer feeling frustrated about his lack of exploration, but now that he was on the move, he couldn't stop worrying about the Blackfeet tribes. After two days he had seen enough of the river to know that it was navigable, and when the horse trail cut inland he told Ugly Head that he needed to get back. They turned around and retraced their steps—up the river, across the portage, and, unbeknownst to Thompson, right beside the headwaters of the Columbia River.

COLUMBIA LAKE, the actual source of the river, lies only a few miles upstream from Windermere Lake in southeastern British Columbia. It is long and narrow, hemmed in on the east by the ponderous, bare-shouldered Mount Sabine and on the west by the Purcell Range. There is no sign of rushing streams or a birthing spring; instead, the lake seems to ooze up from a shallow basin, and swords of sedge grass peek up far offshore. A few years ago the hills along the west side were blackened by a forest fire, and now summer finds them rife with charcoal spikes of Douglas fir and new pink fireweed. Along the lake's shoreline, white hoodoos catch the sunlight, their fluted columns intricately carved by wind and water. A little camping park called Thunder Hill overlooks the south end of the lake, and I was poking about there when a park ranger drove in to pick up the trash.

Unlike a Stateside ranger, this one didn't wear a uniform or ride in an official vehicle. He drove his own pickup, an older, squeaky-clean Dodge, and he was eager to talk. "Oh yes, the fire. Four summers ago, on the hottest afternoon you've ever seen. We sweated it out for a while, but you can see how it just nipped past us. She burned a lot of fine timber, quick and hot. They've found a way to mill a lot of what's left standing. The bad part of it is, though, they've had to cut it all as quick as they can. In four years I reckon they've fallen what it would have taken them twenty if they'd just cut it on their regular cycle. Threw their plans out of whack a bit. But you should see all the elk coming back in on the new growth now."

We looked out over Columbia Lake, and the ranger explained to me how the Columbia River bubbled up here and flowed north. He pointed down at Canal Flats, an open plain about one mile in breadth, which separates the Columbia from another big river that sneaks out from behind Mount Sabine and runs south. This south-flowing river is the one that Ugly Head had shown to David Thompson. At first Thompson called it the Flat Bow, but later he renamed it McGillivrays River in honor of his bosses Duncan and William. Today it is known as the Kootenay River in British Columbia and the Kootenai in Montana and Idaho. Looking down on Canal Flats from Thunder Hill, it was hard not to be amazed at how this one small strip of land in the middle of the entire Rocky Mountain Trench divides the headwaters of the Columbia from the Kootenay. I understood for the first time how David Thompson could make the switch with an easy portage and zip down into what is now the United States. The ranger nodded enthusiastically; he knew he was the steward of a good place, even if most fishermen shunned it.

"Nobody fishes Columbia Lake much. It's what we call a coarse-fish lake—trout, bass, sucker, kokanee, all mixed up together. The sportsmen run up to White Swan. That's because we killed that one out three years ago and fresh stocked it with rainbow trout. But I've heard this lake here used to be something else. There's an old-timer around who remembers salmon coming into the lake. Salmon! And seals too, he said. Seals."

The ranger saw my eyes widen—a harbor seal fourteen hundred miles upriver did sound a little outrageous—and backed off a bit: "That's just what the old-timer said now, couldn't prove it by me. I can see salmon maybe, before the dams. But seals—that's hard to swallow. That's what the old-timer said, though. Salmon and seals. And he was a lot closer to it than we are now."

Later, I got lost up in the eerie landscape of the burn. Scaly outcrops of rock tilted up like furrows in a giant field, and to walk at all I had to keep my eyes on the ground. When I did look up, there was wilderness all around: the massive Rockies across the river to the east, the craggy Purcells straight above me to the west. As I followed the outcrops back and forth, trying to make my way out of an island of charred blackness into the vast ocean of greenery that ringed the mountains, the notion of an animal from another time didn't seem so amazing. The Old Chief told David Thompson a story about a creature who lived up in these woods, an animal that stood eighteen feet tall and could never lie down, but had to lean against big trees to catch a nap. The Kootenais thought this was because it had no joints in the middle of its legs, but they couldn't say for sure since they had never been able to kill one and examine it. "Nurses Fables," Thompson called the tales, and got the Kootenais to admit that they had "rarely or never" seen one. Thompson had heard similar fables from other tribes, and whenever I read one of these tales I couldn't help thinking about woolly mammoths. Weren't mammoths supposed to stand almost eighteen feet tall? And didn't they sleep on their feet? Natives in the East told Thompson that in the old days mammoths lived all over their country and fed on other animals, including people. Eventually the Great Spirit grew tired of their ravenous ways and brought out his thunderbolts to kill them all. One big bull survived the onslaught and, with an enormous leap, escaped the wrath of the Great Spirit. He had run away to the West, they said, and lived there still. I liked the idea of an old kneeless bull leaning up against one of these trees above the Columbia while seals swam around in the lake below. Even more, I liked the fact that David Thompson occasionally found room in his daybooks for the fabulous.

WHEN THOMPSON got back to Kootanae House on October 6, he found Boulard, Buché, and Boisverd busy cutting pickets for a stockade. The surveyor sent the women out to dig watap for tying the logs together and began standing up the heavy posts. Work speeded up two weeks later when word arrived that the Blackfeet and Bloods had declared war on the Kootenais for supplying arms to the Flatheads, and on Thompson's post for supporting the west-side tribes. So far the Piegan bands had not joined their kin in the hostilities, but there was no way to know what might happen. Everyone prepared for an attack; the Kootenais tied their horses to their tents, and the white men quickly put up a bastion. On October 26, working together, they completed the stockade, then held a council to decide on a course of action in case they were attacked. They all agreed to "give them battle the moment they appear," and Ugly Head set off to alert the other bands of the danger. During the next six weeks there were sporadic reports of gunfire and war songs from across the lake, but no war parties materialized.

The salmon run was over now, and the shores were littered with dead fish. The men harvested trout and an occasional loon from their nets and hunted the swans that were gathering on the lakes to winter. Snow in the mountains was pushing the big game back down into the valley, and Kootenai hunters like Chien Faux (Deceitful Dog) and the Gauche (Left Hand) brought in fresh elk and *chevreuil* on a regular basis. In early November Finan McDonald and his crew returned safely with supplies from the east side. In addition to the regular array of trade items and new clothes for the men, Thompson's order included a keg of French brandy, two blank notebooks, a pair of brass candlesticks, a pound each of cinnamon and cloves, a bottle of "Eau de Luce" (toilet water), twenty pounds of marbled soap, twenty-four bottles each of peppermint (for digestion) and Turlington, two papers of black ink powder, and six black lead pencils.

With the warehouse full of fresh goods, Thompson was anxious to trade. He sent Boulard out to encourage the Kootenais to hunt beaver while their winter pelage was at its prime, for these thick pelts brought the best prices at the London markets. But winter was traditionally a time of relative leisure for the Kootenais, because game was concentrated in the valleys and the bands could gather together to socialize. In mid-November the families tenting near Kootanae House were all busy accumulating meat for a big dancing feast, and Thompson had the Old Chief deliver a "Harangue" for them to break camp and get after the beaver.

By December there was plenty of snow in the passes to keep war parties away, and things had calmed down enough for Thompson to get some bookwork done. On December 11 he noted that he had "Transcribed Capn Lewis's account of his journey to the Pacific Ocean." This account was actually a long letter written by Meriwether Lewis about his expedition to the Pacific. Finan McDonald must have brought it back from the Saskatchewan on his supply run, but no one has ever discovered how it fell into the hands of the North West Company. Wherever it came from, Lewis's letter provided information of great interest to Thompson, including a summary of Lewis and Clark's route up the Missouri River, across the Rockies, and down to the Pacific. From the account Thompson would have learned that the lower Columbia beyond the mouth of the Snake River was navigable to the sea.

Thompson copied Lewis's letter into the same notebook in which he had entered extracts of Vancouver's *Voyages* six years earlier, then turned to the lighter task of repairing a hand-cranked barrel organ that had been knocked to pieces on its trip over the pass. During the next week he built a desk,

caught up on his accounting, and finished arranging the
"Barrel of Music." On December 18 five Piegans came across
the mountains with a welcome update: the Blackfeet tribes
were now embroiled in a war with the Crees on the east side
and no longer had any intention of bothering anyone on the
west side of the mountains. During the next few days,
a Flathead chief and four of his men arrived, then the Old
Chief and four tents of his people. The Flatheads and
Kootenais got together with the Piegans to smoke and talk
peace, and spent Christmas night in dancing. The next day
the Piegans left for home, and Thompson made arrangements
with the Flatheads about collecting beaver for trade in the
spring.

It was probably this same group of Flatheads and
Kootenais that brought in a second note from the mysterious
American military officers. This one was dated September 29,
1807, and addressed "To the British Mercht trafficking with
the Cotanaiss." It was signed by "U.S. Lieutenant Jeremy
Pinch," whose name looks suspiciously like the Zachery Perch
who had signed the first letter. Pinch rebuked Thompson for
his failure to respond to the Americans' original proclamation
and stridently demanded that he retreat from his position: "We
have more powerful means of persuasion in our hands than
we have hitherto used, we shall with regret apply Force . . .
You will see Sir the necessity of submitting and with good
grace." The letter ended with complaints that marauding
Piegans had wounded one of the American soldiers, and that
British furmen ought to stop supplying these scoundrels with
weapons and ammunition.

Thompson chose to answer this threat, and on December
26 he sent off a calm reply to "your polite favor of the 29th
Sept." He noted that he was not politician enough to settle
boundary disputes, but that it was his understanding that
George Vancouver's initial exploration of the lower Columbia
gave Great Britain claim to the river. He assured the
Americans that he would forward their demands back East for

consideration by the North West Company. Thompson sent a copy of the note to his partners, adding his own assessment of the affair: "not one of these petty officers but what has as much arrogance as Buonaparte at the head of his Invincibles."

Western historians have driven themselves to distraction trying to figure out the origin of these letters. There are no records of U.S. military expeditions anywhere near the Northwest during this time, nor are there records of any officers in the U.S. Army that match the three names signed on the two letters. The best guess seems to be that they came from a party that left St. Louis in April of 1807, led by independent furman Manuel Lisa. An ambitious man often surrounded by intrigue, Lisa did have forty-two men in his party. He did pick up two veterans of the Lewis and Clark Expedition on his way up the Missouri. He did meet up with a Canadian trader at the Mandan village who could have mentioned Thompson's expedition to the Kootenais. Some of his men did have trouble with the Piegans. But Lisa's fort was on the Yellowstone River, on the east side of the Divide, and quite a ways to the south; it was nowhere near the Columbia as claimed in the letters. The only things that can be said for certain about this incident are that whoever they were, the Americans had their sights on the big river, and wherever they were, the native tribes were keeping track of them and the other newcomers in their territories over thousands of square miles.

January of 1808 found Michel Boulard making an ice house, or "glacier," in which to store the abundance of fresh meat that Chien Faux and other Kootenai hunters were hauling in. Thompson's new year did not get off to such a happy start: he sprained his knee on an icy bank and had to limp around on a crutch for the entire month. While his men made birch pipestems for smoking with the chiefs and gathered aspen wood for a sled, he "arranged the desk for papers and drawing etc." On clear nights he took observations on Kootanae House (latitude 50° 32' 12" N, longitude 115° 56'

15" W) and on clear days he measured the elevations of local landmarks, especially one impressive peak that loomed behind the western shore of Windermere Lake. He named the uplift Mount Nelson, after the admiral whose heroics at the Battle of Trafalgar two years before had thwarted Napoleon's plan to invade England.

At his desk Thompson recopied the long lists of compass courses from his field books into a neat table, arranging them in columns alongside the coordinates from his observations. Many days were then spent reworking mistakes and inconsistencies. When it was finally time to draw an actual map, he used these numbers to re-create the curves of a given river between his fixed points of latitude and longitude. He penciled in the outlines and then inked, tinted, and shaded the topography onto a series of foolscap sheets that measured sixteen by thirteen inches each. Laid together, these sheets filled in a few more sections of the wilderness.

The surveyor also made time to go horseback riding almost every day, the better to learn his new territory. He found the weather on the west side of the Divide mild compared with what he had grown used to in the East—so mild, in fact, that the birch rind growing there was too thin to make good canoes. He hunted elk and antelope and tried going after the mountain goats up in the hills, but without much success; the Kootenais told him they were wicked animals that kicked down stones on hunters.

Aside from his daily entry of "Drawing, etc.," the events that Thompson chose to record over this first winter at Kootanae House almost all took place during the day, and out of doors. But he was living in a latitude that gets barely eight hours of sun in the winter months, and even allowing for his nocturnal observations, the great majority of his time must have been spent indoors. Fur trade journals did not usually dwell on personal matters, and Thompson's was no exception. There is no hint of Charlotte's role. There are no descriptions of furnishings, utensils, or of playing that odd barrel organ.

There is no comment on what it was like to work out several hours of trigonometry by a grease lamp with three kids playing on the rough floor of a small cabin. There is no mention of how his men were entertaining themselves during the long evenings, although his supply order for this season had included a request for two decks of playing cards.

Whatever was going on inside Thompson's stockade at off hours, there was no mystery about how the Kootenai men were spending their spare time.

> Febry 6th   Saturday   Rode 4 Hours – Drawing – Netmaking . . . After a long gambling Match, one Kootanae has gained near the whole. His gains are 17 Red Deer Skins – 24 Chevreuil – 1 Gun – 3 Axes – 10 Knives – 350 Balls – 7 lbs. of Powder – 6 Horses & Saddles – Saddle Stuff etc. – 1 Robe – 1 Blanket & many small Articles besides 2 good Tents. The others have only their Wives, Children, and old leather clothing left.

On March 1, half a dozen Piegans arrived from across the mountains, carrying with them letters that had been sent from Fort Augustus three months earlier. Thompson quickly wrote answers, which the Piegans carried with them when they returned to the east side two days later. Of the hundreds of letters Thompson sent off during his career, copies of the two missives he entrusted to the Piegans are among the very few that have survived. One was a "public letter," addressed to James Hughes, Donald McTavish, and John McDonald of Garth but meant for the eyes of all the partners. Here Thompson tries to explain that the west side of the mountains is "utterly different" from anything they have ever experienced, and says he has had a terrible time finding food over the summer due to a lack of fish and especially rabbits ("Were these plenty I should be at my ease, as I yield to none in the country in the art of killing them"). He has also had trouble convincing the Kootenais and Flatheads that he would rather receive beaver skins than the horses and berries that are their own favorite items. Yet the natives look upon his arrival as a godsend, and if he can induce them to hunt beaver, he is certain the company's investment will pay off. He speaks highly of the prospects of the country he has seen so far and thinks it would be a good idea to send over ten or twelve good Iroquois free hunters to help trap. He hopes he can make thirty packs of furs this season and asks for a two-year trial period on the west side, saying that if his efforts don't show a profit by then, he will be willing to give it up. He closes his letter with a request for a forge, a blacksmith, two good hoes, and some extra blue beads.

Thompson's second letter was addressed to Donald McTavish, an agent in the Athabasca district whom he must have come to know well during his own years there. Thompson thanks his friend for his support, revealing his awareness that other partners of the company are set against his whole enterprise across the mountains. He rails at their short-sightedness and at his own lack of knowledge about the "fluctuating politics" within the company. But he also conveys his excitement about the possibilities of the west side: "I wish to heaven you could be transported by some Geniis to see how this Country is formed and the pains and trouble I have taken to carry on our Business." He adds up all the expenses so far on his expedition to the shilling, tallying the cost of provisions and the men's wages, and figures that he just might come out of it with a profit at the end of the year. "You know that I do nothing without calculation, so that I know fairly what I am about."

Near the end of his letter to McTavish, Thompson makes a personal request: "I must now again beg of you to take my little child under your protection and if possible to get him from his mother . . . you might send him to Fort Augustus or contrive some way or other to put him in my hands – at least see him well clothed and of course charge it to my account." The mother that he refers to cannot be Charlotte, since she is at Kootanae House with him. Apparently at some point

Thompson had a child by another woman in the Athabasca district and left them both behind. This was not an uncommon practice among the furmen; what is unusual is his attempt to get custody of the child. Having asked his favor, Thompson tells McTavish that the Piegans who brought the letters are in a hurry to be off, and bids his friend adieu.

Two days later a North West Company clerk named James McMillan rode in behind a dog team, bringing Kootanae House more news and supplies from the east side. The surveyor dashed off another batch of correspondence and five days later sent it back to the Saskatchewan with McMillan, transported by dogsled. Thompson was trying to keep in close touch with a world that seemed very far away.

CHAPTER FIVE

BORDER CROSSING

SPRING 1808–WINTER 1809

B Y MID-APRIL of 1808, the willows around Kootanae
House were leafing out, and Thompson was ready to
continue the trip he had started with Ugly Head the previous fall. Leaving Finan McDonald in charge of the post, he
retraced his route south along the two source lakes and across
the Canal Flats portage to put into the Kootenay River. While
four voyageurs paddled the canoe downstream, Thompson
the geographer was hard at work, listing compass directions
and distances as usual. He noted the location of rapids and
shoals, the mouths of tributaries, and good camping spots.
And all the time he was scanning the surrounding terrain,
studying the way the country was put together.

As they moved south, the explorer remarked on the
new leaves of gooseberry and aspen, and the appearance of
Douglas fir among the mix of trees. He saw elk and *chevreuil*,
a few wolves, and many ducks. When they put up to camp
on the second evening, one of the men shot a goose and got
eight eggs out of her nest. Thompson wrote glowingly of
the country's prospects: "April 22nd Friday Morning a little

Exploring the Kootenai Country

Cloudy but clear in the afternoon ... the River in general has a very smooth easy Current with a sufficient depth of Water & where we are camped the Points of fine Meadows & the first ground I have seen that I think has sufficient moisture to farm a Garden for Herbs."

It rained the next day and they stayed in camp to re-gum the canoe, which had been badly scraped on some shallow rapids. When the rain stopped, they floated on past the mouth of the St. Mary's River, which was as far as Thompson had made it the previous October on his quick trip with Ugly Head. He had been remarking on the scarcity of beaver sign ever since he left Columbia Lake, but on this stretch he spotted some lodges and set out traps every evening in hopes of catching a meal. The nights were frosty and the current of the river picked up, keeping his senses on alert; he was mesmerized by tiny whirlpools on the surface of the river that made "a hissing noise as if they were full of small icicles."

As they slipped below the 49th parallel on April 25, the canoe began taking on water again, and they stopped to camp in one of the beautiful meadows that lined each side of the river. "This is the place where the Indians speak so much of growing their tobacco; and we named them on that account, the Tobacco Meadows." The Kootenais had told him about this area, and about their practice of burying a dead fish beneath each tobacco seedling at planting time. Looking through his telescope, Thompson could see that the grasslands continued up onto the hills to the east. Now known as Tobacco Plains, these open hills were prime habitat for bitterroot, a low-growing pink flower whose root was an important vegetable food for many western tribes. Bands of Kootenais gathered here every summer, and the women fanned out across the dry hillsides with their pointed willow digging sticks to twist up great mounds of the fleshy bitterroot bulbs. They spread the roots in the sun to dry, then ate them boiled or stewed with meat.

Thompson had made plans to meet some of the

Kootenais here and sent two voyageurs off to look for them. They found a few tracks, a trail leading downriver, a place where six lodges had recently been taken down, and one skunk, which they killed and brought to camp. The men spent the next few days hunting and repairing their canoe while they waited for the Kootenais. Just before they landed, Thompson had remarked on what he thought would be a fine location for a trade house, but he couldn't do much scouting because he had sprained his knee again. He did attempt to go hunting, but was so lame that he needed a stick to walk. "April 30th Saturday A fine Day – Gale at South – visited our traps – nothing . . . our Subsistence this day was a Dram of Rum & half a Partridge [grouse] per man."

The next morning they heard a man calling from across the river. It was Le Monde, a Kootenai who had hunted for them at Windermere Lake, and the Nor'Westers fetched him and his family in the canoe and gave him some balls and powder for hunting. Thompson spent part of that night observing for longitude, but had to skip the next one because he had already used up most of his candles. Two days later Le Monde killed a mountain lion, "His Tail 2 ft. 10 in. – Coulour of a Fawn – Belly white very strong Legged & sharp Claws . . . very good Food & yields as much meat as a Chevreuil."

Thompson decided that he must have missed his rendezvous with the Kootenais and tried to hire Le Monde to go south as their guide. But Le Monde did not want to leave his family, so the furmen continued downriver on their own. Along the way they emulated a common native practice by setting ground fires to clear the brush and attract game to the new growth that would follow. By evening they had left the grasslands behind and passed into a rich forest of big trees; Thompson measured one tamarack that was 13 feet around and 150 feet clear to its first branch and noted what fine masts such trees would make for the Royal Navy. Another day of paddling brought them to an abrupt westward turn in the river's course. The wooded hills began to close in on them, the banks turned to steep cliffs, and within twenty miles they came upon the cataracts of Kootenai Falls thundering through a tight, S-shaped canyon. The only portage they could find around the falls was a long and treacherous animal trail three hundred feet above the river. "The least slip would have been inevitable destruction, as the steepness of the rock allowed no return; or, in once falling, to stop till precipitated into the river."

The men put on two pairs of shoes, but the rocks soon cut them to pieces. Each trip across the portage took over an hour, and it was nightfall before they got all the packs over the path. They made a light supper from the last of their provisions and next morning faced the daunting task of fetching the canoe. Two voyageurs usually carried one boat, but even with some of the timbers removed, it was all four men could do to maneuver the canoe around the cliffs that edged the narrow trail, and "it was with difficulty preserved from breaking against the rocks."

ON THE MUGGY summer day when I happened along, that same nasty portage had the Montana Department of Highways out in force, trying to make a more secure shelf for the road between the towns of Troy and Libby. They had blasted thousands of tons of rock down onto the old roadbed, and flaggers were allowing traffic to creep through the construction zone only once every two hours, day and night. While motorists swore and sweated, yellow bulldozers and front-end loaders pawed away at the bedded purple stone that forms the tumultuous landscape around Kootenai Falls.

I got out of the car to stretch and watched the vehicles stack up behind me. A pickup truck pulled a shiny boat, probably headed for some kokanee fishing on a dammed-up section of the Kootenai River. A muddy logging truck groaned under the weight of big Douglas fir and tamarack.

The twin trailers of a mule-train ore truck were ferrying milled earth from somewhere deep underground to a smelter across the Canadian border. David Thompson had fished the eddies at the base of Kootenai Falls and pointed out the marketable timber as he paddled downstream, but he had no premonition that the rocks that shredded his shoes and tore at his canoe would ever be in demand by anyone. Within seventy years of his passage, however, a mad gold rush was luring the first white settlers into the area. The gold played out long-ago, but in the years since, copper, silver, lead, zinc, and vermiculite have all taken their turns at fueling the local economy.

I wormed my way through the roadwork and on into downtown Libby, where I caught up with Terry Webster just finishing lunch. "I figured you were sitting out there waiting for the pilot car," he grinned. "Everybody else is." Terry works for the Hard Rock Division of the Montana Bureau of Lands, which oversees permits on all mining jobs in the state, and he was in town that day to check on a couple of big mines—one slowly winding down, the other just starting up. He filled me in on the details as we drove down Main Street past the Stitch 'n' Shoot, a needlepoint and ammo supply shop, then over to the office of the Kootenai National Forest. Terry talked with a couple of foresters there, then made sure that I heard the story of the local Howard brothers. Grubstake miners from Libby's earliest days, the Howards got advance word that the railroad was headed their way and came down from their mining claim to stake out the area where they guessed the tracks would have to pass. Railroad officials moving ahead of the track crew arrived in the valley to find a sea of flagged ground and figured the Howard boys had them by the shorts. After long negotiations, the brothers bargained the railroad slicks right out of a pair of round-trip tickets to Chicago, with sleepers, on the first passenger train that steamed out of town.

Back outside the office, Terry pointed up toward a huge

carved hill that dominated Libby's landscape like a stairst-epped Mayan temple, roaded and sculpted over time. "That's where we're headed," he said: "Vermiculite Mountain." After almost a half century in operation, the company that had mined the mountain was shutting it down, and for the rest of the afternoon we wound through a maze of muddy tail-ings and freshly planted fir seedlings as Terry checked on the progress of their reclamation efforts. By the time he finished his inspection it was late in the day. His next appointment was early the following morning in the opposite direction, and he had planned to get a head start by camping out along the way. We drove out of town and soon turned south onto a washboarded Forest Service road that led up into the Cabinet Range.

The Cabinets lie directly south of Libby and the Kootenai River—they are the "right tolerable snowy mountains" that David Thompson faced as he paddled from Tobacco Plains toward Kootenai Falls. The crest of this range was set aside as a National Wilderness Area several years ago, and as we bounced along Terry caught me up on the controversy now swirling around its peaks. Deep beneath the mountains lies a mammoth deposit of copper and silver ore. Many people thought that wilderness status would squelch any plans for extracting it, but an old mining claim on a neighboring ridge provided a foothold in the area, and a consortium of U.S. and Canadian companies called Montanore had obtained a permit to drill an exploratory tunnel. "*Quite* a deal," Terry said. "You can imagine the screaming and yelling over that piece of paper."

We were riding on what would be a main access route for the proposed mine, and Terry kept waving one arm out the window to describe changes of immense proportion: electrical power lines roping through the forest here, the backup from a three-hundred-foot impoundment dam there. Near the top of the drainage, though, his conversation veered away from the effects of the Montanore project and onto which twisted side road he might be able to negotiate with his pickup. "How's that one look? Too scraggly . . . too many tire tracks . . . ah, I'm gettin' hungry . . . what the heck—let's try this one."

He banged his Ford across the gravel pile of some gold prospector's old sluicebox operation, bucking mightily to reach a flat area at the end of the track, and backed up to a spot of tall grass beside the stream. We hopped out and walked a circle around the pickup. "Looks good to me," Terry said. "Let's set up."

Terry doesn't camp out quite like anyone else I know. He clambered into the bed of his pickup and shoved out a wooden picnic table that had spent the day holding down a sizable piece of green canvas. While I got the table roughly leveled, he rolled back the tarp and produced canvas folding chairs, a two-burner propane stove, a milk crate packed with utensils and condiments, a pair of Army-issue air mattresses, two battery-powered lanterns, and three sacks of groceries. "Bring on the grizzly bears," he chortled as a package of hamburger tumbled onto the ground. The next thing I knew, he was revving a little orange chain saw and wading into a patch of beetle-killed pines. Within ten minutes he had whacked out enough firewood for a night's stay in the bush. He switched off the saw, tossed out a rusty double-bitted ax head he had found inside the copse, and then stepped back into the clearing to survey his handiwork. Once again, he approved.

"Some people," he said, "just don't understand how to get set up."

Next morning Terry and I drove farther up Libby Creek to Montanore's base of operations. A section of rough hillside had been completely stripped of timber and enclosed with a tall cyclone fence; an access road carved into the steep hill switchbacked down to a flat area crowded with heavy equipment and wet, fractured rock. Terry swept his arm around the enclosure. "Yep," he said. "Some old-timer patented this forty acres as a claim years ago, and it ends up as a little piece of private land in the middle of the national forest. Now there's

your wilderness area right up there." He pointed across to
the spine of the Cabinets, where long outcrops of bare rock
folded up to form the crown of each summit; the one called
Elephant Peak shimmered like a dancer in the blue air above
the scene.

"So Montanore comes along and—you've got to picture
this now—and they figured that if they start right here"—he
held one fist out and lined up his knuckles with the trio of big
peaks directly in front of us, then wormed a finger sideways
between two of the knuckles to the opposite, hidden side of
his hand—"and bore this tunnel for about three and a half
miles under the mountains over there, they think they'll run
smack dead into their ore body." While I took in the crust of
trees and dirt and crumbling talus, Terry's eyes drilled straight
into the bedrock.

"So here's the deal. We gave them a permit for one exploratory shaft. Now *if* they manage to hit the right spot, and
if they decide the stuff has a high enough ore content, and *if*
there's enough of it, *then* they've got to prove they can pull
this off without screwing up the wilderness area."

Already big mounds of rock were windrowed along the
entire lower edge of the fence line—not surprising, noted
Terry, since the shaft had to be big enough to accommodate
an oversized dump truck alongside the conveyor belt that was
carrying the mountain's innards out to the parking lot. A bat-
tered crew-cab pickup rolled in through the gate, its driver
giving us the once-over as he eased past. Terry told them he
was with the State, just taking a couple of samples, and his
words worked their usual ambiguous magic. The pickup eased
down the roller-coaster road to the shaft entrance and its crew
slumped out to begin their day. The big conveyor was already
going, dropping rocks onto the ground with a steady beat.
One of the new arrivals cranked up a front-end loader and
started pushing the tailings farther away.

"Yep, it's that second permit that's going to be the bitch,"
Terry said, and went on to explain that the plan called for two

more tunnels under a low ridge to the north—one to haul out the ore and the other to carry wiring and plumbing inside to the digging equipment. "This is going to be a room-and-pillar mine—that's where you hollow out the mountain except you leave a few pillars of rock to hold the whole thing up." Terry paused to consider such a structure, describing vast chambers of empty underground space.

"Anyway," he continued, "it's going to be a big deal. One hundred million tons of tailings. Major impact. We're hearing from a lot of people about this one."

I had seen the way people looked at Terry when he told them he worked for the State. I had been to enough town meetings to know the sort of tug-of-war that goes on around new mining permits. I knew that Terry had worked for private exploration companies before, and I also knew that he took his present job as a watchdog for the State very seriously. I was curious to know what he thought about this situation.

"I don't know," he said, shaking his head. "The thing is, *nobody* really asks the right questions when it comes to a deal like this. I mean, everybody just funnels down into their own little crack and that's as far as they can see. The wildlife guys, they're all upset about the dynamite scaring the grizzly bears. The botanists, they've got some plant that's gonna get run over by a bulldozer. The mining guys, they want to get their hands on that ore. Then the folks down in Libby . . . they've got one mine closing down already, and they see jobs. What're they supposed to do? It's hard to know what's the right thing. And I guess I'm just as bad as any of them—I want to find out where the water's going and base every other little thing on that."

Terry is a hydrologist, and he spends a lot of time visualizing the flow of water through rock. Much of his thinking is done out loud, and now he began muttering, half to himself, half to me, as he sent his mind underground, down through the strata of Precambrian rocks beneath the peaks. There was one place in particular that made him a little nervous: on the far side of the crest, the tunnel would pass ticklishly close to a fault. Just above that fault lay a deep alpine lake. "You never know," he said. "They could all come paddling out of that tunnel in a rowboat."

We walked over to the mouth of the exploratory shaft, and I watched the conveyor belt roll while Terry talked to the foreman. The opening was larger than a warehouse, and its blackness swallowed up the puny efforts of the people scrambling around it. Noise, trucks, lights, men, the long conveyor itself, all faded quickly into the gaping hole. When I stepped back outside, the stature of the surrounding peaks seemed to have diminished.

I looked up to the line of flatiron peaks around the Elephant. There were no visible signs of the machines eating their way in among the roots of those giants, but at my back, quite distinctly, I could hear the sound of big rocks plopping down off the conveyor onto the growing pile.

BY NOON on May 7, Thompson's men had bumped their canoe past the last of the rocks on the Kootenai Falls portage trail and set off again. They ran the rest of the canyon, plowing through "violent Eddies that threatened to swallow up the Canoe and People." At one point they put ashore and found a dead *chevreuil*, half eaten by eagles. Ignoring their experience with the wild horse, they loaded the remains into their canoe. "It smelt strongly, but as we were without Food, we were glad to take what remained, altho' we could hardly bear its Smell." They put back in the river and bore the smell while Thompson jotted down twenty-three more river courses before making camp. They boiled the deer for dinner, then spent a sick and sleepless night. Later Thompson theorized that, "had we had time to make charcoal, and boiled this with the meat, the taint would have been taken from the meat."

Early the following day, as the river emerged from the

narrows and calmed itself between broader banks, the furmen spotted a Kootenai man on shore. He climbed aboard to float downstream a short distance to his camp near the present location of Bonner's Ferry, Idaho. The ten lodges gathered here were recovering from a recent scuffle with some Piegans, and as Thompson listened to the details, he realized that two of his men had been involved. At the end of March, he had sent Michel Boulard and Augustin Boisverd south to find the spring camps of the Flatheads and Kootenais and encourage them to work beaver. Somewhere along the way the two voyageurs had met a group of Piegans, who had followed them to the Old Chief's camp. The peace the tribes had agreed to at Kootanae House the previous Christmas did not hold, and a fight had broken out. Three Piegans had been killed, and three Kootenais wounded, including the Old Chief, who had taken a bullet through his thigh. The surviving Piegans had gotten away with thirty-five Kootenai horses, and the turmoil had completely disrupted the spring hunt.

The people at the Kootenai camp were short of food—all they had to offer were a few suckers and some of their moss bread. This "bread" was made not from moss but from the black goatsbeard lichens that hang from old Douglas fir and tamarack trees. The hair-like lichens were cleaned, soaked, roasted-on hot stones, then mashed into cakes. Thompson found the bread "of a slightly bitter taste, but acceptable to the hungry . . . I could never relish it, it has just enough nourishment to keep a person alive." Things looked up the next day when a hunter brought in a *chevreuil*. Then Ugly Head arrived and agreed to go south and fetch the Flatheads with their furs.

Thompson spent a day trading at the Kootenai camp, passing on eight tanned beaver hides to his men so that they could make themselves some new shoes. While waiting for Ugly Head to return, he continued downstream toward Kootenay Lake in search of a good site for a trade house. The wide, lush valley at the base of this lake was the home of the

Flat Bows, so named by the Blackfeet after their particular style of bow. The Kootenai word for this group translates as "the marsh people," and Thompson sometimes called them the Lake Indians. Their language was the same as that of their upriver Kootenai relatives, but their lifestyle was quite different. Although individual members occasionally went east on buffalo hunts, for the most part these people relied on their local resources. Instead of tipis, they lived in lodges covered with mats woven of rushes from the surrounding wetlands. Dried fish was their staple food, supplemented with other meat when they could get it. They had a Fishing Chief who supervised the construction of weirs, as well as a Duck Chief and a Deer Chief to orchestrate communal hunts. They didn't have many horses, for the long-legged animals were not very useful in their wet, woody country. Dogs with miniature saddlebags served as pack animals, and on water they traveled in distinctive pine-bark canoes with elongated ends that sloped back from the waterline. This design made the boats more stable in the wind-driven waves that often swept the shallow lake, and the Flat Bows claimed that the jutting chins tracked better in swift river currents. In a memorandum dashed off on an odd page of his journal, Thompson noted: "Legs of the Lake Indians crooked inwards by sitting cross-legged in their small canoes."

The Nor'Westers had not been on the lower river long before they met four of the Flat Bows riding in one of their sturgeon-nosed canoes, who stopped to trade a few skins. The Flat Bows also had some moose and sheep meat to offer, "but it was too much putrified"—apparently the furmen had finally learned to stay away from meat of a certain age. The next day, May 14, Thompson and his crew paddled through their first mosquitoes of the season into the long shoestring of Kootenay Lake. As they wandered among a series of marshy side lakes in search of anyone who might have some skins to trade, Thompson's compass read NE. When he stopped to observe for latitude, his calculations told him he was at

49° 17' 44" N: he had navigated a long U since leaving
Windermere Lake. If he had continued north along the western shore of Kootenay Lake, he would soon have reached the
Kootenay River's outlet, and from there it was only fifty miles
farther west to its juncture with the Columbia.

But they were fifty long miles. From a letter that he wrote
to the partners later that summer, it is clear that Thompson
realized where he was. The Kootenais had told him that a
series of waterfalls and five portages—one of them twenty
miles long—lay between him and the big river. Even though
the passage sounded unnavigable, Thompson wanted to go
and explore it in person, "but my time and the weakness of
my men prevented me." So the surveyor made the pragmatic
decision to tend to business first. He finished his trading
along the lakeshore, then headed back to meet the Flatheads;
along the way he bought four bows for the personal collection
of Duncan McGillivray.

When he got back to the Kootenai lodges, he found his
old campsite under water and learned that the route south to
the Flathead country was also flooded. Thompson had been
counting on the Flathead hunt to meet his projections, but
now no one from those bands would be able to make it to him
with their furs. He had been expecting Boulard and Boisverd
along with the Flatheads and the main band of Kootenais, but
had heard nothing from them. Thompson tried to make arrangements to go himself to the Flathead country, but no one
would lead him. He couldn't wait for things to dry up, because he had a shipment of pelts waiting at Kootanae House
that had to be delivered across the mountains, ". . . & thus all
my fine hopes are ruined."

With few alternatives left, he set up a makeshift post near
the Kootenai camp and left Beaulieu to man it. Thompson
knew his canoe would never make it back up the canyon
during high water, so he bought a few horses from the
Kootenais and loaded the three packs of furs he had managed to collect. He hired a young Kootenai to lead his party

overland and, possibly anticipating a rugged trip, decided to leave his precious sextant behind. "May 19 Thursday A fine Day – arranged the Skins, Goods etc. & got ready to set off with our Kootanae Guide." All the paths that the Kootenais usually followed to Tobacco Plains and Windermere Lake were flooded, and after two days of floundering through thick forest, their guide abandoned them. Thompson could still barely walk with his bad knee, and he sent Lussier and another man back to the Kootenai camp for help. Time hung heavy for Thompson for the next two days, and on Tuesday he came back after wandering about "in sad reflections" to find that his men had returned with Ugly Head himself to guide them. For his services, Thompson agreed to pay the chief one belted jacket, a yard and a half of red wool cloth, one large knife, one small ax, ten balls, and a quantity of powder.

Even with Ugly Head's local knowledge, it was not a good time of year to be traveling. Bushwhacking along steep mountainsides, "the broken rocks has cut the Legs of the Horses to Pieces, so that we can often trace them by the Blood only – poor Animals." Entire days were spent throwing down trees to bridge the torrents of meltwater; at several crossings, they laboriously chopped down big spars only to watch them be sucked into the current and swept away as if they were jackstraws. They lost one fur bundle and Lussier's personal belongings while trying to line them across a roaring stream. But Ugly Head was able to kill an occasional antelope and elk to vary their diet of moss bread ("which gave us all the belly ache"), and after twelve days brought them out of the dripping wilderness back on the upper Kootenay, not far from the Columbia Lake portage. Here the men helped Ugly Head strip out a new canoe, and on the afternoon of June 5 they "bid a kind adieu to our humane Guide, without whose Perseverance & Attention, we had certainly not been able to have reached this Place."

By the time Thompson got back to Kootanae House, it

was time to head east with the season's fur packs. Finan McDonald had already started downriver in the big cargo canoe with the women, children, and furs. When the sur-veyor caught up with them on June 8, he learned that "they have fared but poorly at times & have eat most of the dogs." Thompson canoed on downriver while the rest of his men brought the horses through the woods. At the beginning of the portage trail, they cached the canoes and loaded the horses, substituting pack saddles made out of well-smoked leather for the standard wooden frames. Thompson was trying to pamper his pack animals, and had also made belly bands for them out of some linen cloth, because when the old leather straps got wet they cut the horses' sides severely. It was mid-June, and although spring runoff had swollen the river, there was still snow in the woods. The trail up Blaeberry River had not improved since the previous spring, and Charlotte was well along in another pregnancy. Game remained scarce, forc-ing them to kill some of their horses for meat. As they neared the Divide, Thompson had a scare: "One of my horses nearly crushing my children to death with his load being badly put on, which I mistook for being vicious, I shot him on the spot and rescued my little-ones." They stripped the meat from the dead horse, then pressed on. The next day they marched up very close to Howse Pass:

> June 20th Monday A frosty Morning, but very fine Day. by 6½ A.M. we were ready and set off . . . unloaded our Horses to refresh them & ourselves – at 3 P.M. we re-loaded, but missing my little Daughter & nowhere finding her, we concluded she was drowned & all of us set about finding her – we searched all the Embarrass [logjams] in the River but to no purpose. At length Mr. McDonald found her track going upwards. We searched all about & at length thank God at 8½ P.M. found her about 1 Mile off, against a Bank of Snow.

This would have been either seven-year-old Fanny or, more

likely, two-year-old Emma. These perilous days on the way
up the Blaeberry mark two of the very few appearances of
Thompson's children in the field journals.

With no further mishaps, the pack train made its way
over the pass the next day and on to Kootenay Plains, where
it was met by James McMillan and five Iroquois free hunters. Following Thompson's suggestion, the partners had
hired the Iroquois to hunt beaver across the mountains and
had equipped them with two steel traps each. Steel traps were
a relatively new innovation and, when baited with castorum
from a beaver's musk gland, had proved a deadly efficient
way to capture beaver. Thompson accepted some fresh sheep
meat from the Iroquois, then arranged to take their boat as
well when he found that winter snows had crushed his own
cached canoe beyond repair. The Saskatchewan was running
fast, and as they flew downstream, Thompson had to give up
all attempts at taking compass readings. He did note that the
women went ashen as the voyageurs ran the canoe through
the swift rapids.

They stopped to shoot a bison and enjoyed their first meal
of fresh buffalo in over a year. On June 25 they camped just
below the empty Rocky Mountain House, where they found
Jaco Finlay tenting across the river. Jaco was working the area
as a free hunter, and whatever grievances Thompson harbored
about the trail work of the previous summer, he was always
willing to buy furs. By the next evening, he had arrived at
Boggy Hall, a new post in the Fort des Prairies Department—
trade houses seemed to spring up like mushrooms along the
Saskatchewan.

Charlotte's brother Patrick Small was working at Boggy
Hall, so Thompson dropped his family there and kept right
on going east. By August 2, sometimes paddling all night, he
and his men had made it all the way down the Saskatchewan
and through Lake Winnipeg and Lake of the Woods to Rainy
Lake House. The North West Company had set up this
supply depot for the far-flung Athabasca canoes, which could

SHIPPING THE FURS EAST

never make it back and forth to Fort William during the open season, and now it would also service David Thompson's newly designated Columbia Department. Thompson's friends Donald McTavish and James Hughes were already at Rainy Lake when he arrived, along with several other North West partners. Here, if he hadn't heard about it already, Thompson would have learned of the death of Duncan McGillivray the previous April. Less than forty years of age, McGillivray had been one of the most vigorous proponents of Thompson's Columbia venture and had spent the last few months of his life petitioning the British government to send a ship to the mouth of Columbia to protect the North West Company's interests. In a letter written shortly after he heard the news, Thompson said that he had named the Flat Bows' river after William and Duncan McGillivray, "in honor of the family

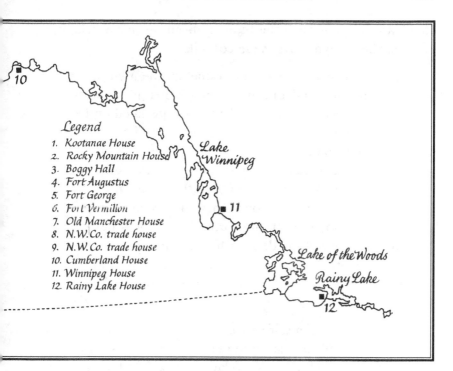

Legend
1. Kootanae House
2. Rocky Mountain House
3. Boggy Hall
4. Fort Augustus
5. Fort George
6. Fort Vermilion
7. Old Manchester House
8. N.W.Co. trade house
9. N.W.Co. trade house
10. Cumberland House
11. Winnipeg House
12. Rainy Lake House

who may be justly attributed the knowledge and commerce we have of the Columbia, one of [them] as is now no more, yet sacred be his memory." The surveyor didn't say what he did with the four Lake Indian bows he had brought with him for Duncan's artifact collection.

Thompson stayed at Rainy Lake for two days, just long enough to unload his furs and pack up new trade goods. By October 3 he and his two supply canoes had made it back to Boggy Hall, where Charlotte had recently given birth to a baby boy, named John. The family did not travel west with Thompson that fall; it was obviously easier for them to remain on the Saskatchewan with Charlotte's brother than to labor across the pass again. Trying to beat the onset of winter, Thompson left Boggy Hall after another two-day stop and-moved quickly upriver. While his men dragged the loaded canoe upstream, he hunted ahead on horseback, and one day he brought down a big cow elk.

> As she was dying the Canoes came up, the Men began skinning her, and one man cut off her head, upon this-the Deer arose and for half a minute stood on her feet . . . The Men became Frightened, said she was a devil, and would have nothing more to do with her . . . I cut a piece of meat for my supper, put it in the Canoe, and marched on; when we camped, I expected my piece of meat for supper, but found they had tossed it into the River, and my servant said to the Men, "Does he wish to eat a piece of the devil, if he does, it is not me that will cook it." Instances of this nature are known to the Indians, who call them Seepanee, that is strong of life.
>
> *Narrative*

Strong of life himself that season, Thompson pressed on through rain and sleet and the season's first snowstorm. The bad weather forced the party to lay by for a day, during which the men made socks, mittens, and winter jackets for themselves. The next morning they cleared the snow off the canoes and tracked on up the river, but layers of ice began to form on the birch bark, turning the boats into "unwieldy Masses of Snow and Ice." Finan McDonald and James McMillan came to the rescue with horses from Kootenay Plains, and after a day's shuffling of supplies the weather moderated and the pack train set off. A pair of buffalo cows ambled ahead of the party all the way up the Howse River and across the Divide, and the Columbia brigade made it back to Kootanae House by November 10. Their supply run to Rainy Lake, a round trip of over three thousand miles, had taken a little more than five months.

The day after their arrival, Thompson was hanging new doors on his warehouse when Jaco Finlay and his family stopped by with the five Iroquois free hunters. They had already trapped eight packs of pelts, and after James McMillan took some rum to their camp that evening, "they drank and fought the whole night" in celebration. Thompson spent the next two weeks refurbishing the post: he mended the chimneys, put up his bed, and whitewashed his room. Finan McDonald and four voyageurs had gone down to the Kootenay Lake country to set up an auxiliary post for the winter trade, and in late November the clerk returned with discouraging news: his canoe was frozen fast in the ice on the Kootenai River. He rounded up a dozen horses and went back south with two men to try again. They made it only as far as Kootenai Falls before the horses were "knocked up" in the deep snow, and they decided to set up two leather tents and hunker down for the winter nearby.

For his part, Thompson passed the cold months of 1808–09 at Kootanae House in a state of relative tranquillity. "My mode of passing the day is to 10 A.M. writing my journal, calculations etc. To 2 P.M. Exercise in walking, Riding etc. From thence Indian & horse affairs – in the evening my Letters on the Country." He made drawings of the east slope of the Rocky Mountains and found time to indulge his interest in the local bird life. He watched magpies gather around open holes in the frozen lake in search of fish fry, "of which they make great havock." The men were working on another ice house for meat, the ravens "most cordially helping them finish." On a clear sharp day in January, Thompson walked over to a large gully and came upon a flock of what, from his description, sound like pine grosbeaks: "the Cocks of a beautiful brick Red in the Head Back breast & Belly & some parts of the wings – with stripes of white in the wings & lower part of the Belly – Thighs and the rest a blueish color – three claws before & 1 behind." He watched the wary trumpeter and tundra swans that wintered around the lakes and succeeded in bagging one of each. "The former is a large species . . . weighing thirty-two to thirty-five pounds; the inside fat filled a common dinner plate."

Thompson also spent time chasing after some of the feral

horses that grazed in the foothills above the lakes. The
Kootenais told him that these horses had once belonged to
the many members of their tribe who had been wiped out
by smallpox. The French Canadians called them *marrons*
(chestnuts), their slang word for something domestic gone
wild. Upon learning that Jaco Finlay had captured and tamed
eighteen of them, Thompson and Bercier decided to try their
luck. On the first excursion they tracked the *marrons* with
their most long-winded horses on "a wild steeple-chase, down
hills and up others." The next day they again dashed after
them on their swiftest steeds. Two of the mustangs fell dead,
but they were able to hobble a third. "I passed my hand over
his nostrils, the smell of which was so disagreeable that its
nostrils and the skin of its head became contorted." On the
third day he led the mustang back to the fort, where it was
broken to the bit and saddle and before long came to find the
smell of its captor's hand agreeable.

On the same day that Thompson caught up with his first
marron stallion, Michel Boulard and Augustin Boisverd arrived from the Flat Bow country, where they had been trading. They brought with them a letter from Finan McDonald
and must have also carried the sextant that Thompson had
left at the Kootenai camp the previous spring—on the next
clear night, the surveyor was out taking observations for the
first time in months. Boisverd had accumulated a handsome
total of eighteen packs of furs, and apparently had acquired
a Kootenai wife as well. Most of the voyageurs had native
wives—they were the ones taking care of the endless busy-
work that kept the operation going—but they were rarely
mentioned in fur trade journals. Boisverd's "country wife,"
however, would become well-known to both natives and
whites over the next few years.

HER STORY BEGINS down in the Flat Bow country around
Kootenay Lake. Her given name was One-Standing-Lodge-

Pole-Woman, and she was apparently a healthy girl, large and heavy-boned. In the 1930s, Kootenai elders told anthropologist Claude Schaeffer that as she reached maturity she wanted to marry, but no man showed any interest in her. They said that Lodge-Pole-Woman was a teenager when white traders first came to her country, and when they left she went away to live with one of them. Her people thought that the girl soon grew unhappy and was ready to return home, but it was more than a year before she reappeared at her tribal camp. This part of her story fits with Boulard and Boisverd's visit to the Flat Bow country, and with David Thompson's memory of his first meeting with the woman as Boisverd's wife. When he wrote about her two years later, he did not remember her fondly—her conduct had become so loose, he said, that he had asked Boisverd to send her back to her friends.

When Lodge-Pole-Woman did return to her own people, she announced that her white husband had transformed her into a man. She changed her name to Gone-to-the-Spirits and began to dance out the story of her sexual transformation for everyone she met. She wore men's shirts, with leggings and breechcloth; she began to carry a gun along with a bow and arrows. It wasn't long before she was claiming to possess great spiritual power. In the Kootenai scheme of the world, a person might claim such power but would not use it without a need. Some of the Kootenai people believed that she had lost her mind, while others, especially the younger women, grew afraid of her.

The voyageurs used the word *berdache* to describe a person who chose to live out the role of the opposite sex. The notion was not an unfamiliar one to the North American tribes, but almost all of the recorded berdache stories deal with a man living as a woman. Now Gone-to-the-Spirits declared that since she was a man, she wanted to marry a woman. She approached several available girls and was rebuffed each time. Some people mocked the berdache, but stories began to circulate that she would use her new powers to harm any girl who might refuse her.

After a time Gone-to-the-Spirits found a woman who had been abandoned by her husband and was willing to share a tent. The two became constant companions, and curious Kootenais tried to catch the new "wife" alone to discover the intimate details of their relationship. Gone-to-the-Spirits' companion only laughed at these intrusions, but a rumor went around that the berdache had stitched together a leather phallus. There was also talk of jealousy and unfaithfulness. Loud arguments were heard between the two, and soon Gone-to-the-Spirits was openly beating her wife. The berdache had taken up gambling, and in one costly session she lost a bow, quiver, and canoe. Her wife, upset at the loss, picked up a bow that lay nearby, shot an arrow through the side of the canoe, and left her "husband" for good.

Around that same time, Gone-to-the-Spirits accompanied her brother on a raid to capture horses. The party made a long trip without locating the enemy camp they were looking for. Over the course of their journey, they had to cross several streams and creeks, and they would always undress for the crossing and carry their clothes across on their heads. The berdache's brother noticed that his sister was holding back at each crossing, and hid himself to watch her at the next ford. In the middle of the stream he saw his sister standing in water well below her waist. She was clearly still a woman. When she noticed her brother, Gone-to-the-Spirits quickly squatted down in the water to hide herself, pretending that her foot was twisted between two rocks. A while later she caught up with the raiding party, complaining of a sprained ankle.

When the party arrived at their home camp, Gone-to-the-Spirits announced that she was changing her name once again. Her injury had forced her to sit down in the stream, she said, as her own brother had witnessed. From this day on she wished to be known as Qánqon kámek klaúla (Sitting-in-the-Water-Grizzly). Her brother said to his friends that he was going to call her Qánqon instead, a derisive nickname that referred to the squatting posture she had assumed when he spied her in the middle of the stream.

Shortly after the raid, Sitting-in-the-Water-Grizzly found a woman from the marshlands around the south end of Kootenay Lake who was willing to be her new wife. They hadn't lived together long before the berdache became jealous, and one night the two began to quarrel. The quarrel turned into a noisy beating that roused the berdache's brother from his nearby lodge. He came out and denounced her to the village in a loud voice, saying that he knew her sex had not been changed, and that was why he would only call her Qánqon. After her brother's revelation, all the Kootenai people called the woman Qánqon, but she endured their ridicule and continued to camp with her tribe. She associated with a number of other women, but there were no more stories of arguments or beatings. Finally she took a long journey with one of her companions, and was gone from her people for several years.

WHILE RUMORS about Qánqon circulated around the Kootenai country, the man who had booted her out of his trade house was himself the subject of discussion on the other side of the Divide. James Bird, the Hudson's Bay Company agent at Edmonton House, next door to Fort Augustus, kept an eye on the rival furs that floated past him and an ear to the whispers of the voyageurs. Bird had been trying to decide whether to risk sending a party of his own across the Divide, and followed Thompson's movements with interest. He was not quite sure what to make of the latest reports: "The expedition across the mountains does not seem to be quite relinquished by the NW Co [North West Company] though their success last year appears not to have been encouraging."

In February of 1809, North West Company trader Alexander Henry, wintering near Bird on the Saskatchewan River, offered an updated reckoning of his partner's position in a letter of his own:

We have not heard from Mr. Thompson since last
October when he was taken in the Ice in the first ridge
of the Mountains about a month's journey short of his
wintering ground. He was then preparing to proceed
with the property on horses and was in hopes of reaching his destination in due time. The snow in the mountains is the only obstacle he had to surmount; once over
that he comes to a warm climate & a fine country, when
all his troubles are at an end. He gives us great hopes of
making at least 40 packs of beaver.

Forty packs of beaver, almost two tons of furs, would be a
respectable haul—enough to attract the attention of James
Bird and the Hudson's Bay Company. Henry remarked that:
"Should the Philosopher David Thompson succeed in making
good returns in Beaver on the Columbia, we may rest assured
that Bird will attempt sending them the ensuing summer."
    When Henry spoke of David Thompson as the
"Philosopher," he was paying tribute to his unusual status
among the furmen. Thompson was an explorer, making a historic push west. He was a trader, bent on good returns. And
he was also a philosopher—that is, in the usage of the time,
someone well versed in a particular area of natural science,
such as botany, zoology, or, in this case, astronomy. He was
a man who could navigate by the stars and chart a course for
others to follow.

CHAPTER SIX

TOUCHING
THE CIRCLE

SPRING 1809–SPRING 1810

AS MIGRATING TUNDRA swans passed above Kootanae House in March of 1809, Thompson finished drawing Mount Nelson and began preparing for spring. He sent men out on the never-ending search for good birch rind and dispatched James McMillan down the Kootenay River to help Finan McDonald bring up his winter trade. He gave Boulard and his wife supplies and sent them south to pass the summer with the Flat Bows at Kootenay Lake. While his men pulled meat out of their glacier to make pemmican and began pressing the furs into packs, he put a handle on his hoe and planted some turnip seeds. Everything was almost ready for their trip east by late April, when their final preparations were interrupted by sickness in the camp.

> APRIL 24 MONDAY A very fine hot day . . . Passed a sad
> night with Lussier's wife, who is dying.
> APRIL 25 TUESDAY A fine day. At 2 A.M. it pleased
> Heaven that Lussier's wife should depart this Life –
> she has left four small Children – the youngest only 6

months old, which much distresses me. At 1 P.M. the
men returned & we buried the poor woman & take the
best care we can of her Children.

A few days later the Nor'Westers left Kootanae House
with their fur packs. On the way to the Blaeberry River, they
stopped at Jaco Finlay's camp and made arrangements to leave
Lussier's children in the care of Jaco and his wife. Thompson
spent the next two weeks ferrying horses downriver to the
portage trail and sowing turnip seeds at promising sites along
the way. He set up camp near the mouth of the Blaeberry
to wait for Finan McDonald, and there he met Martin and
Jacques, two of the Iroquois who had spent the winter trapping with Jaco. They had been "on discovery," looking
for beaver to the north on a section of the Columbia that
Thompson had not yet seen. Martin and Jacques reported bad
rapids, few beaver, and generally unfavorable country. They
traded Thompson a good beaver and some bear fat, then collected the pelts they had stored at Jaco's camp and brought
them back to Thompson's tent. He gave them part of their
payment in rum, and somehow an argument ensued. "Martin
insolent & dislocated my right thumb in thrashing him which
will render me incapable of doing anything for a few days."

Two days later he was able to use his thumb enough
to hobble horses and write a little, and that evening Finan
McDonald and James McMillan finally arrived from the
south, carrying thirty-two packs of good furs. These, com-
bined with twenty-two packs from around Kootanae House
plus a half-pack of the skins of white goats, swans, and a large
grizzly bear, meant that the Columbia Department had more
than met Thompson's projection, and he was pleased: "Thank
God for this great Success."

He set off as soon as possible for his trip across the mountains, topping Howse Pass with relative ease and arriving at
Fort Augustus in late June. James Hughes was manning the

post, and Charlotte and the children must have been in residence there with him. Hughes was family now, for his daughter had married Charlotte's brother Patrick Small. In the flurry of drying and re-pressing furs, finishing out two new canoes for the trip east, and giving the men a dance, it was three days before Thompson discovered that over the course of the winter he had somehow lost a day. "June 27 Tuesday. A fine day . . . The Gentlemen here hold this to be 28th June Wednesday."

Thompson sent James McMillan on to Rainy Lake with the fur packs and spent the next three weeks at Fort Augustus, visiting with his family and catching up on news. Here he probably learned that the previous summer, Simon Fraser had completed his run down the Tacoutche Tesse (later named the Fraser River) to its mouth just above the 49th parallel— three full degrees too far north to be the Columbia River. Alexander Mackenzie's dotted line had been wrong: the Tacoutche Tesse and the Columbia were not the same river after all. The Tacoutche Tesse would not work as a trade route, either—its lower canyon was even wilder than the upper section that had turned Mackenzie away. Any hope for a navigable path to the sea now lay with the still unexplored Columbia. But apparently the North West Company no longer considered tracing that river a high priority. As Thompson later summarized the situation: "1809. The Partners of the Coy. allow of no further discoveries but only trading posts upon a small scale, and I have means for nothing else."

But Thompson was to prove himself a master at working within tight limits. As a partner in a profit-sharing company, he had to bring in furs, and his movements for the next year combine the rounds of a determined trader with an explorer's steady advance. During his two years across the Divide, through assiduous questioning and many stick-drawn maps, he had gleaned information from every tribe he met. He had shaped a coherent sense of the tangled geography of the

TRADE ROUTE OF THE COLUMBIA BRIGADE

region, and knew where he wanted to build new posts to expand the trade and prove to the partners that the Columbia Department was economically viable.

Hoping to get a jump on winter, Thompson and Finan McDonald left Fort Augustus in mid-July with a few supplies and headed west on their familiar route up the Saskatchewan. A few miles above the old Rocky Mountain House, the surveyor experienced "a violent palpitation of the Heart" and had one of his men bleed him for relief. They traveled on through Kootenay Plains and soon afterward met Joseph Howse of the Hudson's Bay Company, returning from a quick scouting trip up into the mountains. As Alexander Henry had predicted, the Bay Company was preparing to make a move. Thompson breakfasted with his rival, gave him a letter to deliver to James Hughes back at Fort Augustus, and continued on his way. Just across the Height of Land, the Nor'Westers met Jaco Finlay and his wife and children, all traveling on foot. Two weeks earlier a group of Piegans had crossed the mountains and raided their camp near Kootanae House, robbing them of their whole string of horses and most of their personal property. Thompson loaned Jaco a few horses to carry his family, and the Finlays turned around and continued down the Blaeberry with the Nor'Westers.

The surveyor had decided to abandon Kootanae House for the present and concentrate on the more populated area farther south. Moving quickly, he and his men passed by the empty trading post, portaged across Canal Flats, and launched their canoe in the Kootenay River again. As they traveled downstream, they frequently noticed places where the Piegan horse thieves had forded the river with Jaco's animals only a few days before. Their tracks finally turned east at the Elk River, which marked one of their "War Roads" across the mountains; after that, Thompson and his party breathed a little easier. At Tobacco Plains they stopped to check on the progress of a garden Finan McDonald had planted the previous spring; they found "nothing of the Peas, the turnips only

in Leaves & their very small roots worm-eaten." Five or six
stalks of barley were faring well.

Near the top of Kootenai Falls, the men stayed for a day
waiting for Michel Boulard, who had spent the summer in the
Flat Bow country and was supposed to meet them here with
horses to carry their cargo around the falls. When he didn't
show up, Finan McDonald went off to search for him and
instead found several Kootenais who agreed to come and help
them across the portage. After working their way through the
tight canyon, the party continued downriver to a trail they
called the "Great Road of the Flat Heads," where Thompson
dispatched a man to find some horses to carry them overland.
A week later sixteen Flathead men arrived with mounts to
collect the furmen and their baggage. Everyone got busy wid-
ening the "Great Road" and headed south.

On September 9 the pack train arrived at present-day
Pend Oreille Lake, where a large camp of several different
tribes welcomed the Nor'Westers with berries, fresh *chevreuil*,
and dried salmon. The next day Thompson and two Flathead
men explored around the lake until they found a location that
he deemed acceptable for a trade house, even though "the soil
was light, and had no blue clay, which is so very necessary for
plaistering between the logs of the house and especially the
roof." His crew got to work setting out fishnets in the lake
and digging postholes in the rocky ground while he traded
with the natives who kept arriving with quantities of furs. The
men dubbed the new post Kullyspel House, after the local
people's name for themselves (spelled Kalispel today). The
French Canadians called this tribe the Pend Oreilles, while
Thompson sometimes referred to them as the Ear Bobs or
Ear Pendants. According to several sources, Finan McDonald
married a daughter of a Kullyspel chief.

When Jaco Finlay and his family wandered into the new
post on September 21, the men were hauling in trout and getting ready to roof the warehouse; Finan McDonald hung the
doors in the middle of a thunderstorm. A week later, leaving

his men to frame a second floor in the warehouse, Thompson set off west on horseback: "My view was to see if we cannot change our Route to cross the Mountains, as at present we are too much exposed to the incursions of the Peeagan Indians." By this time, the surveyor had figured out the general course of the upper Columbia and knew that he had built Kootanae House either on the big river itself or on a main branch of it. Now he hoped to find a route that would follow its northerly loop and bypass the country frequented by Piegan raiders. Accompanied by his man Beaulieu, he rode across the top of the lake and followed a good trail down the Pend Oreille River through yellowing leaves, taking meals from among the migrant ducks, geese, swans, cranes, and plovers that covered the water. The second day out, the surveyor pulled out his compass and found that the glass had fallen off and the needle had been lost; for the rest of the trip he had to eyeball their courses.

After four days they reached the extensive marshy plain around the modern town of Cusick, Washington. The friendly Kalispel Indians camped there were so completely untouched by white culture that they lacked iron tools of any sort, even an ax. There were plenty of beaver about, which the Kalispels killed for their winter clothing, but they had nothing more than pointed sticks and snares to hunt them with. One of their elders presented Thompson with dried salmon, a basket of camas bulbs, and two cakes made from camas roots that had been pounded to a pulp and then baked on hot stones. The surveyor reciprocated with tobacco and a steel and flints for starting fires. Then he asked his usual question: "I enquired of the Road before me. They say there is only another Fall to go to the Columbia of which they drew the Chart." This was good news, and very different from what he had been told by the Flat Bows, who had described a series of heavy falls that required a long portage of one and a half days. Thompson indicated to the Kalispels that he would like to go and have a look for himself.

They told him that the trail downstream along the Pend Oreille was no good for horses, but they did offer to loan him a pine-bark canoe and a guide. Thompson, Beaulieu, and the Kalispel guide put in the river next morning in a drizzling rain, in what turned out to be a very leaky canoe. At first the river was wide and placid, but as they proceeded it narrowed and picked up speed. Around midmorning on the second day, Thompson asked how far it was to the falls, and the guide confessed that he had never been on this stretch of water before. The surveyor reluctantly turned around, his appointment with the Columbia postponed again.

"THAT'S WHAT I like about those old guys," said Steve Zender from the bow of the canoe. "They'd take off down some unknown river to see where it was going, and I mean a bedroll and a compass was about it. We go out for one night and fill up a truck with air mattresses and hot dogs and— whoooa, look out to your right there. Deadhead."

Zender feathered his paddle to ease up on a fat fir log that was bobbing vertically in the water. It slipped away from his oar and dawdled in the current, pogoing up and down in the murky Pend Oreille River. Steve is the state wildlife biologist for northeastern Washington, and he was out to check a bald eagle nest on one of the river's grassy islands. From my seat in the stern he had a dark, compact presence, and he approached his job with dogged concentration. Leaning forward on his knees, he studied the deadhead to see where the river's slow current was pushing it.

We had put in just below Cusick, near the spot where David Thompson had his first taste of dried camas roots. Camas flowers still turn these bottomlands blue each May, and the pumping gulps of bitterns fill up the low, marshy expanse. The wildest of the downriver canyons that stopped Thompson's progress toward the Columbia have been dammed, and the edges of the river are dotted with pilings for yarding up sawlogs. Some of the disused poles are topped with the ragged twigs of osprey nests or nesting cans set up for Canada geese. Steve looked downstream and pointed to a cluster of spars where a handful of cormorants, sharing the oily creosote color of their perches, stood on tiptoe and spread out their stubby wings to dry.

"Don't you wonder what these pole-sitters did before we stuck poles in the mud?" he asked. "I mean, do you think they really belong here?" As a matter of fact, cormorants have always been a part of the local scene. The Kootenais attributed weather-changing powers to these long-necked birds. During hard winters, they said, you could shoot a cormorant through the head, fetch the body and dip it in an unfrozen pool, then throw water from the pool three times to the sky. If after all that the dead bird was thrust into a snowbank, warm chinook winds were sure to blow up soon.

The eagle nest Steve wanted to check was a bulky pile of sticks atop a tall yellow pine. While the male sat in a roosting tree about a quarter of a mile off, the female flew circles between nest and roost and us. We tied up our canoe and, using an alder thicket for cover, quietly worked our way close enough to watch one jet-black chick stand up for a look around. We stared through our binoculars until we were sure there weren't two chicks, then quickly backed away to stroll down the gravelly shore of the island and see how the ospreys at the south end were faring. On the way we smelled dead suckers—David Thompson's carp—along the beach, and Steve commiserated with the explorers who had to eat such ugly fish. A male bobolink uncoiled its long, metallic song across the field above.

When some willows blocked our way, we scrambled up onto a rolling field of timothy grass well beyond the whistling eagles. There was raven noise coming from a stand of cottonwoods ahead, so we aimed for the trees and talked about where we were. Steve said that later in the summer, when the

Corps of Engineers drew the river down, the island's owner could drive a tractor over from the mainland and cut the grass for hay. The place was not a full-time island, but it stayed separate and safe at just the right time for the eagles.

Then we walked right up on a spotted fawn in the grass. Dry and pretty, it lay so still that at first we thought it was trusting its camouflage to protect it. When it finally stretched up on its front legs, afraid, the line of spots on its neck winked like eyes. It bawled a bit, then got quiet. When we looked around we could see where it had been flopping through the timothy, and that it was exhausted from pulling itself along by the forelegs. Its hind legs didn't work at all. The only sign of injury was a slash beneath its left hip. Steve guessed it had gotten caught on a fence, but I spent some time imagining an eagle attack. Either way there was nothing for it: the fawn was paralyzed, and the ravens were all around. Steve snapped off a stout fir branch and whacked the little deer across the snout. It went down immediately, breathing easy, and I knelt on its chest the way trappers do when they want to protect a pelt.

Canoeing back across the river, we came up on the deadhead again, still wallowing in the middle of the current. Steve thumped at the butt end of it with his palm and considered the fiberglass body of his canoe. "This thing's dangerous," he announced. "Think she'll pull?"

We managed to loop a line over one end, then found that we had harnessed ourselves into a very awkward paddle, with the current dipping and snapping the log against the weight of the boat. Steve joked about good deeds, but the hard row reminded him of those early fur traders again, how they lived out here, all year, with nothing extra.

"Those guys amaze me," he repeated. "Do you think they were that much tougher than us? I mean, I like being out as much as anybody, but after a few days I'm ready to go home and get a hot shower."

SCRUBBING UP was a luxury that occasionally occupied David Thompson's mind as well—his supply order for the previous season had included twenty pounds of soap, "for without soap, there is no effective cleanliness; this we know very well, who too often experience the want of it." One of the things that impressed him about the tribes he had met on the west side was that they were "as neat in their persons as circumstances will allow." He found the ones around Kullyspel House industrious as well. When he and Beaulieu got back to their new post on October 6, Finan McDonald had just finished trading with a band of Coeur d'Alenes (Pointed Hearts) for three horses and almost two hundred pounds of good furs.

By the end of October, Thompson had met James McMillan coming from Fort William with trade goods and led him back to Kullyspel House. The surveyor had decided that the Flatheads to the east (whom he also called the Saleesh) needed a post of their own, and that it would be a good idea to reach them before the Bay Company or the Americans did. Leaving Finan McDonald in charge at Kullyspel House, he and McMillan led a pack train up the Clark Fork River along the "Saleesh Road to the Buffalo" to a location near the modern town of Thompson Falls, Montana. There, opposite the mouth of a fine creek, they built Saleesh House. The surrounding open country promised plenty of game, but during that first week in November nobody could find any food. The weather was rainy, and when McMillan and Thompson did get out, they didn't do much to improve their situation.

> November 12th Sunday. A fine mild day – As we are all quite hungry and much in want, Mr. McMillan, Forcier and myself went a hunting but without Success. By the accidental going off of his Gun Mr. McMillan had both

the forefingers of his Hands shot through by a Ball &
much lacerated with the Powder, both of his Fingers are
broke & seemingly will with difficulty be kept from falling off – I dressed them the best I could.

Two days later Jaco Finlay and his wife showed up with
twenty-eight beaver tails and forty pounds of dried meat.
Steady work on Saleesh House resumed, and eight daily entries about meals and construction matters passed before
Thompson returned to the matter of his clerk's damaged
digits. "Mr. McMillan's forefinger of the left hand having a
bad appearance & no hopes of its joining with the stump I
separated it."

Saleesh House was on a route used by several tribes on
their way to hunt buffalo or trade with the Flatheads, and it
proved to be a magnet that attracted its own diverse community. Thompson was still unpacking his baggage when a man
whom the voyageurs had nicknamed Le Bon Vieux (Good Old
Man) stopped by with his band, on their way to join a large
hunting camp upriver. Ugly Head arrived with his compatri-
ots Large Kidney and Deceitful Dog at the end of November,
and all three stayed to hunt for the company. Several groups
of Kalispels and Kootenais stopped to smoke and trade on
the way to their winter camps in the Flathead Valley. Six free
hunters, independent trappers who had crossed the mountains on their own and were working beaver in the area, came
in to get supplies. Hoping to bring in tribes from even farther
afield, Thompson sent Boulard and Beaulieu to spread the
word of his new trade house.

The rest of the men continued to work on the post compound. While they covered the walls and roofs of the buildings with clay, Thompson built himself a desk, fashioned a
cupboard, and put in paper windowpanes for want of the
parchment skins he usually used. On December 19 the men
split out rough planks for their beds and slept in their own
house for the first night. Over the next few days, warm

weather brought rain, and all the buildings started to leak. Thompson traded for some mats that the local women wove out of rushes and covered the roofs with them, but they didn't do much good. "December 24 Sunday – not withstanding the Matts the Rain is so incessant & smart that the Houses drip everywhere, especially the Warehouse in which hardly anything is dry. Our Matts flew off with the Storm."

Thompson found the bands that clustered around his post most compatible; they in turn dubbed him Koo-koo-Sint, Star-Looker, and he gained a reputation among them for both integrity and curious interests. One of his interests was their language; he made a long list of English words and phrases and began filling in his phonetic approximations of the Flathead equivalents:

What do you say?	*Stem soon annouer*
Where is my horse?	*Chane sin chits arks kar*
I speak the truth	*Oa na uf*
Where are you going?	*Et chin oo e*
You have lost it	*Host a*
What do you call it?	*Stem thloo, tarn oo*

Among the families tenting near Saleesh House were two tribal leaders—Thompson called them Cartier and the Orator—who often came over in the evening for a smoke. In his *Narrative*, Thompson tells of a February night when the two chiefs entered wearing such grave expressions that he asked if there were rumors of war afoot. In reply, the Orator asked if the white men knew that his people's penalty for adultery was death for both parties. It turned out that the Orator had a married daughter, and one of the furmen had apparently been bringing beads and rings to her while the men of her family were out hunting. Thompson looked around in surprise at his voyageurs—"the men and myself were every day too much fatigued to think of women"—then noticed that one of them had slipped from the room. The surveyor told the Orator that he wouldn't think of protecting the offender, that the chiefs could deal with him however they thought fit. But if they killed him, he would need a strong warrior as a replacement to return east with him and pick up more guns and steel. The chiefs looked at each other and said that they could not send one of their men so far away among strange people where he might be killed. Thompson replied:

> Very well, then if you kill my man I cannot return to you, but shall stay with the Peeagans, your enemies; then what is to be done exclaimed the Orator. I replied, let him live this time, and as you are noted for being a good gelder of Horses; if this Man ever again enters your Tent, geld him, but let him live; at this proposition they laughed . . . after smoking they retired in good humor.

Narrative

Toward the end of February, Thompson and Michel Boulard started out on a winter sojourn in search of birch bark for two canoes. Along the way they stopped to visit the Old Chief and his Kootenai band, who were hunting in the valley where the Clark Fork and Flathead Rivers meet. A few days later word came that Thompson was needed at a large Flathead camp nearby. He and Boulard immediately set off and arrived to find a group of white free hunters and several Kootenais waiting for them. These men had with them the property of an American trapper named Courter who had recently been killed in another Piegan attack somewhere in the vicinity. Thompson took responsibility for settling affairs as best he could, giving out credits to one Kootenai for rescuing Courter's body and to another for helping with the burial. He purchased all of the trapper's furs that had been brought in, even though they were of poor quality, and paid the hunters who had loaned horses to the rescue effort. But beyond saying that Courter was an American, Thompson provides no information on what had happened. Some historians think that Courter must have been Charles Courtin, a French Canadian naturalized as an American citizen who was known to have trapped with other American free hunters far up the Missouri River. In his *Narrative*, Thompson added that he had spent the rest of the afternoon with the Flatheads, asking about birch rind and discussing the fatal folly of those American trappers who were hunting around the headwaters of the Missouri. They had a habit of wandering about in Piegan and Blackfeet territory alone or in small parties and setting their traps without asking permission, imagining that "the Natives of the Plains were all skulkers in the woods, and never dared shew themselves on open ground, and they suffered accordingly, being frequently attacked in open ground and killed."

Thompson was not so naive about the Piegans, whom he characterized as "those ever watchful people, ever alive to what is passing," and whom events of the last five years had caused him to consider as adversaries rather than friends. He never underestimated their strength or volatility, but he knew that much of their power lay in intimidation, and he encouraged the west-side tribes to stand up to them. The second week in March found him on another visit to the big Flathead camp, and while he was there Jaco Finlay rode in to report a suspicious-looking group of horsemen nearby. A hundred men quickly gathered up their new guns and iron-tipped arrows and rode off to do battle. The invaders turned out to be the Old Chief with a Kootenai hunting party, but Thompson was gratified by the quick response of the Flatheads.

He was also gratified by the results of his trading that winter. He had chosen a good location for Saleesh House, in a rich beaver area where several tribes traditionally wintered. He had found natives he could work with and trust, who had kept him supplied with dried meat and pemmican. The growing number of free hunters in the area had helped him accumulate an impressive haul of furs. Thompson liked this rich territory, especially the stretch to the east, along the Flathead River:

> The impression of my mind is, from the formation of the country and it's climate, it's extensive Meadows and fine Forests, watered by countless Brooks and Rills of pure water, that it will become the abode of civilized Man, whether Natives or other people; part of it will bear rich crops of grain, the greater part will be pastoral, as it is admirably adapted to the rearing of Cattle and Sheep.
>
> *Narrative*

FROM THE TOP of a lookout ridge above that same section of the Flathead River, I scanned the slopes for animals poised in the grass. At my feet, sharp sunbeams lit up a woolly slope of balsamroot sunflower; to the northeast the ice-scraped walls of the Mission Range shimmered in the summer air. This is a good place to watch for hawks or whistle up a ground squirrel. It's also a good place to get a feel for just how close the country looks today to the way David Thompson predicted it would almost two centuries ago. The land remains under the care of the Flathead Indians, and over the years the tribe has bucked several proposals for dams within its territory. The river still flows freely through the flats, and beside it farmers grow oats and barley. The hills that roll up in huge swells are dry but grassy, spotted with cattle and sheep.

Along the western base of the ridge, a little tributary named after Jaco Finlay creeps secretly in the shade of cottonwoods and willows, then bursts with reflections as it meets the Flathead River out in the open. Together they wind west across the foot of the reservation to pour into the Clark Fork forty miles downstream. That was the trade route, a path Jaco must have followed many times: a day's canoe ride east to Saleesh House, then another day or two downstream to the Kullyspel post.

Back in my car, I drove the other way, along the main road north, and soon passed a giant sign announcing the many attractions of Doug Allard's Flathead Trading Post. The parking lot crawled with tourists and revelers on their way to the annual Pow Wow of the Confederated Salish and Kootenai tribes—a grouping that includes most of the peoples who lived around David Thompson's west-side trade houses. Doug Allard sat on a wooden bench on the front porch of his substantial peeled-log structure, comfortable in his position between a poster commemorating the Declaration of Independence and another announcing the Pow Wow Rodeo Finals. His long ponytail shone raven in the sun; the broad features of his face complemented his powerful bronzed hands. A big eagle chain-sawed from a yellow pine butt guarded the rail beside him, its vanilla scent still hanging fresh in the air.

At the moment Allard was talking about farming. A friend of his had just spent a whole week trying to make hay, riding the back of a baler fiddling with knotters that refused to tie. "Couple hundred bales for a whole week's work," he laughed. "Pitiful." Allard flashed his teeth as the stream of people flowed past. A stretch van with Washington plates slid up to the railing and deposited a contingent of native women. Allard began hooting about their homeland on the Spokane Reservation before they were clear of the van. Five of the ladies mounted the boardwalk and approached Allard in a swirl of fawnskin, and when he noticed that one of them brandished a huge roll of raffle tickets, he slapped his forehead and turned away, pretending to look for a place to hide. Then he turned back to greet each of them by name, deferring to age, before he started moaning about the unreasonable demands on proper braves and small business-men. As I backed out of my parking place, I saw one of the Spokane women stuff a sizable loop of tickets into Allard's shirt pocket.

The Pow Wow at Arlee was just hitting its stride when I got there late in the evening. License plates from every western state filled the rodeo ground's mammoth parking lot, which was dotted with cardboard signs giving directions and cautioning that a prohibition against alcohol would be strictly enforced. Many of the vehicles were large and made for living in; I eased in next to a bubble-windowed conversion van and picked my way through the tipi village near the gate.

In the center of the grounds, three long tents shaded a group of stick game players. Two lines sat facing each other in folding chairs, enmeshed in the same guessing game that used to exasperate David Thompson so. The idea of the game is very simple: the leader of one side shuffles short sticks behind his back, then holds out his closed fists for the other side to guess left or right. The guessing team sings a special song that helps them visualize which hand holds the prize, and if they are right, they collect the wager and then take their turn at hiding the sticks. I watched a few rounds, yet I never could see exactly who was holding the sticks, or what the guess had been, or even who had won. But it was impossible not to bounce to the rhythms of the family chants. Two women with their eyes closed, an ancient grandmother, giggling sisters, a pimply teenage boy, a man in overalls—their voices trembled like aspen leaves in a breeze, gradually rose in pitch and intensity, then suddenly dove to a halt. When they stopped, I thought I saw one poker-faced elder in a faded Stetson make the merest twitch of his left forefinger. His brethren beside him broke into cheers. While the old man calmly lit a cigarette, the line opposite him launched into *their* song, and the winds blew through another many-leafed tree.

Behind the stick game was a marketplace of exotic booths. The crowd in the dusty pathways moved slowly, stopping to examine strips of leather, little cylinders of colored beads, trays of jewelry. A bunch of boys gathered around a hide seller to rub their hands along a black skunk pelt hanging from a pole, then moved on to a pile of wolfskins. As the boys thumbed through the stack, oohing and aahing at the swirls of wolf pelage, I found myself studying their profiles, looking for the kind of oddly clipped Welsh nose that David Thompson was supposed to have had. Although most historians write about Thompson's lifelong faithfulness to Charlotte, rumors about his time at Saleesh House have circulated among the local people. In the 1930s Duncan MacDonald, a man of mixed blood who grew up in the area, told a newspaper reporter that "David Thompson was a great man. He lived among my people . . . He had a woman among the Salish. His descendants still live on the reservation." Duncan's sister Christine told another interviewer that Thompson had a daughter by a Pend Oreille woman. Neither Duncan MacDonald nor his sister ever identified any descendants, however, and Thompson's own writings contain no hint of any involvements on the west side of the mountains.

Across the way from the booths, tiers of bleachers surrounded a covered pavilion, which rocked with the furious rhythms of the Pistol Creek drummers. Two or three hundred dancers of all ages and attires jostled around the ring. There were toddlers and grandfathers, a blond modern dancer in Los Angeles garb, and a high-schooler wearing a plain black cowboy shirt. Feathered headdresses and elaborate animal masks were everywhere. A warrior with an armband of beaten tin shook his eagle-claw medicine stick playfully in my face. I had missed the performance by the Fancy Dancers, but several of the little girls bounced around the ring with the crowd, their fringed buckskin dresses and entry numbers flapping with each move.

The Pistol Creekers put down their sticks, and the caller cleared the ring and ordered up the five finalists for the Clown Dance competition. The crowd hooted lustily when the first contestant, Ms. Canada, pranced out. She was a big, muscular woman with wild black hair, and she wore a deerskin dress, swiped with grease, that stretched from her shoulders clear down to the ground. A few snatches of lewd, showy bumps evoked a round of catcalls from the grandstand. A small boy crawled out from under the bleachers at my feet; he was crying, and clambered up my sock. I picked him up and toted him around in back of the crowd until a woman tapped me on the shoulder to claim him. As I returned to my place, the last dancer was being announced: I-Am-a-Horny-Person. She entered the sawdust ring as a whirling mass of burlap, lumped in all the wrong places and clanking with several beer can belts and bandoliers. She shrieked like a witch and let her long hair fly; she ground her wide hips; she mocked the mocking crowd for the time of a rodeo ride and then backed away to furious applause. It wasn't until Ms. Canada was announced as the winner half an hour later, and a healthy young man in blue jeans and a T-shirt strutted out to collect his trophy, that I understood the dance's sexual inversion and could laugh along with the crowd. As the grinning Ms. Canada held his prize up for approval, the Pistol Creekers burst into a fanfare of rimshots and staccato shouts; the victor answered with a twisted kick.

DAVID THOMPSON finished gathering furs from the Flathead and Kootenai camps in late March, just as the first foals were born in the valley. The tribes were preparing to pitch away for a place they called the Root Plains to dig the first of the season's bulbs, but many of them were sick "with a violent Cold which generally ends in a Rash breaking thro' the Skin. A Purge of Salts with a little Paregoric Elixir soon eases them entirely." Spring snow squalls hindered the furmen's trip back to Saleesh House, and by the time they arrived, many of them were also ill.

At the post, Thompson found he had too many furs to fit into the warehouse, so he stored the surplus in his own quarters and moved outside into a tent. Within two weeks he had pressed and packed his winter take and headed west to Kullyspel House, where he arrived in time for an uncharacteristic journal entry: "April 22nd Sunday. A very fine Easter Sunday – rested all day." The next morning he dispatched Finan McDonald to manage Saleesh House while he was away. He had recently rehired Jaco Finlay "in his old Capacity of Clerk & Interpreter" and now gave him orders to follow the "Skeetshoo Indian Road" southwest to a busy salmon-fishing camp on the Spokane River. Thompson wanted Jaco to build another trade house there, to serve the Colville and Spokane tribes as the next link in his supply line. Once it was completed, his network of posts would cover the main native routes in the region, and the traders would be able to visit them all in two weeks' time. He would also be one step closer to the Columbia River.

Thompson now had a clear picture of how that big river arches far to the north, then suddenly turns back on itself to rush almost straight south before bending toward the sea. He now understood how the Kootenai's neat horseshoe nests into the long parabola formed by the Flathead–Clark Fork–Pend Oreille system, which he had the good sense to call simply the Saleesh River. He now knew how both of those large tributaries oddly mirror the Columbia's course as they flow south from the Rockies, then twist north and west to meet their mother just above the 49th parallel. Like an astronomer who factors in the invisible effects of gravity, he had made his deductions about the country by keeping the elusive Columbia on a tangent to his expanding circle of trade.

Thompson had arrived at Kullyspel House with a little time to spare. Still hoping to reach the Columbia and pioneer a more northerly route back across the Divide, he sent Le Bon Vieux to buy him a pine-bark canoe so that he could make another try at navigating the Pend Oreille's northward swing. With a different guide this time, he probed deeper into the canyons, but kept getting penned in by steep rocks until he was finally stopped cold by the sudden drop of Metaline Falls, thirty miles from the spot where the Pend Oreille spills into the Columbia. His Kalispel guide explained the difficulties of the portage in clear detail: "Highly dangerous & passable only to light active men & they obliged to go on hands & Feet up the steep Crags, which he assured us was continued for a distance of 2½ days." The Kalispels only came to the falls to gather red ochre, he said, and never went far beyond them. Leaving his canoe, Thompson scrambled up a mountain that offered a view to the north. From there he could see exactly how the big river was flowing down to intersect his route, and he couldn't do a thing about it.

> I now perceived the Columbia River was in a deep valley at the north end of these rude Hills, and its west side the high rolling lands of Mount Nelson, round which it runs. Attentively surveying the country, and considering all the information I had collected from various Indians, I concluded that we must abandon all thoughts of a passage this way, and return by our old Road, till some future opportunity shall point out a more eligible road.
>
> *Narrative*

The guide described a path overland through the Colville Valley that his people followed to reach the Columbia, but Thompson had no more time to scout it out; once again, his pendulum of duty swung east. He turned back toward Kullyspel House and on the way passed his fortieth birthday without remark, his dinner "a good Meal of swan, Geese, and Roots." A day's ride from his trading post, he came upon Beaulieu and Boisverd splitting wood. "Boisverd is very ill, having been ruptured by a violent Fall from a Horse 3 days ago, & his foot hanging in the Stirrup the Horse hauled him a considerable distance before he could be extricated. He has thrown up much blood which has relieved him considerably."

With Le Bon Vieux helping to transfer packhorses, Thompson left Kullyspel House on May 9 to begin the trip along his established route north to Kootanae House. On May 17th he had a set-to with one of his men, who "declared himself unable to do his duty & upon my attempting to oblige him, deserted." Left short-handed, the surveyor had to send back the cargo of one of his canoes for later delivery, but he still had such a load of furs that it took the men five trips each to portage around Kootenai Falls. As they shuttled back and forth, Thompson stopped to watch a dipper, or water ouzel, that worked the swift water:

> He was in the Cascades of the Brook plunging & fishing for Worms boldly – often letting himself drive upon the foaming little Waves of the Brook & seemed always quite at his Ease – his plunging was always while he kept firm foot on the bottom – the moment he lost his footing he dove down, but in an instant always brought himself up with amazing dexterity & agility – he brought for his young a small Kind of Insect out of the Water something like a very small frog – his food seemed to be in plenty, he is not in the least web footed – & with all his plunging in the little Cascades his Feathers never in the least appeared either Wet or ruffled.

Farther up the Kootenay River, at another rapids, one of the voyageurs took a dunking, and when they tried to coax the horses across the river, several were swept away and nearly drowned. All the cargo went into the water. The time that was lost drying things out and re-gumming the canoes turned out to be a stroke of good luck, for at Canal Flats they found the fresh tracks of Piegans and an aspen branch that had been broken and stripped of its bark only a few hours before—had Thompson's canoes arrived a little sooner, there might have been a much longer delay. Pausing only for a quick shave and wash, "of which we stood in much need," the men put into Columbia Lake and paddled past Kootanae

House toward the ascent of Blaeberry River. At the beginning of the portage trail, they stopped at their "Hoard"—a stout hut constructed of logs and covered with pine bark, where they had cached saddles and dried provisions. Inside they found a wolverine: "He had cut his way thro' the door of our little House & eaten 25 pounds of Pemmican, ½ a dressed Skin, 3½ pairs of Shoes, & cut to pieces 6 or 7 large Saddles." They caught the carcajou and killed it, then made do with a swan and a goose for dinner.

CHAPTER SEVEN

OMEN OF THE RED STICK

SUMMER 1810–SPRING 1811

THE NORTH WEST Company had a policy of giving its wintering partners a furlough every few years, and in 1810 it was David Thompson's turn to "go down on rotation." He left James McMillan to bring the fur packs and a parcel of his books over the pass and sped east in a light canoe with Augustin Boisverd and two other voyageurs. On June 23, running downstream on the Saskatchewan, they crossed paths with a pair of well-stocked Hudson's Bay Company canoes under the charge of Joseph Howse, bound for the west side: the Bay Company was finally making its move over the mountains. Thompson paddled on, docking that same evening at New White Mud House, a post that had just been completed by Alexander Henry and James Hughes near the present-day city of Edmonton.

Henry and Hughes had passed a rough winter. The Blackfeet tribes were still at war with the Crees, and traders on the upper Saskatchewan found themselves caught in the middle of the feud: both sides wanted the furmen to quit selling guns and ammunition to their enemies. Hughes had begun the year in charge of Fort Augustus, while Henry manned another establishment downstream, but repeated threats against both posts, plus news that Henry's scalp was in great demand by a band of Crees, had convinced the men to consolidate their forces at a central location. The neighboring Hudson's Bay Company traders, equally frightened, followed the Nor'Westers, and the two companies built their posts side by side within a single stockade. This show of force had prevented violence so far, but the situation remained tense. Alexander Henry's journal entry for the day after Thompson's arrival captures the mood:

> We got an alarm from the Children taking up a lock of horse hair, tied to a piece of Red Cloth and Feathers, that was found drifting down the river, and four of them at the same time declared they saw a human arm tied to a log pass down the stream. I sent a boat in pursuit of it, but to no purpose . . . Dumont's woman arrived and declares she saw a party of Indians concealed in the Woods, who had made a fire and were drying their Buffalo robes. All this spread a great alarm at this place.

Some of Thompson's children were probably among those who saw the phantom arm, since his family had moved up to White Mud House along with James Hughes. During the five days Thompson spent at the new post exchanging news and information, Alexander Henry would have told him what he knew about another recent Blackfeet attack on the upper Missouri: "They fell upon a party of Americans, murdered them all, and brought away considerable booty in goods of various kinds, such as fine cotton shirts, beaver traps, hats, knives, dirks, handkerchiefs, Russian sheeting, tents, and a number of banknotes, some signed New Jersey and Trenton Banking Company." This incident sounds similar to one that the Flatheads later related to Thompson, involving a Piegan attack on an American fort near the headwaters of the Missouri. On the subject of Americans, Henry also may have loaned Thompson his copy of Patrick Gass's newly published *Journal* from the Lewis and Clark expedition, which included a day-by-day account of the Americans' trip down the lower Columbia.

On June 28 Henry reported that "Mr. Thompson embarked with his family for Montreal in light canoe with five men." At this point the surveyor's family included Charlotte and three children: Samuel, six; Emma, four; and John, two. Their oldest daughter, Fanny, was already in Montreal attending a boarding school. The Thompsons passed a typical trip down the Saskatchewan, paddling through buffalo herds, rain, and relentless mosquitoes. In mid-July they stopped at the company post on Lake Winnipeg, and "here I left my little Family with her Sister in Law to the care of good Providence." Apparently Charlotte and the children were not going on to Montreal with Thompson for his furlough.

While the surveyor had been herding his fur packs and family across the continent, Finan McDonald had taken off from Saleesh House on a different mission. Before leaving his Flathead post, Thompson had asked his clerk to lay in a large supply of dried buffalo meat for the next winter. When the Flatheads and other neighboring tribes began gathering for one of their summer hunts, McDonald and two French Canadians went along. As always, the Flathead bands were on alert for enemy scouts, and they were barely across the pass when they met up with a party of Piegans. In a battle that lasted all day, the three Nor'Westers fired off many shots of their own ("I have noticed that the Indians allow no neutrals," wrote Thompson), and the losses at sundown tallied seven Piegans and five Flatheads. The west-side peoples counted this as a great victory, whereas the Piegans were mortified. The balance of tribal power was shifting again.

ON JULY 22 Thompson arrived at Rainy Lake House, where
something happened that changed his plans to continue on to
Montreal. Only a few days before, at their annual meeting in
Fort William, the partners had reappointed him as the proprietor in charge of the Columbia Department for the upcoming
year. There are no surviving minutes from that meeting and
no record of any specific orders to Thompson, but in a letter
written a few months later he explained that "the critical situation of our affairs in the Columbia obliged me to return."
The critical situation involved New York entrepreneur John
Jacob Astor, who was dispatching parties by land and sea to
establish a fur-trading base at the mouth of the Columbia.
Astor had done business with the North West Company
before and, realizing the importance of Thompson's interior
posts, had offered it a stake in his latest enterprise; the partners gathered at Fort William had voted to accept a one-third
interest in the American's project. The partners forwarded a
copy of their resolution to Thompson at Rainy Lake, and they
must have also sent a dispatch asking him to finish exploring the Columbia down to the Pacific. They were planning
to send their own supply ship around the Horn the following year and needed to make sure there was a workable route
from the coast to their inland posts.

Some historians have inferred that Thompson was supposed to race Astor's men to the coast, but in that case, the
partners would surely have sent Thompson ahead and put
someone else in charge of ferrying the trade goods west.
Thompson's journals are of no help here, because no notebook survives for the three months following his arrival at
Rainy Lake. Judging from his later comments and from an
1811 letter written by William McGillivray, it seems clear
that his mission was to cross the mountains and distribute
his trade goods as usual, then tackle the Columbia. Given the
absence of any field notes between his arrival at Rainy Lake
on July 22 and the end of October, Thompson's only account
of the fall's events is in his *Narrative*, and there he completely

ignores the breaking political situation. Instead he describes an incident involving a woman he had encountered some six years before in the Muskrat Country, who was now in the possession of a marvelous long stick.

> The day after my arrival a Lady Conjuress made her appearance. She was well dressed of twenty five years of age, she had her Medicine Bag, and bore in her hands a conjuring stick about 4½ feet in length 1½ inches at the foot and three inches at the top, by one inch in thickness, one side was painted black, with rude carved figures of Birds Animals and Insects filled with vermilion; the other side was painted red with carved figures in black, she had set herself up for a prophetess, and gradually had gained by her shrewdness, some influence among the Natives as a dreamer, and expounder of dreams, she recollected me, before I did her, and gave me a haughty look of defiance, as much as to say I am now out of your power.
>
> *Narrative*

This woman and her conjuring stick were apparently involved with a religious cult of the Ojibway tribe who lived around Rainy Lake, but without recording any of her prophecies, Thompson got directly back to work and by the end of his next paragraph had loaded four supply canoes and paddled off up the Saskatchewan.

Alexander Henry noted in his journal that the explorer made it back to White Mud House on September 6, 1810: "At 2 O'clock Mr. Thompson arrived from Lake la Pluie in a Canoe with six men, bound for Columbia. He brings us the long-wished-for news from the civilized world, for which we have been anxiously waiting for this some time past." Much of the news from the civilized world was unsettling. Napoleon was trying to isolate Great Britain with economic blockades. The Royal Navy was impressing sailors from U.S. merchant ships into its own service, and the Americans appeared ready to fight over the matter. There was also sentiment in the United States to try and drive the British out of Canada, and tensions at the fur posts on the Great Lakes were running high.

None of these international crises affected Thompson's plans. When his three other canoes arrived the next morning, Henry had his blacksmith put up his bellows to make iron tips for their poles, then hosted a dance that lasted until daybreak. It was late the next afternoon before Thompson directed his voyageurs on upriver. A couple of days later, he followed on horseback with two Iroquois hunters and Alexander's cousin William Henry, who was on his way north to a post on the Athabasca River. According to Thompson's *Narrative*, they killed three elk about a day's ride above Rocky Mountain House and camped beside the river to dry the meat while they waited for the canoes. The next morning the oldest Iroquois stared at the drying racks and announced: "I have had bad dreams, this meat will never be eaten." He then saddled his horse and rode off. The voyageurs were overdue for their rendezvous with Thompson, who, somewhat worried, sent William Henry and the remaining Iroquois to look for the boats. What they found was a camp of Piegans only a few miles downstream. When Henry returned with this news, Thompson deduced that the Piegans were on the lookout for his party, and fearing that a rifle shot had revealed their whereabouts, the three men took off cross-country at daybreak in a fall snowstorm.

> We rode on through the Woods until it was nearly dark, when we were obliged to stop; we remained quiet waiting our fortune, when finding all quiet, we made a small fire, and passed the night with some anxiety; my situation precluded sleep, cut off from my men, uncertain where to find them, and equally so of the movements of the Indians, I was at a loss what to do, or which way to proceed.
>
> *Narrative*

Meanwhile, Alexander Henry was traveling upriver from White Mud House to reopen Rocky Mountain House for trade with the Blackfeet tribes, who wanted to avoid any contact with the Crees at the trading posts downstream. Relations with both nations were still strained, and the traders were making every effort to keep peace on the river. When Henry approached the supposedly empty fort on October 5, he was surprised to see smoke rising from chimneys within the stockade and to find Piegans and white men standing at the gate. The white men turned out to be voyageurs from Thompson's Columbia brigade, who had been stopped by a group of Piegans a few miles upstream and told that they could go no farther upriver. The Piegan Blackfeet, upset about their summer defeat by the Flatheads, had determined not to allow another shipment of guns and ammunition across the mountains to their enemies. The voyageurs reported that the group that detained them had been cordial but had kept them under an unrelenting watch. The voyageurs also told Henry that they had decided to return to Rocky Mountain House in hopes of finding Thompson, whom they had not seen since he parted from them to go hunting on horseback over two weeks before. "Sadly perplexed to know whether Mr. Thompson was above or below," Henry broke open the trade goods and began to placate the Piegans with rum.

It wasn't until the following day that Henry had a chance to walk around the post. To his distress, he found that the Piegans had dug up the graves of two Crees who had been buried on the premises a few years before and scattered their bones—"a certain Omen of their bad intentions." That afternoon more Piegans came in to trade and informed Henry that four tents of their tribesmen were keeping watch on the river a day's ride upstream, in order to make sure that no traders got past. Next evening several Piegans from the blockade arrived on horseback, and Henry recognized one of Thompson's steeds among them. When he asked about the horse, the Piegans replied that they had found it at a camp upriver, along with a pair of blue leggings that Henry knew belonged to his cousin William. The Piegans said that they had tried to follow tracks leading away from the camp, but that a snowstorm had buried them. Henry pretended non-chalance, saying that the horse and pants must have belonged to a party of free hunters after beaver. From the information on hand, Henry had to assume that Thompson was some-where upriver from him, probably at Kootenay Plains, and he determined to send the supply canoes on up to him as soon as possible. But "this could not be done while any Indians were at the fort; they are suspicious of our every movement. However, I kept everything in readiness, until a favorable op-portunity should present."

On the sixth afternoon all the Piegans departed, and the canoes were about to launch upriver when a group of horse-men was sighted in the distance. Henry quickly instructed the voyageurs to paddle downstream a ways, as if they were going to another post for supplies, then tie up and wait until mid-night to sneak back upstream, "when whatever Indians might arrive I would keep dead drunk." He kept his word, and by 2:00 A.M. the canoes had lined their way past the fort and the group of Blackfeet were snoring in Henry's tent.

The next evening, cousin William showed up. Henry "was astonished to hear that he came from below," *downriver*, from a campsite he and David Thompson had set up after fleeing the Piegans. Thompson had already sent an Iroquois mes-senger up to Kootenay Plains to tell Bercier, who had been waiting there with horses for the portage, to bring the horses down to him by a trail through the woods on the north side of the river. Alexander Henry quickly sent a man upstream to stop the canoes, and the next morning he paddled down him-self to see Thompson.

At 4 Oclock arrived at the spot where Mr. Thompson was camped on the North side of the River, upon the top of a Hill about 300 feet from the level of the water, where tall Pines stood so thickly planted that I could [not] see his tent until I came within ten yards of it. Here he was starving, and waiting for his people – both his own Canoes and those men who were coming down with his Horses. This affair of his Canoes being stopped by the Peagans has induced him to alter his route and endeavour to open a new road . . . It is therefore determined that the Canoes should be ordered to return below in as private a manner as possible, to avoid all misunderstanding with the natives.

Henry returned to Rocky Mountain House and, three nights and several quarts of rum later, accomplished the redoubling of the cargo back downstream: "As the Piegans were roaring drunk, the canoes got away unperceived & my Cousin went with them . . . I was happy to get clear of those canoes, that had caused me so much worry and anxiety ever since my arrival." A few days later a Cree hunter arrived from across the mountains with the news that the Piegans had also set up a blockade across the pass; even if Thompson had somehow gotten his canoes around the barricade on the Saskatchewan and made it across the Divide, he would have been stopped by this second blockade. His oft-expressed desire to find a way around the Piegan Blackfeet had now become imperative.

For years Thompson had been thinking about some alternative route, and he and Henry had both heard about a pass near the headwaters of the Athabasca River. The upper Athabasca River runs about eighty miles north of the Saskatchewan and roughly parallel to it; the country between them is wooded and marshy, and the Blackfeet tribes seldom ventured that far north. Though pioneering a new route this late in the year would require precious time, Thompson obviously felt he had no choice but to try—not only did he have the exploration of the Columbia to complete, but he also had men at three trade houses waiting for supplies. By the time his next journal notebook resumes at the end of October, Thompson has reassembled his men, gathered twenty-four

CROSSING ATHABASCA PASS

horses, and signed on a pair of Iroquois hunters. He sent two men to a post downstream to obtain dogs that could pull sleds over the pass. He found another Iroquois, named Thomas, who professed to know the way over the Athabasca River pass. On October 29 the revamped expedition set off for the Athabasca along an old hunting trail.

A week later two of the voyageurs made their way back to Alexander Henry at Rocky Mountain House with a request for more supplies, and their account of the journey so far prompted Henry to express concern about Thompson's well-being: "They had left him on his way to the Waters of the Columbia, cutting his road through a wretched, thick, Woody country, over Mountains and gloomy Muskagues, and nearly starving with Hunger, Animals being very scarce in that quarter . . . in fact, their case is pitiful."

Thompson's case was not so pitiful that he meant to waste his winter on the east side of the Divide. By the first week in December, he had reached the Athabasca River and followed it to the foot of the mountains. He stopped at Brule Lake and quickly built sheds for provisions, then scattered his men in search of birch trees to make snowshoes and sleds. A few of the men had brought their wives this far, and Thompson assigned them to cutting line and netting snowshoes. He complained that the women made an awkward job of it, but did allow that the temperature had not risen higher than twenty below zero for several days. From this campsite, just before Christmas, Thompson wrote a letter to Alexander Fraser, the old friend whose post had been his first stop when he joined the North West Company almost fourteen years before. Fraser had recently retired from the field and was living in Montreal, where he had visited Fanny Thompson.

21 Dec. 1810, Athabaska River
Foot of the Mountains

My Dear Fraser,
I received your esteemed favour the 9th Sept. and am

obliged to you for the traits of civilized life and the information of my daughter. She costs me 62£ 10s. at present, and I think 50£ a year would do her all the good that the present sum costs me. It is my wish to give all my children an equal and good education; my conscience obliges me to it, and it is for this I am now working in this country.

I intended to have paid you a visit at Montreal last summer, but the critical situation of our affairs in the Columbia obliged me to return. The Americans, it seems, were as usual determined to be beforehand with us in the Columbia in ship navigation. As the Peagans killed an officer and 8 soldiers out of a tribe of 12 ditto, if this accident has not drove them back, they will probably get the start of me.

My canoes were also drove back by the Peagans, but no lives or property lost and I have changed our route from [illegible] to the Athabaska River and am now preparing in this hard season to cross the mountains and gain my first post near the head of the Mississourie [Saleesh House], a march of about 34 days, and a part of it over a dangerous country for war. I hope good Providence will take care of us and bring me safe back again.

I am always in such distant expeditions that I cannot write to my friends regularly . . . I am getting tired of such constant hard journeys; for the last 20 months I have spent only bare two months under the shelter of a hut, all the rest has been in my tent, and there is little likelihood the next 12 months will be much otherwise.

Your humble servant,
David Thompson

On December 29 Thompson left his Brule Lake camp with twelve men and eight dogsleds loaded with over seven hundred pounds of supplies. Four horses carried two hundred pounds of pemmican, thirty-five pounds of grease, and sixty pounds of flour. A temperature of minus thirty-two degrees made for solid sledding, but they had a rough climb ahead. On January 1 the dogs could not pull their loads, and Thompson stopped to cache a third of his goods. The men frittered away most of the day repacking, "during which time they cooked twice a four gallon Kettle of Meat, which they devoured, although they had had a hearty breakfast . . . upon my reproaching some of them with their gluttony, the reply was 'what pleasure have we in Life but eating?'" Most of these voyageurs were new to Thompson and to his methods of travel; even before they reached the mountains, several had shown that they did not share his zeal for exploration.

That evening the hunters brought down two buffalo bulls and a mountain sheep, so the party stopped for a day to split and dry the meat. When they started again, they forked off to follow the Whirlpool River, moving among thick, stunted trees and marshy lakes. The horses, helpless in the deepening snow, were left to fend for themselves in a small meadow around some little ponds. But the heavy snow did not impede all animals; soon afterward the men came across a set of tracks that gave them quite a start: each footprint had "4 large Toes, about 3 or 4 inches long & a small Nail at the end of each; the Ball of his Foot sank about 3 inches deeper than his Toes; the hinder part of his Foot did not mark well. The whole is about 14 inches long by 8 inches wide." At the time Thompson surmised that the track must have belonged to a big grizzly bear, although his hunters had a different idea. In his *Narrative* he remembered their qualms: "Strange to say, here is a strong belief that the haunt of the Mammoth is about this defile, I questioned several, none could positively say they had seen him, but their belief I found firm and not to be shaken."

It was Thompson's habit to travel for a few hours every morning before stopping to eat, but on the march up the Whirlpool his crew continually exasperated him by cooking breakfast before they set out. On January 8 the voyageur Du Nord beat one of his dogs senseless, and tossed it to the side of a trail with a broken sled. "He is what we call a 'flash' man, a showy fellow before the women but a coward in heart, and would willingly desert if he had the courage to go alone." The next day the temperature climbed to thirty-two degrees, and the snow turned to slush: "Very bad hauling: the Sleds I may say stuck to the Snow." Despite the conditions, the party made its way above timberline and began the final ascent to the Divide. Just short of the pass, Du Nord refused to haul his sled any farther. Thompson had had enough of the man's obstreperous behavior and ordered him back down the trail. But Du Nord apologized and the surveyor allowed him to continue "although, in my opinion, he is a poor spiritless wretch."

That afternoon they crested Athabasca Pass and made camp on the west side. Thompson went out to look at what lay before them, and when he returned found his crew probing the snow with a twenty-foot pole, trying to measure its depth. There was too much to clear away, so they had to build their fire on top of the snowpack. That night a storm blew through, and the few logs they had brought with them for firewood were soon consumed.

> In this exposed situation we passed the rest of a long night without a fire, and part of my men had strong feelings of personal insecurity. On our right about one third of a mile from us lay an enormous Glacier, the eastern face of which quite steep, of about two thousand feet in height, was of a clean fine green color, which I much admired . . . My men were not at their ease, yet when night came they admired the brilliancy of the stars, and as one of them said, he thought he could touch them with his hand.
>
> *Narrative*

Thompson and the Iroquois Thomas led the way down

the Rockies' western slope along the Wood River, which the surveyor called the "Flat Heart" in memory of his men's low spirits. Several members of the crew continued to balk at the task before them. They seemed to find comfort only in food, and in thirty-six hours consumed fifty-six pounds of pemmican. One morning Du Nord went out hunting for a couple of hours and when he returned chastised the cook for not having any moose meat ready for him. "What, said he, do you take me for a Horse to go for so long without eating?"

The snow was waist deep, and the warmer west-side temperatures made for slushy, wretched traveling. When Thomas shot two moose, the expedition halted again for a day to dry the meat. Thompson, short on paper, scribbled a letter to the partners on wooden boards. Their guide had completed his job, and on January 13 he set off with another man to start the message on its journey east. In the face of the continued mild weather, Thompson decided that in order for the dogs to get down the mountain he would have to further lighten their loads. He stripped his supplies down to the bare essentials, hung up the rest to come back for later, and set off through the wet snow. "The Courage of part of my Men is sinking fast. They see nothing in its proper Colour – the soft Weather is a thing, it seems, they never felt before . . . but when Men arrive in a strange Country, fear gathers on them from every Object."

On the 18th of January they camped within a mile of the Columbia, close to the mouth of the Canoe River. In heavy rain, Thompson pushed the party south toward the refuge of Kootanae House. After three days they had made only twelve miles, and some of the men refused to go on. Thompson knew that he was more than two hundred miles north of his post and decided to retreat back to the Canoe River to wait for breakup. There Du Nord and three others, "having long been dispirited & useless as old Women, told me he would return." The surveyor gave the deserters forty-five pounds of pemmican for provisions and gladly let them go.

The handful of remaining men built a twelve-by-twelve hut and settled in for a long winter with few amenities. Thompson found a big birch knot and carved himself a bowl, "as I have no Kitchen Furniture other than a Kettle." He had happened into the midst of a big snow winter, in a forest that contained the largest timber he had ever seen—cedars up to thirty-six feet in circumference, larches just as large that "rose full two hundred feet without a branch, and threw off very luxuriant heads . . . on the west side we were pigmies; in such forests what could we do with Axes of two pounds weight?"

What they had to do was build a canoe. For several days he and his men searched for birch bark without finding any thick enough to make even a dish. In early March they decided that they would have to fabricate a wooden boat. Thompson drew up a plan, then they threw down a cedar three feet in diameter and split out nine timbers thirty-one feet long. The next five weeks were devoted to a maddening process of trial and error, as they transformed those rough cants into a twenty-five-foot clinker-built canoe. Frozen boards had to be thawed for the drawknife and carefully scraped down. The men had to keep redesigning the frame as they went along, sometimes replacing sections of boards that had ended up too thick or too thin. They overlapped the planks like clapboard and sewed them to the frame with spruce watap that they dug out of the icy ground. Cracks from their auger holes ran too far in the brittle wood, ruining whole pieces. Often the cedar turned out to be too green, and they had to unsew their day's work and redry it by the fire. One version of the boat broke in half under its own weight.

The trials of this project inspired Thompson to name the place Boat Encampment, but finally, on April 16, the tedious job of heating gum and calking the seams was almost finished, and he was busy packing. He had made a cedar box for his sextant and another for his clothes and papers, but there wasn't much else to load: "We have abt. 3 pieces of Goods, 180 lbs. of poor dried Meat & 30 lbs. of Grease – 10 lbs. of

Pemmican & a little Flour." They left behind the hides of seventeen moose they had killed for food; "all the skins were useless, there being no woman to dress them."

The Canoe River flows into the Columbia right at the tip of the big river's northern elbow, just as it turns decisively to the south. Thompson knew where he was, and in his *Narrative* says that he toyed with the idea of going straight down the river, but it would have been foolish to take off with only three men over several hundred miles of unfamiliar water in a jerry-rigged canoe. So he resolved to pole and track his way up the Columbia toward his trade houses, where he knew he could find more voyageurs.

The first night out, a storm dumped heavy snow on the four men as they slept under the canoe, and Thompson thanked Heaven that the cedar boards didn't split under the drift. Fighting through five feet of snow around the portages, or dragging their outfit on a makeshift sled across iced-over sections of river, it took them three weeks to cover the two hundred miles to the mouth of the Blaeberry River. When they met a canoe of free hunters along the way, Thompson hired an Iroquois named Charles to go south with him as canoe foreman on the Columbia trip. All the hills and mountains were still completely snow-covered, and the late thaw kept the river at the lowest level Thompson had ever recorded. What elk and mule deer they managed to shoot were in very poor condition due to the persistent winter, and at Columbia Lake the surveyor sampled one of the black cormorants that had just arrived for the breeding season: "They are very fishy tasted and their eggs almost as bad as those of a Loon."

From Columbia Lake he crossed Canal Flats and headed down the Kootenay River. Near Tobacco Plains he found a group of Kootenais and free hunters, including another Iroquois named Ignace who had traded at Saleesh House. Thompson knew Ignace to be a skilled canoe hand and hired him to serve as his steersman. One of the Kootenais told the surveyor that Finan McDonald, after a dispute with some Piegans, had abandoned Saleesh House and built another post twenty miles farther down the river. The Hudson's Bay Company agent Joseph Howse had also had trouble with the Piegans; during a short winter of trading near Flathead Lake, he had been so harassed that he and his party returned to the east side for good. Howse reported to James Bird at Edmonton House that the Piegans had warned "that if they again meet with a white man going to supply their Enemies, they would not only plunder and kill them, but that they would make dry meat of his body."

It was a wary group of Nor'Westers who continued on overland to Saleesh House, expecting to find a letter from Finan McDonald giving them his new location.

> May 27 Monday A cloudy Day and much heavy Rain in the afternoon & Night. I examined the old Ho[use] – but found no Letter nor writing of any kind to inform me what had become of the people who had wintered there – wrote a few Lines in Charcoal on a Board in case the Americans should pass – purporting that we had left the Ho[use] on account of the War with the Peeagans – Killed a Mare for Food – Killed 2 Rattlesnakes – I was near treading on one of them.

It is unclear for whom the surveyor intended his charcoal note—it might have been for the independent American trappers in the region, but he might also have been thinking of the expedition that John Jacob Astor had sent west from St. Louis that summer, bound overland for the Pacific. In either case, Thompson himself kept moving. He and his men rode west to Kullyspel House, which was also deserted, then continued down the Pend Oreille River to the camas plains near modern Cusick. There they found a group of Kalispels preparing for war. "Every warrior puts white Earth on his Head as a kind of Mourning for those who are to fall & Penance for himself, that the Great Spirit may give him success." The Kalispels reported that Finan MacDonald had joined Jaco Finlay on the Spokane River, and Thompson sent word that he needed horses. While he waited, Le Bon Vieux dropped by with twelve mullet and some elk meat.

Finan McDonald and Michel Boulard arrived on June 12 with a string of pack animals and led Thompson's party south to Jaco's new post, nicely situated on a yellow pine flat beside the Spokane River. Thompson spent his first day there calculating its position (latitude 47° 47' N, longitude 117° 27' W). He traded for some carp from the Spokane families camped nearby and sent gifts to the neighboring chiefs. Then, since the Spokane River was unnavigable downstream from Spokane House, he rode north on a trail through the Colville Valley with his voyageurs. On June 18 they met two Canadian free hunters living in the valley. Thompson shot a curlew near Blue Creek, then moved on toward his rendezvous with the Columbia.

CHAPTER EIGHT

WANAPAM

JUNE 19–JULY 14, 1811

THE COLVILLE RIVER empties into the Columbia just below Kettle Falls, and David Thompson reached their junction on June 19, 1811. Near the falls he found a village of square cedar sheds, built from boards split out from driftwood cedars and roofed with rough shakes and woven mats. The interior of each hut was criss-crossed with poles for drying salmon. The natives here (known today as the Colvilles) set up big woven baskets at the bottom of the falls to capture fish, and Thompson called both the place and its-inhabitants "Ilth koy ape," a local phrase meaning kettle trap or net.

After all of his detours and delays, Thompson had finally made it to a launching point for the Pacific; now all he needed was a canoe to get him there. The ponderous local boats, made from burning out half a drift pine or cedar trunk, would never do, so he fanned out his men with some villagers to look for clear cedar or serviceable birch bark. They searched for two days without success and finally backtracked seven miles up the Colville River to a hummock of branchy cedar they remembered from the ride up. The wood was of poor quality, but they managed to piece together the parts for a boat from several trees.

The Nor'Westers had gotten to Ilthkoyape Falls at the beginning of the first salmon runs of the summer, only a few days too late to witness the ceremonies and dances that ushered in the fishing season. For several days after they arrived, a single spearman worked alone from the rocks, although there were enough fish to keep many spears busy. "The salmon are about from 15 to 25 to 30 pounds weight here, well tasted, but have lost all their fat, retaining still all their meat. Their flesh is red and they are extremely well made." Later on, once the Salmon Chief announced that the prescribed number of salmon had ascended the falls, other men set out nets and baskets to begin the harvest in earnest.

Thompson studied the complex rituals that these people attached to one of their most important food sources—"Deep attention is paid by them to what they believe will keep the Salmon about them." He was intrigued by the salmon's mysterious ability to switch from fresh to salt water and then back again for their spawning journey, and he cut open stomachs to confirm that none had eaten anything on their long trip from the sea. He puzzled again over the fact that dogs, which could eat other fish, were poisoned by the flesh of raw salmon. He grappled with the natives' explanation of the salmon's birth, migration, and death: "It is the popular belief that all the Salmon that enter the River die and not one ever returns – this is perhaps almost true of all those that go to the very sources of the River to spawn, when exhausted by their long Journey, weakened by spawning, they become so emaciated as to have no strength to return and die in great numbers of very weakness." He had witnessed the hordes of dead salmon around Windermere Lake at Kootanae House but found it hard to believe that this phenomenon was repeated lower on the Columbia. "But this is only at the very sources of the River as all the water of the River is perfectly clear, and were the whole to die, their amazing numbers would cause such a putrid odor as would soon bring on a pestilence to cut off Mankind."

The Colvilles told Thompson that the salmon had an aversion to any water tainted by humans or animals, and could taste if others of their kind had been cleaned in the water. The explorer watched them sweep the river's edge of all debris and clean their catch well away from the banks; he saw how fish parts down to scales and drops of blood were kept strictly away from the river. One morning the appointed spearman, on the way to his post at the falls, passed near the skull of a dead dog. He immediately returned to his hut, for "to have speared fish with such unclean Eyes would have driven all the Salmon away, and he purified himself with a decoction of the scraped Bark of the Red Thorn [hawthorn]. Thus cleansed he proceeded to work."

Thompson thought this and other taboos pure superstition until one of his men carelessly tossed a horse bone into the river after a meal, and all the salmon instantly spooked back downstream. One of the villagers took to the water and dived for the bone, bringing it up within a few minutes, but fishing was done for the day. The more Thompson watched, the more he became convinced that there was more to these practices than hocus-pocus: "Experience has taught them the delicate perceptions of this fish."

THE CANADIAN artist Paul Kane visited Kettle Falls thirty-five years after Thompson. In his painting of a fall salmon run, fish leap straight up at a series of cataracts that pour over the bedded pitches of rock. On the river's edge three spearmen stand waiting while a fourth man, out on a ledge, leans forward to club a nice-sized chinook that seems to dangle from a short cord attached to the point of his lance. Woven traps, supported by trussed tree limbs and twisted lines, are set up in three different eddies. People are gathered on the columns of stone that edge the falls, but they are not in a fishing frenzy—they stand or sit quietly, eyes on the great numbers of salmon that flash up from the white water. At the edge of the painting, one man lies belly-down on the stone, his head propped on his forearms in the posture of a sphinx. He studies the fish.

A hundred years after Thompson's visit, the Colville and other tribes still gathered at Kettle Falls to capture and prepare salmon in much the same way. A Colville woman named Mourning Dove wrote about camping out at the falls early in this century at her family's traditional place, on the west side of the river. She describes the big fishing baskets they wove from red willow with rims of limber serviceberry. She details spears made with detachable deer-horn prongs held in place with pine pitch and secured by a line; when a salmon was struck, the point came loose, allowing the spearman to play the fish and bring it close to shore for a deathblow. Only men could catch the fish; it was the women's job to split and dry the salmon for winter food.

Mourning Dove says that her great-grandfather, See-whehl-ken, was Salmon Tyee when David Thompson came on the scene. The people of See-whehl-ken's band had never seen a white man before, but they had heard stories of Lewis and Clark from people downstream, and welcomed the strangers. The Salmon Tyee's job was to distribute the salmon caught each day, and Mourning Dove maintains that her grandfather gave the whites the finest fish caught. She says that Thompson couldn't pronounce her grandfather's name very well, so he called See-whehl-ken "Big Heart."

WHILE THOMPSON ate salmon at Ilthkoyape Falls, he tried to find out everything he could about the rest of the river. The Colville people told him that the Columbia upstream was quite rocky, with sparse trees, and that hunting was poor except in the winter months. Of the world downstream they knew little beyond the next village, whose people were called the San Poil. During the week that it took to put the new canoe together, he watched as people from all over the area gathered at the village, "a kind of general rendezvous for News, Trade, and settling disputes." On June 27 five San Poils arrived from a weir they had set up nearby, along with his Kootenai friend the Old Chief and a free hunter from the Flathead country. They presented the surveyor with a bushel of roots, and that wasn't all. "They brought me also from Boisverd's wife a present of 2 pieces of Iron, 5 dressed Skins, 1 Beaver skin & 2 Horses to be paid for when I see her." Thompson does not say whether this is the same wife of Boisverd whom he had sent home from Kootanae House and who later became known to her people as Qánqon. Nor does he explain why this woman would be sending him presents, or where he expected to see her again.

By the first of July, the voyageurs had finished their canoe and were rendering gum to take with them. The men had tired of their salmon diet, and Thompson ordered a horse butchered for provisions along the way. The tribes for some distance downstream spoke languages of the same Interior Salish group as the Colville, Kalispel, and Flathead peoples, and a young San Poil couple fishing near the falls agreed to go along and help interpret for the first part of the trip. The explorer's crew also included a French Canadian free hunter, two of the voyageurs who had come over Athabasca Pass with him, the Iroquois canoemen Charles and Ignace, and his old hand Michel Boulard.

"July 3rd Wednesday After arranging several small affairs, we in number 8 Men with 2 Simpoil Indians set off on a voyage down the Columbia River, to explore this River, in order to open out a Passage for the Interiour Trade with the Pacific Ocean." As the Nor'Westers floated south from Ilthkoyape Falls, the comfortable humpbacked mountains faded behind them, and they watched the landscape dry up before their eyes. Beyond the mouth of the Spokane River,

THE MIDDLE COLUMBIA

the Columbia turns west to make its big bend, passing through country that varies from scattered stands of ponderosa pine to open sage rangeland to vast flows of basalt scoured bare by a series of glacial floods. Powered by the runoff of the same deep snows that had dogged the furmen all winter, the canoe flew downstream for that whole first day. From his vantage in the boat seat, Thompson had time to note little more than "high rocks on the right" and "high rocks on the left." Later he described steep cliffs of columnar basalt, with deep ravines and monstrous stacked rocks "often in step like Stairs." Voyageurs traditionally loved fast water and fewer portages, and Thompson let them run while he plotted courses in his notebook as best he could: "The Courses are not so correct as I could wish. The strength of the Current caused many eddies and small whirlpools which continually toss the canoe from side to side so that the Compass was always vibrating. I hope by the mercy of Heaven to take them much better on my return."

This part of the river was totally new to white men, and Thompson made a point of stopping at every little fishing camp he passed in order to introduce himself. It was a practice that slowed his progress but, as he pointed out in his *Narrative*, seemed politically astute: "My reason for putting ashore and smoking with the Natives, is to make friends with them, against my return, for in descending the current of a large River, we might pass on without much attention to them; but in returning against the current, our progress will be slow and close along the shore, and consequently very much in their power ... "

The party spent the first night at the home village of the San Poil, a poor but friendly tribe who lived in pole huts covered with rush mats. They subsisted mainly on salmon, roots, and berries; they possessed no stone or clay pots for storage, no forged tools or weapons. Thompson passed out tobacco and sat down for a session of smoking and speechmaking— first the chief, then Thompson, who delivered a message through his two interpreters that he would repeat many times over the next ten days: "I then explained to them my object to know how this River was to the Sea, and if good, very large Canoes with Goods of all kinds would arrive, by which they would be supplied with Clothing and all they wanted if they were industrious hunters." The San Poil, like nearly all the tribes he sat down with, were very responsive to his offer of trade. After matters of state were taken care of, a man asked if the women could bring the furmen a small present. Thompson consented, on condition that the present didn't include any *eetoowoy* roots. These eetoowoys were probably camas lily bulbs, which at other times the surveyor enjoyed but at the moment had most of his party doubled over with colic. The women proceeded to shower him with baskets full of eetoowoy and other assorted roots, and the voyageurs asked for a dance. The San Poil, without any musical instruments beyond their expressive voices, performed so eagerly that they raised a cloud of dust that "often fairly obscured the Dancers, tho' we stood only about 4 feet from them."

The next day, July 4, Thompson and his men stayed in the San Poil camp talking and taking observations until noon, then put back into the river. Late in the afternoon, they stopped to scout a rapid, and the voyageurs decided to portage their cargo and ride down in the empty canoe, "but in doing this they run too close to a drift Tree on a Rock, which tore part of the upper lath away & struck Ignace out of the Stem of the Canoe – Altho' he had never swam in his Life he swam so as to keep himself above the Waves, 'till they turned the Canoe around & took him up." That night in camp Thompson bled Ignace to help him recover from his dunking, then got busy splitting a driftwood log to make replacements for the two paddles they had broken during the day.

Afloat again next morning, the Nor'Westers stopped to parley with the Nespelim, a prosperous group with many horses. The elders presented the furmen with five horses, five roasted salmon, three bushels of roots and berries, and four

small dried animals that Thompson thought must be mar-
mots but declined to taste. He also declined another basket of
eetoowoy bulbs. He repaid the gifts with three feet of tobacco, ten plain and four stone rings, eighteen hawk's bells,
a fathom of beads, four papers of vermilion paint, four awls,
and six buttons. In return the Nespelims performed a dance
to wish him luck on his journey. An old man sang for the
dancers, who seemed to jog in place along a curving line.
Both men and women wore decorations of brilliant white
shells—armbands, bracelets, headbands—and a few had
copper baubles hanging from their clothing, ornaments
brought from far away through an active trade relay. While
they were exchanging presents and smoking together,
Thompson counted a chief and sixty men. It was his custom
to number the men who showed up to pass the pipe, then
multiply by seven for an estimate of the size of the band,
thus providing a consistent first census for the native peoples
he-encountered.

The next tribe downstream was the Methow, who greeted
the white men with another dance. Afterward the women sat
down outside the circle of men and joined in the smoking.
Thompson noted that the ladies were entitled to only one
puff, whereas the men got between three and six. The
Methow said that they didn't have any knowledge of the river
beyond their nearest neighbors, and the travelers didn't tarry.
That afternoon, as the river curled south through the rude,
wild country around the base of the Cascades, they saw the
first mountain sheep and rattlesnakes of the trip; they killed
two rattlers but missed the bighorn.

"July 7th Sunday A fine day but cloudy Morning . . . We
came to a large Band of Indians at 10½ A.M. – They received
us all dancing in their Huts, one of which was about 80 yards
long and the other 20 yards." These were the Wenatchee
people, a large tribe of about 120 families. They had heard of
the white men but had never seen them before. One of their
elders came and sat beside Thompson to feel his shoes and

his legs, "gently, as if to know whether I was like themselves." Many of the Wenatchee wore shells in their noses and
sported fine goat-hair blankets. In the mountains to the north
they were able to hunt goats as well as sheep and mule deer,
and Thompson pronounced them hearty in health. Their settlement marked the last of the tribes who belonged to the
same language family as the San Poil; the Columbia Plateau
tribes to the south spoke Sahaptin tongues. By chance a chief
of one of the Plateau bands was visiting the Wenatchee, and
he offered his services as interpreter. Thompson accepted,
and the chief and his wife replaced the San Poil couple in the
canoe.

It was still early in the afternoon, and despite much plead-
ing to stay the night, Thompson was determined to push on.
As he paddled away, the Wenatchee people stretched their
arms heavenward in a prayer for his safe return. A few hours
later the furmen entered country that was "all steep rock and
fine low meadows. It is curious to see fine meadows as it were
springing out of the feet of steep rocks, and spreading along
the river, at times fine knolls of sand." That night proved
fitful, with mosquitoes and a high wind.

In the morning the men decided to take advantage of the
breeze and rigged up a mast and sail. They had made only
a few miles under their sheets when they came to the high
waves of Priest Rapids and shot through them. There was a
sizable native camp at the bottom of the rapids, but the current was so strong that the canoe was a half-mile below it
before the paddlers could put ashore. A chief from the camp
rode down to investigate, followed by "an old white headed
man with the handle of a tea-kettle for an ornament about his
head. He showed no signs of age except his hair and a few
wrinkles in his face, he was quite naked and ran nearly as fast
as the horses. We could not but admire him." When
Thompson wrote up this meeting in his *Narrative*, he focused
on the chief rather than the athletic old man: "The chief on
horseback now rode down to examine us, he appeared very

much agitated, the foam coming out of his mouth; wheeling his horse backwards and forwards, and calling aloud, who are you, what are you?"

IT WAS HIGH noon, midsummer hot, when Gene Hunn and I knocked on the door of James Selam's modest house on the Yakima Indian Reservation in central Washington. As we waited for an answer, the fragment of a bird call drifted around the corner of the house. "Oriole?" Gene asked, corking his head around for a better listen. The grating blackbird notes sounded out again, in series this time, and he affirmed his guess with a nod. "Oriole. James has a pond back there."

Gene is an anthropology professor at the University of Washington in Seattle with a serious side interest in birds. I had first watched him in action on a frigid November afternoon in an apple orchard not far from where we now stood, as he cheerfully explained to half a dozen bewildered people peering through binoculars that they were looking at a wayward yellow-headed parrot. "Has to be," he had said. "See how it's flying with its fingertips?" Gene had been living on the Yakima Reservation at the time, studying the Plateau tribes' view of the world as revealed through their language and natural history. Now, two decades later, he continues to make frequent trips to the Columbia Basin, still mapping out the Plateau culture. James Selam is a tribal elder who has served as Gene's main contact throughout his study.

After a few more knocks on his door, James ushered us inside to a room lit only by the glow of a television. Gene was excited to see his friend and began rattling off plans for the weekend. James punched off the television with a grunt and nodded occasionally at Gene's flow of words, but did not voice his thoughts. His blue jeans were new and stiff; so was his geometrically patterned rayon shirt and brown bandana marked with yellow arrowheads. Only his dark brown cowboy boots seemed seasoned and comfortable. He had the soft, round face of an old woman, coppery smooth with a broad expanse of cheek and forehead. A sparse mustache prickled out from beneath his generous nose. His silvery temple hairs were plaited into pencil-thin braids that fell down over his shoulders and were in turn plaited into two thicker and darker braids pulled forward from the back of his head. These pigtails disappeared inside the bandana tied cowboy-style around his neck, then reemerged from beneath the flap to fall down over his chest to his ample belly.

Gene handed James a compact camera he had brought for him; James touched all the prominent buttons and took two pictures of his wall. As Gene introduced me, mentioning my interest in David Thompson's trip through the Plateau country, James moved over and carefully chose a black baseball cap from a collection on a dresser. It was only when we bumbled together in the narrow doorway that he spoke to me.

"David Thompson, huh? I remember that guy. I remember David Thompson." James pursed his lips into an oval and let his deep eyes flash—not exactly a smile, but an expression that allowed Gene and me to smile. "You ready to go?"

We drove east, away from the Yakima Reservation and up over the Rattlesnake Hills, then down into a vast desert basin. For their latest project, Gene and James were working on a map that would cover the range of all the various tribes of the Sahaptin language group, detailing their traditional place names and cultural sites, and this area had yet to be thoroughly covered. As Gene drove, he kept looking down at an old book balanced on his lap, written by a reporter named Click Relander who had befriended several local Sahaptin clans during the 1940s. With one hand on the wheel and one eye on the road, Gene flipped to marked pages, scattering questions out to the horizon. Was there any special legend connected with that low ridge to the south? Do you know of any word that sounds like this? What could he have meant by this spelling? James burped out a small laugh as he took a picture out the window with his new camera. "I don't know, Gene," he said. "It all depends on how you pronounce it."

Sailing dreamily into the heat waves, we cut across one corner of the Hanford Nuclear Reservation and slowed to a crawl as we approached the Columbia River at Vernita Bridge—Gene didn't want to miss any shorebirds that might be out wandering after their nesting season. Across the bridge we turned upstream, making for the Priest Rapids Dam. A road runs across the top of the huge dam, and when we arrived there in early afternoon, a work crew had parked a crane directly in our path. We got out to walk around on top of the dam, and James directed our sight to the base of the fish ladders, where a lone sturgeon flapped idly against the current. Then we lifted our eyes to stare downstream at the deep channels cut into the ancient layers of basalt by river and wind. Except for sage and rabbit-brush and a green swipe down each side of the river, the land looked entirely empty. This was once the hunting and root-digging territory of the Wanapam tribe; today it is mostly the domain of the U.S. Government. Downstream lies the Hanford Nuclear Reservation. To the east stretches an expansive national wildlife refuge. To the west the Yakima Firing Range occupies another large tract, set aside as a bombing range for the military.

The crane moved, and we crept over the dam and down into a narrow, dusty flat squeezed between the river and a rugged basalt ridge. This was the village of Priest Rapids, home to a remnant of the Wanapam tribe that chose to stay on the river rather than live on a reservation. We had come here to find an elderly woman named Margaret and her nephew Lester Umtuch, who had helped Gene identify local plants some years before. A handful of prefab houses surrounded a Quonset hut that served as longhouse and community center, and it took only a couple of minutes to walk their circle. No one answered the door at Lester's house or at Margaret's. We were wondering what to do when a young boy rode up on his bicycle and started petting a tired dog that lay beneath a planted spruce tree, one of the few green things in the village. The boy wore a T-shirt with a yellow number 77 on it and allowed Gene to engage him in conversation. The dog was either his or Margaret's. It had just had eight or ten puppies. He either had one or none or all of the puppies for his own. He had no idea where Lester or anybody else was.

The boy's attention drifted to a group of wasps around the drip of a hose in Margaret's yard. We followed him over and examined the insects as they touched down in the wetness, honeybees and yellowjackets and dirt daubers and one all-black solitary wasp. The boy had a keen eye for the different patterns on their backs and could follow a single wasp's flight across the yard. It was a sweltering day, and Gene decided that Margaret wouldn't begrudge him a drink. He traced the hose over to a faucet, turned it on just a tad, and walked back toward the trickle. Number 77 made his own way to the faucet and, the moment Gene put the hose to his mouth, turned the water on full blast. Wet and sputtering, Gene pointed the hose at the boy, who immediately cut back the pressure. Gene put the hose back to his mouth, and Number 77 cranked it back on. James and I howled as the game went on for several rounds, until finally Gene grabbed up a loop of the hose and ran straight at Number 77. *"I can't get wet!"* squealed the boy with delight. *"I can't get wet! Don't touch me! Momma told me I can't get wet!"*

Lester Umtuch heard the commotion and came out of his trailer to talk to us in the sun. He was a wide man of perhaps fifty years, with an imposing head and teeth that glowed brightly when he grinned. His crow-black hair was cut close to the scalp, and he frequently reached up to rub the little spikes with one big palm. James stepped forward and tried to explain to Lester about the information he and Gene were after. Gene pitched in with a little encouragement, pointing down the river. Lester shuffled and touched his hair.

"Well, I dunno, ya know, I went away from here when I was just a little fella. They moved us off our regular campsite, so I went to White Swan School on the reservation from the third grade on. I remember twice riding the buckboard from White Swan through Moxie spending the night at the old windmill—sleeping on some people's kitchen floor—and then riding on up here to our family's campsite."

Lester shook his head and picked at his teeth; Gene asked a couple of gentle questions that only made him shake his head more.

"I don't really know much about that kind of stuff, I didn't see it after I went off to reservation school. I remember after I got my license, driving my grandmother around to visit, and she would be singing the songs and then trying to explain to me the meanings behind the songs and I'd be down here listening to the radio"—Lester leaned forward and reached his right hand out to fiddle with imaginary knobs—"and her words went *poof!* In one ear and out the other. I remember lying down on the bed beside my grandfather and maybe plucking his whiskers or something while he would tell me his stories and he'd talk for a while and then he'd say *tsup tsup:* we go on from here tomorrow or whenever."

After each memory, Lester backed off and opened his mouth wide for a burst of laughter. Gene stood facing him with his hands cradled around his book, rocking on his heels. James only nodded. Lester kept on swearing he couldn't remember, then stepping back to touch his burry head, and then stepping forward again.

"My grandmother said how they used to go up to the swallow nests and pick out the naked baby birds even before they had grown their feathers and roast them under the ground—*tamaksh*—and then pop them in their mouths whole. They didn't even have no bones yet, it was all still gristle you might say, and man she said them was good—you could hear their fat just dripping into the fire while they was cooking down there."

He licked his lips and began to talk about the rock pictures that had been buried by the dam, how they were all up
and down the river: "They saved a couple of those rocks I
guess, you can see 'em up in our graveyard. But there was lots
more. Man, we used to watch them pictures when we was
kids. Some of those things would change overnight you know.
I saw 'em. I was little and I'd go out there at night and look,
go back out there again the next morning, and they'd be
changed."

Lester laughed at the charmed foolishness of children. He
remembered a kid who was out digging roots with his aunts
and saw the Little People—impish little beings that inhabit
Sahaptin mythology—and came screaming back to camp. "If
he just could have kept it to himself," Lester said. "If the boy
hadn't talked about Them out loud, he would have been able
to use some of their power.

"That's like me," he continued. "When I was a little
fellow we was camping up in the Naches and my father gave
me two buckets and told me to get some water and I went
up to the spring and a frog there told me *Go away* that was
his water and I couldn't have any. If I hadn't gone back to
camp with two empty buckets and talked about the frog as an
excuse, maybe he might have shared some of his power with
me. Huh?"

Big grin. Lester waved at some people in a station wagon
that had just pulled up, but they stayed in their car, invisible
in the glare of the sun, leaving Lester free to ferret through
his mind for another memory. This time he came up with a
special white clay from the other side of Saddle Mountain.
His uncles used it like putty to secure sticks and feathers, or to
chew on—nibble-chalk, they called it. Lester smiled, and then
stopped as one of the station wagon's doors popped open. He
shook his head without any smile. "Oh well," he said. "Now I
guess you got to talk to this guy for a while."

A tall, lean man with long, black braids rolled out of the
car and stomped straight over to us, a can of beer in one

hand. The arm that held the can bulged with veins and sinewy muscles. He addressed himself directly to Gene.

"What you want, man?" he asked, his face inches away from Gene's. Behind heavy black-rimmed glasses his eyes were bleary, as if he had been crying. He had on a red T-shirt with a small photograph of Chief Joseph and letters that spelled out WANAPAM: LAND OF THE COLUMBIA. He looked to be around thirty years old, but it was hard to tell for sure.

"I said what the hell you want, man?"

I suddenly wished that Gene hadn't chosen to wear his new red Audubon Bird Ambassador cap to the village, but he calmly met the man's gaze and said that he was working on a map project and wanted to see if Lester could help him.

"I'll tell you what you want," interrupted the Wanapam, supplicating toward the rock cliffs with his arms. "You want our names. And why should we give you all our names? What do we get out of that?"

Gene clasped his hands together at his belt, still holding his book. He cocked his head to look at his adversary, but kept quiet.

"I'll tell you what we get. We get nothin'. And we ain't telling you nothin'. Those names, them's the only things we got left. Why should we give those away? You tell me that. Why?"

Gene coughed to clear his throat and tried saying that he certainly didn't want to take anything away, but the Wanapam wasn't listening. His tirade grew loud and profane. He was drunk, but lucid—he knew all about Gene, and about his research. Gene coughed a couple more times without attempting a sentence, simply taking the abuse. He held his head up, his eyes locked on the man.

"And this old man here," the Wanapam said, pointing at James. "What you got him up here for? He wants our river and we ain't giving it to him. *Our* river. These Yakima want everything when they already got everything. Why should we give them something when we don't got nothing except that dam right there, and that bomb factory down there? We're the ones that live here! We're the ones who know this place! I know what's here and *I ain't tellin' you*. Go home, old Yakima man."

"He's Warm Springs," Gene said, as the Wanapam swept his beer can through the air. "Not Yakima."

The Yakima were the most populous of the Sahaptin-speaking tribes in the Columbia Basin; James Selam had been born into the smaller Warm Springs tribe. While it was true that James did not live in the Priest Rapids area, his dad had been raised just downstream and had told young James many stories about the land and its people.

James offered none of this information out loud, and Gene heeded his cue to keep quiet. The Wanapam looked hard at both of them as he shouted on.

Lester had disappeared inside his trailer soon after the drunk man arrived. Now James evaporated also, back to Gene's van. Gene stood his ground, assuring the Wanapam that he didn't want anything that the people didn't want to give, that he was after simple knowledge.

"Forget your knowledge," said the Wanapam. "Look what you done for us so far." He waved again, at the dam that changed the river. The cliffs where jets flew too close to the ground. The big factories that leaked death.

His companions began honking the horn of the station wagon. A new person emerged from the trailer beside Lester's and made a beeline for our depleted circle. He was about the same age as the Wanapam but larger, with a bigger belly, and dressed all in black. He faced up to Gene, his face even closer than the Wanapam's had been. He held that pose for-several seconds, then burst into words: "*Gene Hunn!* Haven't seen you in a while, man." He shook hands, clasped fingers, tweaked thumbs with Gene, then moved on to me. "Donald Blackbird," he announced. I shook, clasped, and tweaked with Donald before he continued on to the station wagon to see what the horn-honking was all about.

The Wanapam raged on. "You ain't gonna get nothin', man. You stand here with your stupid books and notepads and you don't know nothin'. Now Click Relander, he knew. Click listened when we said something. He wasn't afraid to put down the truth."

This was an odd turn in the stream of invective, and for a moment I thought I was hearing things—Click Relander was the white reporter whose book Gene had been quoting from all day. Now Gene simply unclasped his hands and held up Relander's book, *Drummers & Dreamers.* The Wanapam stepped back in surprise. In the silence that followed, Gene told him he had every right to be angry, and that he agreed with much of what he had said. The Wanapam listened for the first time since his arrival and stood quietly for a moment. He turned in a half circle and started back toward the station wagon, then stopped and reversed the maneuver to replant himself in front of Gene. "So," he said, not as loud this time. "I'm going to get myself a sip of whiskey from the car. Need one for yourself?"

Gene rocked on his heels. "No thanks," he said. "I guess I'll hold off for now."

ONCE THOMPSON'S Sahaptin interpreter assured the foaming chief at the Priest Rapids camp that all was well, the men of the village collected for the usual smoking and talking. After one dance the Nor'Westers took their leave, heading due east now at the base of the Columbia's Big Bend. Late the same afternoon they put up at a camp of about 150 men belonging to the Yakima tribe. The salmon these people offered as gifts showed a little fat, and peering into the kettle, Thompson saw that traces of fish oil had risen to the surface of the water—something he had not seen happen with any of the salmon he had eaten upstream. He thought this camp had a very favorable situation and promised to build a trade house on the site sometime in the future. When he went out during the night to make some observations, he discovered that his sextant had been shaken out of adjustment in the rapids.

On July 9 Thompson's canoe arrived at the mouth of the Snake River, where the Columbia again turns west for its final run to the sea. This was the point at which Lewis and Clark had entered the big river, and Thompson knew where he was from his knowledge of Meriwether Lewis's letter and Patrick Gass's journal. Both of these accounts clearly noted that the Americans had named this large tributary Lewis's River, but Thompson chose to call it the Shawpatin River after the people who lived in the vicinity. Near the front of his notebook, Thompson had copied a short memorandum from Gass's journal that gave Lewis's calculation of the latitude of this point as 46° 15' 14" N. Thompson took his own reading at the junction and came up with the slightly more southerly conclusion of 46° 12' 35" N. This was the farthest south the surveyor had ever been; he was now in the same latitude as the mouth of the Columbia.

At the confluence of the two great rivers, the surveyor put up a small pole with half a sheet of paper tied around it, claiming the territory for the British Crown and stating that the North West Company merchants "do intend to erect a factory at this place for the commerce of the country around." Five miles farther downstream he came upon the claims of the United States in the form of a miniature American flag in the possession of Yellepit, a chief of the Walula tribe. Yellepit wore a peace medal decorated with Thomas Jefferson's portrait, also given to him by Lewis and Clark in 1805. Thompson found the chief "intelligent, he was also very friendly, and we discoursed a long time." Yellepit complained that his tribe had been accustomed to travel across the Blue Mountains to hunt buffalo, but in recent years the Snakes had chased them off. He was very willing for the Canadians to come and supply his people with guns, and he and Thompson decided that the place where the Snake met the Columbia would be an excellent spot for a trading post.

When the Nor'Westers put back in the river after their talk with Yellepit, they faced up to one of the afternoon gales for which the Columbia is famous. Even though they were moving with the current, the men had a difficult time making much headway against the wind. During the course of their struggle, they had their first sight of one of the Cascade volcanoes, probably Mount Hood, a "conical mountain right ahead alone and very high, seemingly a mass of snow." Thompson's journal for the day ends with an offhand sentence sandwiched among observations of Antares and Saturn: "Passed in all about 80 families in small straggling camps." These were bands of Umatilla people, and when he sat down to write his *Narrative*, that simple statement touched off the memory of an unsettling encounter:

> We embarked and proceeded thirty two miles down the River, and passed about eighty families in small straggling lodges; at one of which of ten families we put ashore to smoke with them, but they were terrified at our appearance. My men stayed on the beach, and I went forward a few paces unarmed, and sat down with a pipe and stem in my hand; they sent forward two very old Men, who lying flat on the ground and in the most pitiful manner; crawling slowly, frequently lifted their heads a little as if imploring mercy; my Native Interpreter would not speak to them, and all the signs I could make gave them no confidence; close behind the men three women crawled on their knees; lifting up their hands to me as if supplicating for their lives; the men were naked and the women nearly the same, the whole, a scene of wretched destitution, it was too painful, they did not smoke with us, I gave to each of the

men two inches of Tobacco, and left them. They appeared as if outcasts from the others . . . when I spoke to the Interpreter when we camped to learn the state of these people, he gave me no answer, and both himself and his Wife did not wish to be spoken to about them.

Lewis and Clark recorded a similar incident at a small encampment some miles below the mouth of the Snake, very near where Thompson stopped. Clark had landed at a group of lodges and had been greeted by silence. When he entered one of the huts, he found three dozen people hiding inside, "in the greatest agutation, Some crying and ringing there hands, others hanging their heads." When his interpreters arrived, they learned that the frightened people had seen Clark shoot a flying sandhill crane and thought that the white men had come from the clouds and were not human. Only the presence of the young Shoshone woman Sacajawea in one of the canoes finally assured them that all was well.

The next day Thompson stopped at a camp near what is now called the John Day River for a more familiar reception. He counted another eighty families here and measured a dugout canoe thirty-six feet in length by a full three feet wide. He noticed that in addition to setting seine nets to capture salmon, this band had crafted long poles with hoop nets on the end. When the furmen put back into the river, another afternoon gale had blown up and "the water was swept away like snow." Forced ashore, they spent the evening watching the most dexterous curved-line dances they had seen so far. Dance, song, and step were measured out by an old chief, and all the young people of both sexes took part. Thompson's journal for this day ends with the line, "Heard news of the American ship's arrival." John Jacob Astor's men, coming around the Horn, must have already made it to the coast.

On July 11 the Nor'Westers came to a long set of rapids called The Dalles, or the Narrows, a famous fishing and trading spot for far-flung tribes, as well as the rough

THE LOWER COLUMBIA

boundary between the Sahaptin-speaking tribes of the middle river and the Chinookan groups of the lower Columbia. Near the top of the rapids the furmen almost cracked up on a big rock, and when they put ashore to drop off their Sahaptin interpreter, they were surrounded by hordes of large crickets. Thompson and his crew camped at the top of the portage with over three hundred families, and that evening they were treated to a dance that almost got out of hand: "The respectable men among them had much trouble to reduce them to order, and they were the least regular in their way of behavior of any we have yet seen – at Night they cleared off with difficulty & left us to go to sleep."

The next day the furmen had to make the long portage around The Dalles on foot, since the horses that the natives had promised the night before never materialized. At the bottom of the rapids, they came upon bunches of harbor seals chasing after the migrating salmon—a sure sign that the ocean was near. They fired a few shots at the seals, but missed. Sixteen miles later they floated into the tight, luxurious growth of the Columbia Gorge, and everything about the countryside changed. As they passed through veils of hanging clouds, the men saw their first extensive forest since the Spokane country, gigantic trees, more harbor seals, and smoky huts filled with curing salmon. The local Chinookan people who came out to greet them babbled English words, "some of them not the best," learned from trading ships. Thompson worked at picking up phrases of their language and listened as they described to him the five species of salmon that annually passed by on their way upriver.

On the evening of July 13, the Canadians camped for the night "a little above Point Vancouver." This was a landmark whose name Thompson had copied into his notebook at Rocky Mountain House during the winter of 1800 as he and Duncan McGillivray planned their trip to the western sea. Twelve years later Thompson knew that he was finally drawing close. The next morning he recorded a tidal fall of two feet overnight, then pressed on. "July 15th Monday A very fine day, somewhat cloudy. Staid 'till 6:25 A.M. shaving & arranging ourselves, when we set off . . . the Fog all along prevents me seeing well."

CHAPTER NINE

SITTING IN
THE WATER

JULY–SEPTEMBER 1811

ONE YEAR EARLIER, at about the time David
Thompson departed from Rainy Lake House, a large
birchbark canoe had swept down the Hudson River toward
New York City. The paddlers were all Canadian voyageurs,
fresh recruits for John Jacob Astor's Pacific Fur Company.
One of the passengers was Gabriel Franchère, the son of a
Montreal merchant, who had signed on with the company
as a clerk. Sensing that he had hooked into an adventure, the
young man kept a journal of the trip: "The Americans took
our voyageurs for Indians . . . we sang as we rowed, and our
singing, along with the sight of the bark canoe, drew a crowd
of people to the wharves." Another new clerk, an opinion-
ated Scot named Alexander Ross, had left behind a teaching
job in Upper Canada for "the gilded prospectus of the new
Company." Ross had already traveled south and was on hand
for the dramatic arrival of the voyageurs in their birchbark
canoe. He too had a pencil in hand.

The appearance of this unusual kind of craft on the

American waters, with the cheerful chantings of its crew, their feathered caps and sylvan appearance, as they approached the gay city of New York, attracted such a crowd of spectators of all classes around them, as left but little space to land; but what was the astonishment, when, in the twinkling of an eye, two of the crew were seen to shoulder their craft, capable of containing two tons weight, and to convey it to a place of safety on terra firma. Mr. Astor, who happened to be present, was so delighted with the vivacity and dexterity of the two men, that he gave them an eagle to drink his health.

On September 6, 1810, as David Thompson and his Columbia brigade beached their canoes in front of Alexander Henry's post on the upper Saskatchewan, Astor's ship the *Tonquin* set sail from New York Harbor, bound for the Pacific via Cape Horn. The expedition leaders were all from Canada, as were most of the twenty-nine voyageurs, clerks, and artisans under their charge; several were former employees of the North West Company. Alexander Ross wrote that they were scarcely out of port when the captain threatened to "blow out the brains of the first man who dared to disobey his orders." His bluster incited a running feud that percolated for the rest of the journey. During a stopover in the Sandwich (Hawaiian) Islands to take on supplies, several crew members deserted. When the *Tonquin* left Hawaii in early March of 1811, she was loaded down with an extra complement of islanders, plus a variety of livestock and chickens to help feed the new post. Two weeks out, huge seas washed most of the animals overboard, and cold winds coated the rigging with ice. When they finally reached the mouth of the Columbia, it was a cloudy, stormy day, and the ship lost a dory and five men before making it across the river's notorious bar and into safe harbor. When they touched land, David Thompson was still more than a thousand miles upstream, struggling to finish his cedar plank canoe at Boat Encampment.

Once ashore, expedition leaders Duncan McDougall and
Robert and David Stuart took charge. By mid-April they had
chosen a spot for their intended fort a few miles in from the
bar and put their men to work hacking at the thick coniferous forest. Gabriel Franchère reported that "the weather was
superb and all nature smiled. We imagined ourselves to be in
an earthly paradise—the forests looked like pleasant groves,
the leaves like brilliant flowers . . . we set ourselves to work
with enthusiasm and in a few days cleared a point of land."
Alexander Ross was less enthusiastic—the way he tells it, it
took four men two days to chop down each tree, and it rained
constantly. In his opinion they had landed in the worst spot
on the planet for an establishment. He was sick of boiled fish
and wild roots, and McDougall, whom he dubbed "the great
pasha," did not meet with his approval: "He was a man of but
ordinary capacity, with an irritable, peevish temper; the most
unfit man in the world to head an expedition or command
men." McDougall's journal is more evenhanded—among the
routine business of building shelters and keeping his crew
fed, he reports meetings with leaders of the local Clatsop and
Chinook tribes and outbreaks of venereal disease among his
men; he also tries to sort out a variety of rumors about the
presence of white men in the unknown territory upriver.

Franchère, Ross, and McDougall do agree that by the
end of May the men had laid the foundation for a store-
house and had named their rudimentary post "Astoria." The
three of them also reported that an unusual pair of visitors
arrived on June 15. According to Franchère, "some natives
from up the river brought us two strange Indians, a man and
a woman. They were not attired like the savages on the river
Columbia, but wore long robes of dressed deer-skin, with leggings and moccasins in the fashion of the tribes to the east
of the Rocky Mountains." The man spoke some Cree and
was found to be-carrying a letter, which McDougall promptly
perused. Dated April 5, 1811, it had been sent by a Mr. Finan
McDonald from Spokane House and was addressed to Mr.

John Stuart, Estekakadme Fort, New Caledonia.

This was a curious occurrence. John Stuart was a partner with the North West Company, working on the Fraser
River in the section of British Columbia then known as New
Caledonia. There was no fort called Estekakadme there, but
Finan McDonald was a most adventurous speller and could
have scrambled any number of words to come up with the
name. At the time there was no charted route between New
Caledonia and the Columbia country, so Finan McDonald
could not have given his messengers very detailed instructions, but he certainly would have indicated to them that
Stuart's post was several hundred miles to the northwest of
Spokane House. Yet here was his letter in Astoria, which was
decidedly southwest. All the letter-bearer had to say was that
he and his wife had lost their way and had ended up following
a big river down to a falls, where they had learned that there
were white men farther downstream. Assuming that the ad-
dressee would be among them, the pair had continued on.

The message that Finan McDonald was trying to communicate to John Stuart remains unknown, for Duncan
McDougall did not record its contents in his journal, only
his puzzlement at the messenger: "We cannot make out
the motive of his journey hither either from his conversation or the tenor of the letter he brought." By the next
day McDougall was beginning to suspect that the "inland
stranger" was a spy for the North West Company. Alexander
Ross thought that the husband "was a very shrewd and intelligent Indian, who addressed us in the Algonquin [Cree]
language, and gave us much information respecting the interiour of the country." So encouraging was this information
that David Stuart immediately began planning a trading expedition upriver. A month later, on July 15, Gabriel Franchère
reported that preparations were almost complete:

> All was ready on the date planned, and we were about
> to load the canoes, when, toward midday, we saw a large

canoe, carrying a flag, rounding what we called Tongue Point. We did not know who it could be . . . The flag she bore was British, and her crew was composed of nine boatmen in all. A well-dressed man, who appeared to be the commander, was the first to leap ashore; and addressing us without ceremony, he said that his name was David Thompson, and that he was one of the partners of the North West Company.

By all accounts the unexpected callers were well received by the Astorians. Franchère speaks of "the usual civilities" and says they invited Thompson back to their quarters at one end of the warehouse, where he told them all about his winter's travails. McDougall noted the arrival of the Nor'Westers in his straightforward manner, commenting only on the unusual construction of their cedar canoe. Alexander Ross sounds a more discordant note, wondering if the surveyor was not being treated a little too kindly: "M'Dougall received him like a brother; nothing was too good for Mr. Thompson; he had access everywhere; saw and examined everything; and whatever he asked for he got, as if he had been one of ourselves."

As far as Thompson knew, there was no reason why he shouldn't be greeted like a brother—not only were many of these men fellow Canadians and former Nor'Westers, but he had left Rainy Lake in the belief that the North West Company held a one-third partnership in Astor's Columbia venture. According to McDougall, Thompson told the Astorians "that no doubt remains with him, but ere now a coalition of the two companies had taken place, regarding which he handed us an extract from a Letter on the same subject." That letter was a copy of the resolution passed by the North West partners at Fort William the previous summer, giving their consent to the deal with Astor. Thompson had no way of knowing that Astor's agreement with the North West Company had disintegrated months before. McDougall and the Stuarts should have learned about this before they sailed from New York, but if they shared the news with Thompson, none of the witnesses mentions it. Maybe the partners' letter convinced them that the deal was still viable. This would actually have been good news for the head Astorians—as British citizens working for an American company, they were all very much aware of the hostilities brewing between the United States and England, and they knew that Astoria would be an easy target for the King's navy if war did break out. In that event, it would certainly be to their advantage to be allied with the Nor'Westers.

For whatever reason, all four of the leaders acted as if the deal were still on, and at some point on the day he arrived, Thompson wrote the sort of formal letter that would serve as an official notice of intent. He congratulated the Astorians on their new establishment and expressed his hope "that the respective parties at Montreal may finally settle the arrangement between the two Companies which in my opinion will be to our mutual benefit." The next day McDougall and the Stuarts responded with an almost identical letter, seconding Thompson's wish "that final arrangements may take place to the mutual satisfaction of both parties, which would inevitably secure to us every advantage that can possibly be drawn from the Business."

Alexander Ross, who tended to see intrigue all around him, theorized that there was a double-edged game of cunning going on:

> How could we account for the more than warm and unreserved welcome Mr. Thompson met with from Astor's representative. Unless, as some thought at the time, M'Dougall was trying to pay Mr. Thompson back with his own coin, by putting on a fair face, so as to dupe him into an avowal of his real object. This is more than probable, for in point of acuteness, duplicity, and diplomatic craft, they were perhaps well matched.

There is no doubt that hidden sentiments lurked between the lines of the two high-minded epistles written that
day. At the end of their letter, the Astorians stated that when
Thompson arrived they had just been preparing to go upriver and meet their expedition coming from St. Louis. Since
the overland party was not due for at least three months, this
was an outright falsehood. But if the Astorians' attempt to
disguise the true mission of the boats being readied by their
wharf was disingenuous, so were Thompson's exaggerated
descriptions of "the dangers and difficulties" of conditions
inland. His efforts to keep the Astorians from going upriver
were quite transparent to Franchère: "The description this
gentleman gave of the interior of the country was not calculated to leave with us a very favorable impression, and did not
perfectly accord with that of our two Indian guests."

The two guests, Finan McDonald's stray letter-carriers,
were still at Astoria when Thompson arrived, and at some
point they caught his eye. According to Ross's account, "Mr.
Thompson at once recognized the two strange Indians and
gave us to understand that they were both females." Franchère
echoes the schoolteacher: "He [Thompson] recognized the
two Indians, and told us that they were two women, one of
whom had dressed herself up as a man in order to travel with
greater security." This woman dressed as a man was none
other than the Kootenai berdache called Qánqon, the former
wife of the voyageur Boisverd—the same woman Thompson
had asked to leave Kootanae House three years earlier for
her loose conduct, and a woman that he had obviously heard
more of after he sent her home:

> The Kootanaes were also displeased with her; she left
> them, and found her way from Tribe to Tribe to the Sea.
> She became a prophetess, declared her sex changed, that
> she was now a Man, dressed, and armed herself as such,
> and also took a young woman to Wife, of whom she
> pretended to be very jealous; when with the Chinooks,

as a prophetess, she predicted diseases to them, which made some of them threaten her life.

Narrative

Qánqon and her "wife" had been camping at Astoria for a month when Thompson arrived, and had caused Duncan McDougall considerable anxiety during their stay. Apparently the berdache had been claiming to possess "the power to introduce the Small Pox" on her trip downriver; since epidemics of the pox had already swept the Pacific Coast, such a declaration terrified the natives. Qánqon, so ridiculed at home, must have intended to impress these people by boasting of supernatural powers, but she had seriously miscalculated the effect of her message. Several times the Chinook and Clatsop chiefs had demanded that McDougall turn over the two "inland visitors" to them for slaves; he had repeatedly refused, saying that he wanted to keep them as his own slaves. McDougall knew that the pair would be killed if they fell into the hands of the chiefs, and he wanted to save their lives so that they could guide David Stuart and his party upstream. The berdache had drawn several maps of the interior for Stuart and had been anxiously waiting to leave under his protection when the unexpected appearance of David Thompson delayed their departure.

Thompson's own journals for his stay at Astoria contain no word of surprise at finding Madame Boisverd in disguise at the fort, and no wonderment as to why Finan McDonald would have entrusted a letter to the berdache. There is no thrill at the historic import of his arrival at the mouth of the Columbia, or any expression of disappointment that he did not get there first. There is no puzzlement about the fate of an important deal, no hint of deception in dealing with the Astorians. Rather, his entries for the week, minus his usual survey notes and astronomical observations, sound like nothing so much as a man on holiday:

JULY 15TH MONDAY . . . At 1 P.M. thank God for our safe arrival, we came to the House of Mr. Astor's Company – Messrs. McDougall, Stuart & Stuart – who received me in the most polite manner, and here we hope to stay a few days to refresh ourselves.

JULY 16TH TUESDAY A fine day. Observed for Latitude, Longitude & Time – Latitude 46° 13' 56" N . . . Longitude 123° 48' ¼" W.

JULY 17TH WEDNESDAY A very fine day, if we except an appearance of Rain with a few Drops of ditto. A steady Gale from the Sea as usual.

JULY 18TH THURSDAY A very hot calm Day. I went across to the Indian Villages with Mr. Stuart and my men – after visiting the Houses, we went up a great Hill where we gratified ourselves with an extensive view of the Ocean and the Coast South'd.

JULY 19TH FRIDAY A fine hot day.

JULY 20 & 21 SATURDAY & SUNDAY Fine weather.

THE WEATHER AROUND the mouth of the Columbia is hardly ever fine; it is too powerful a place, too wild a conjunction among the peaks of the Cascades, the draining waters of the whole Inland Northwest, and the massive weather systems that spiral across the Pacific. Below the modern town of Astoria, the river still races to meet the ocean head-on; wide and rough, its reeking sea smells steal attention from the sodden green land. Tongue Point licks out into the current just east of the port, a narrow lacework of hemlock that reclines steeply to the river. In the lee of the point, a marshy flat has been transformed by river dredgings into fennel-covered fields and the town sewage ponds.

As I walked toward Tongue Point along a railroad track that parallels the river, white wooden buildings began to emerge from the green curtain of trees, the nucleus of a Job Corps center and Coast Guard installation. Where the steep slope meets the water, a pier juts out from the shade of the hemlocks, forming a second forest of creosoted pilings spotted with tool shacks, incandescent lights, and ramps for rescue boats. Lined up along the pier, rolling like king-sized amphoras from some ancient dig, red navigational buoys awaited repair.

Two teenage boys in shorts came toward me on the track. They were barefooted, and choosing steps between the splintery ties and sharp gravel had them hopping like chickens. Still, they managed to swagger a little bit. One of them carried a belly-board with two fins, as if he were getting ready to fight his way through the cold outgoing tide that lapped at the riprap beneath us. We grunted to each other, and I asked them if the walking wasn't a little rough today. My voice might have been lost in the wind; they stared back without answering, then padded on.

As I continued down the tracks, an outgoing freighter appeared from around the point. It was of a modern design, with bulbous bow and stern, and slid through the water like a melon-headed beaked whale. Its wide-mouthed stack puffed out a plume of diesel smoke that hung in the hemlocks above the Coast Guard station. The Columbia's dredged channel angled the ship in toward the railroad tracks; as she came closer, I watched her sprout wiry antennae and the clear eyes of bridge windows. Then she straightened out her course for the Pacific, and I spelled out the huge white letters spaced down the length of her black hull—D A I O   P A P E R.

The leviathan glided toward me in utter silence. Gulls and cormorants on nearby pilings sat tight, watching the wake from her shapely bow slap up against their perches. Her great bulk obscured the clearcuts across the gray river, and only when the vessel was right upon me could I hear the clanks and grinds of her inner speech. She plowed right past me and then was gone, off for the Far East with a belly-load of logs from western forests, plying the same trade route that Alexander Mackenzie and the McGillivray brothers all dreamed of, and that David Thompson inaugurated when he scraped ashore at Tongue Point that July day of 1811.

"JULY 22 MONDAY A fine day. Arranged for setting off for the Interior . . . I pray Kind Providence to send us a good journey to my Family and Friends. At 1:24 P.M. set off in company with Mr. David Stuart and 8 of his men. They are to build a Factory somewhere below the Falls of the Columbia [The Dalles]." Apparently McDougall and David Stuart had dropped their pretense about meeting Astor's overland party and replaced it with a half-truth about building a post on the lower Columbia. According to McDougall's journal, however, Stuart's party intended to accompany Qánqon and her companion at least as far as a river they called the "Wahnaaihye," which was probably the Wenatchee and was certainly much farther upriver than The Dalles.

Alexander Ross says that the Astorians had decided to travel upriver in company with the Nor'Westers "for the sake of mutual protection and safety." Ross and two other clerks were among Stuart's crew, and they embarked with style: "After our canoes were laden, we moved down to the water's edge—one with a cloak on his arm, another with his umbrella, a third with pamphlets and newspapers for amusement, preparing, as we thought, for a trip of pleasure." The wind was brisk and sails went up, but Stuart's two dugout canoes proved unwieldy to his paddlers. Loaded with over a ton of trade goods, the heavy boats began to take on water and soon ran ashore on the rocks of Tongue Point. The men lugged baggage and dugouts across the narrow isthmus to the other side, where Thompson's men, having successfully negotiated the point in their cedar canoe, sat waiting. The Astorians loaded up again and made a few more miles before a sandbar

CLOSING THE CIRCLE

arrested Ross's boat: "Down came the mast, sail, and rigging about our ears . . . cloaks and umbrellas, so gay in the morning, were now thrown aside for the paddle and carrying strap, and the pamphlets and newspapers went to the bottom."

The two parties made better progress on Tuesday, but as evening came on, they couldn't find a place to camp. Thompson wrote that at seven o'clock "on a very steep Shore, we put up; with difficulty we could place the Goods, & all slept as I may say standing." They found more comfortable campsites for the rest of the week as they sailed and paddled toward Columbia Gorge, stopping occasionally to dry out baggage or trade for berries and more salmon. Thompson charted the river's courses, fretting now and then that his distances were off or that he couldn't get his bearings because the sail was in his way. One afternoon they passed eight canoes seining for salmon and tried to buy some of their catch, but the fishermen were "inhospitable" and refused to sell any. On Saturday evening, soon after the parties stopped for the night, two natives brought a blind chief from a nearby village to their camp for a smoke. As they were passing the pipe, two more canoes paddled by on their way to a village upstream; David Stuart called out and asked if they would bring back some salmon, to which they agreed. When they never returned, Thompson began to worry that some sort of treachery was afoot, and through the night he kept his canoe loaded and ready to shove off.

No one bothered him until very early the next morning, when the Kootenai couple, who had been riding with the Astorians, appeared at the door of his tent. Qánqon, still dressed as a man, was carrying a bow and a quiver of arrows. She must have lost faith in David Stuart's ability to defend her and her companion, because she asked Thompson for his protection. He does not say whether he made room for the couple in his canoe, only that his party set off at 5:50 A.M. and rowed half a mile through rapids. At the top of the shoals, they spied four men who offered to share some of their salmon. The canoes put ashore, and while the fish were boiling, the four fishermen approached Thompson. Giving the berdache a stern look, they "enquired about the Small Pox, of which a report had been raised, that it was coming with the white Men & that also 2 Men of enormous Size [were coming] to overturn the Ground." Thompson assured the men that there was no truth to this tale and that the Great Spirit would continue to watch after them and their grandchildren. They appeared to be relieved, he wrote, but "I saw plainly, that if the man-woman had not been sitting behind us they would have plunged a dagger in her."

With breakfast concluded and Qángon safe for the moment, the men faced up to the long portage around the boisterous flume of the Cascades of the Columbia. Lewis and Clark called this series of rapids the Great Shute; to Thompson it was the Great Rapid. His seven voyageurs had no problem scurrying over with their minimal load, but the Astorians needed some extra manpower, and Stuart hired several men from a nearby village to help. Most worked with goodwill, while others were more interested in seeing what was inside the small mountain of packs and parcels that emerged from the boats. Several flaunted short, double-edged daggers, reminders of the coastal tribes' long contact with European and American trading ships.

By midafternoon the goods were across the portage, and as the porters gathered around to be paid, so did a number of men who had served only as spectators. Stuart, who could not distinguish those who had helped from those who had not, wound up passing out a great deal of extra tobacco. Thompson wrote that some of the natives remained "highly discontented; they all appeared with their 2 pointed Dags, and surrounded us on the land side, their appearance very menacing." Several of them pulled out whetstones and began sharpening the blades of their long knives and waving them in the white men's faces. Thompson grew impatient with their posturing and drew his pistol; the troublemakers quickly dispersed, but there was no way of knowing if they would return with reinforcements.

Since the Nor'Westers had already gotten their canoe to the top of the rapids, they probably could have escaped an attack, but Stuart's dugouts were still back at the other end. They were too heavy to carry, and none of the local men would help him drag them across until he promised them better pay. Thompson "spoke to the Chiefs of the hard usage they gave Mr. Stuart, & reasoning with them, they sent off all the young Men." Eventually Stuart got his boats over, and they all paddled upstream a short distance to camp. Recapping the day's events in his journal, Thompson concluded: "These people are a mixture of Kindness & Treachery. They render any Service required, but demand high payment, & ready to enforce their demands, Dag in hand. They steal all they can lay their Hands on, & from every appearance only our Number and Arms prevented them from cutting us all off." Canadian and American travelers up the Gorge would write variations on these sentiments for years to come; the proximity of a native village and the logistics of this portage provided a frequent stage for conflict between residents and visitors.

THE COLUMBIA GORGE, where the fully formed river makes a tight squeeze through the Cascade Range, has always been a bottleneck. Tens of thousands of years ago, when the ice dam of glacial Lake Missoula crumbled, the Gorge absorbed an incredible torrent of floodwater. And it was only a few centuries ago, within the memory of man, that a huge landslide crashed down from Table Mountain into the heart of the Gorge, temporarily plugging the river and giving rise to a wealth of local myths such as "The Bridge of the Gods." In one version of this legend, demons from the mountains were at war against the river spirit, and erected a stone dam to block the course of the river. The river spirit cut a long tunnel through the barricade, creating a stone archway that people who lived on opposite sides of the river used as a bridge. A bloody war between these peoples caused the demons and spirits to band together and destroy the Bridge of the Gods. In another story, Thunderbird murdered five of Coyote's sons. Coyote in turn killed Thunderbird, and it was the mangled body of the monstrous bird that formed the rapids.

The same topography that worked for Coyote, that made this spot such an ordeal for generations of boatmen, also made the Gorge at the base of Table Mountain an ideal site for a hydroelectric dam. In 1934 the rocks of the Cascades of the Columbia became the foundation for one of President Franklin Roosevelt's first big WPA projects: Bonneville Dam. On this lower stretch of the river, the politics of salmon carried weight even back in the thirties, and public pressure forced the Corps of Engineers to keep an eye on the fish when they designed the dam. Beginning well below the main structure, a long series of fish ladders winds upriver, skirting the concrete buttresses at the outside base of the dam and the humming turbines within. The original fishway consists of even cement stairsteps, mossy and black with age. On the July morning that I stopped to visit, I had to stand at the bottom of the ladders and stare into the water for several minutes before I could discern any silver ribbons moving along the slabs. The fish drew me up a path into a newer, more random system of groins and vaults designed to mirror the rocks of a real river bottom. A set of stairs mounted to a catwalk that ran above the ascending waterway; from above, the protruding groins looked like letters in a concrete alphabet, no two alike, each one subtly altering the swirls of water. At the base of each letter were eddies where introduced shad steadied themselves comfortably, noses to the current. The walkway ended atop an observation deck with a view out over the surrounding landscape. There was Table Mountain on the

Washington side, dominating the whole scene; there was a spot where the old portage trail might have started; there were the deep pools where harbor seals used to strike at the circulating fish.

I took an elevator down into a basement viewing room, where a thick wall of glass glistened with more shad. At first I could see nothing beyond them but a rainbow of spume. Then a couple of big steelhead muscled their way through the tanks, shiny missiles that whipped smoothly from section to section up the line. A shadow that lingered for a moment in the green darkness was part of a wave of summer king salmon. I followed one of them for the length of the aquarium, through all four tanks, until I was stopped by a wall at the end of the room. Behind a door in the wall was a separate cubicle reserved for the Game Department's official fish counter. In shifts around the clock, employees sit in a chair in that special room and tick off the species as they come through: chinook, coho, sockeye, chum, steelhead. A chart outside toted up the count for each kind of fish for yesterday, and last week, and for the whole season so far.

As I turned away from the chart and back to the fish windows, I saw the raspy mouth of a lamprey eel clasped against a lower corner of the glass. The water rippled past the comb-toothed ridges on its lips while the rest of the creature, all tail, swung out into the bubbles. These eels that are really fish also return upstream to spawn, using their sucker mouths to grip the rocks and pull themselves against the current. The tribes along this part of the Columbia have long made good use of the lamprey, gathering them alongside the salmon; James Selam's friend Elsie Pistolhead still runs poles across the rafters of her garage in the summer to dry their snaky bodies for winter food. When David Thompson compared the taste of rattlesnake meat to that of eels, he was paying the land serpents a compliment.

THOMPSON ATE BREAKFAST with the Astorians on Wednesday, July 31, two days upstream from their troublesome portage around the Cascades of the Columbia. They were in the general area where David Stuart had said he intended to build a trade house, and Thompson prepared to take his leave. He left behind Qánqon and her companion, as well as the voyageur Michel Boulard, who had been part of his crew off and on ever since their first foray into the mountains to meet the Kootenais eleven years before. In his *Narrative*, Thompson explains that he had arranged with Duncan McDougall to swap the forty-year-old Boulard, "well versed in Indian affairs, but weak for the hard labor of ascending the River, for a powerful well made Sandwich Islander" called Coxe. Boulard's experience in the country would make him very useful to the Astorians, whereas Thompson intended to send Coxe to Montreal and then on to London to act as interpreter on the North West Company supply ship that was supposed to sail to the Columbia the following year. Alexander Ross, in his account, added that Coxe "was looked upon by Mr. Thompson as a prodigy of wit and humor, so that those respectively acceptable qualities led to the exchange."

With David Stuart tagging along to scout The Dalles a short distance upstream, the Nor'Westers paddled through thick smoke from a local grass fire until they reached the base of the big rapid at around eight-thirty in the morning. On their way downriver they had been kept awake by the rowdy camp here and had not been able to get horses for the five-mile portage, but this time their interpreter was back in time for lunch with plenty of horses and fresh salmon, and everything went smoothly until they reached the end of the carrying place. There they heard a rumor that one of the chiefs was gathering men to come and steal their guns. Thompson defused the situation with some "sharp words," then asked for another dozen salmon. He presented most of them to David Stuart, and the two men parted ways.

Traveling against the current, Thompson had time to notice much that had flashed past on the way downstream. Early on the morning of August 1, the Nor'Westers came upon a burial island near Celilo Falls. "There were many sheds under which the dead bodies were placed, all of which I wished to examine, but my Interpreter begged of me not to do it, as the relations of the dead would be very angry." The surveyor turned his curiosity instead to the eroded basalt pillars and fractured bluffs along this part of the river, whose shapes he compared to castles and pipe organs. They stopped several times during the day to smoke at friendly camps, and Thompson noted that the river level had fallen at least ten feet in the three weeks since they had passed. Back in the desert now, they had trouble finding enough wood for a fire to boil their salmon. The wind was blowing, and everything was full of sand. After a rattlesnake crawled into one voyageur's bedroll on a cool evening, the men learned to leave their blankets in the canoe until the dew was on the ground and they were certain the serpents were down in their holes.

Near the mouth of the John Day River, the furmen bypassed by a couple of small villages and pushed on upstream. When they stopped to line the canoe up a rapid, Thompson had a chance to measure one chinook salmon at four feet, four inches in length and over two feet in girth. They stayed to eat the fish and were about to reembark when two fishermen crossed the rapids to see them. "They seemed hurt that we did not stop at their villages and give them the news of our voyage, of which they are all very fond." From then on he made sure to stop and smoke with the natives he had met on his way down and recount the events of his trip: "Every trifle seemed to be of some importance to them, and the story of the Woman that carried a Bow and Arrows and had a Wife, was to them a romance to which they paid great attention and my Interpreter took great pleasure in relating it."

The evening of August 5 found Thompson back at the mouth of the Snake River. Months before, he had sent a letter

to Alexander Henry requesting that his winter trade goods be
sent across Athabasca Pass for an October 1 rendezvous, and
now he would have to move smartly to meet them. He was
out of gum to patch the leaks in his canoe, and there were
no trees around to tap for more. Since the Columbia's Big
Bend would take him well out of his way to the west, the surveyor decided to try a shortcut. He sent a messenger off for
Spokane House to tell Jaco Finlay to bring packhorses
south to meet him, then left the Columbia and ascended the
Snake River for two days to the "Shawpatin and Pilloosees
Road," a trail that led north into the Spokane country. The
Nor'Westers put ashore near a camp of Palouse tribesmen,
who "danced till they were fairly tired and the Chiefs bawled
until they were hoarse. They forced a present of 8 horses
on me, with a war garment." Thompson insisted on leaving
an IOU for the horses, then he and his men took off riding
through the rough scablands of the Palouse, choking on
dust from the fine volcanic soil. On August 13 they reached
Spokane House; Jaco and his horses turned up that evening,
having missed them on the trail.

ON THE SAME evening that Thompson pulled into Spokane
House, the Astorians made camp near the mouth of the Snake
River. When Alexander Ross and his companions arose the
next morning, "what did we see waving triumphantly in the
air, at the confluence of the two great branches, but a British
flag, hoisted in the middle of the Indian camp, planted there
by Mr. Thompson as he passed." Ross was not amused at this
symbolic gesture, especially when the chiefs at the big camp
indicated that they would not let the boats pass any farther up
the Columbia,

> saying that Koo-Koo-Sint—meaning Mr. Thompson—
> had told them so, pointing at the same time to the south
> branch [the Snake], as if to intimate that we might trade

there. The chiefs likewise stated that Koo-Koo-Sint had given them such and such things and among others, the British flag, that they should see his commands respected, but if Mr. Stuart would give them more than Koo-Koo-Sint had done, then he would be the greater chief, and might go where he pleased.

It is hard to know just what Thompson was up to here. He had obviously suspected that the Astorians' talk about building their post below The Dalles was a ruse, and maybe this was his way of suggesting to his new partners that a fair division of the business would be for them to turn up the Snake and trade in the territory Lewis and Clark had explored, while leaving the country he had charted to the North West Company. But he was certainly not so naive as to think that a British flag was going to turn them on their heels. Under the rules of joint occupancy, American and British companies had equal rights to the lands west of the Rockies known as the Oregon Territory, and the Astorians could build trading posts wherever they chose, no matter how many Union Jacks Thompson planted in their path. After a council with the chiefs the next day, Stuart's boats continued up the Columbia.

According to Alexander Ross, Qánqon shadowed the Astorians all the way, but not from any seat in a dugout canoe. She and her companion, "bold adventurous amazons they were," shot ahead or hung back from the main party like pups on a hunt, and were "the objects of attraction at every village and camp on the way." It was only later that Ross discovered the reason for all this attention. It seems that Qánqon had judiciously altered her prophecies, and was now showing off a letter (probably Finan McDonald's original note) and claiming that she and her mate

> had been sent by the great white chief, with a message to apprize the natives in general that gifts, consisting of goods and implements of all kinds, were forthwith to be

poured in upon them; that the great white chief knew
their wants, and was just about to supply them with everything their hearts could desire; that the whites had
hitherto cheated the Indians, by selling goods in place of
making presents to them, as directed by the great white
chief.

This new prophecy, though it might make David Stuart's life
awkward in the future, helped make the berdache and her
companion very popular figures among the Plateau peoples,
"who loaded them for their good tidings with the most valuable items they possessed—horses, robes, leather, and higuas
[shells]; so that, on our arrival at Oakinacken [the Okanogan
River], they had no less than twenty-six horses, many of them
loaded with the fruits of their false reports."

DAVID THOMPSON had no such distractions to impede his fall
business. After only three days at Spokane House, he was off
again, this time on horseback, carrying the fur packs that Jaco
Finlay had collected. Back north through the Colville Valley
he went, meeting Le Bon Vieux on the way to Kettle Falls,
where he paused for twelve days to build yet another clin-
ker-sided cedar canoe. His old acquaintance Cartier was there
with his band of Kalispels, ready to present him with a basket
of dried berries. On September 2 the Nor'Westers put into
the water above Kettle Falls and set out on the only stretch
of the Columbia left uncharted. The first night they camped
with the Old Chief and his Kootenai band, in country surrounded by hills of hard white limestone. Over the next three
days, they poled and paddled their way around the mouths of
the two big tributaries that Thompson had spent the past four
years exploring: first the "Saleesh River" (the Pend Oreille,
just north of the 49th parallel), then "McGillivray's River"
(the Kootenay, near Nelson, British Columbia). Here the
men were relieved to buy some fresh fish, because their diet

of dried salmon and berries had made all of them somewhat ill, and Coxe very much so. A few nights later they witnessed a celestial event: "Observed a Comet this evening, we had seen it these few nights past, but having a cloudy hilly horizon took it for a misty cloud then. Its place is nearly in a right line with the 2 guide Stars at 8:25 P.M." Within another week the party had lined its way up the Dalles des Morts (near modern Revelstoke), one of the most treacherous rapids on the whole river. Thompson knew he had almost closed the Columbia's circle, and along the way he watched as Coxe absorbed a whole new world:

> He had lived wholly on an Island, and knew it's extent, but had no ideas beyond it, as we proceeded up the River, and passed the great branches, the stream became lessened, and not so wide, as he did not know from what cause, every day he expected to get to the end of it; as we approached the cold increased, and the first shower of snow, he was for some time catching in his hand, and before he could satisfy his curiosity it was melted: the next morning thin ice was formed, which he closely examined in his hand, but like the Snow it also melted into water, and he was puzzled how the Snow and ice could become water, but the great Mountains soon settled his mind, where all became familiar to him.
>
> *Narrative*

It was September 18, 1811, when Thompson reached the Canoe River and revisited his winter hut at Boat Encampment, thereby completing his end-to-end survey of the Columbia's sinuous course. He had proved that the Great River of the West did run from the mountains to the sea after all, and the route that he pioneered across Athabasca Pass and down the Columbia to the Pacific served as the Northwest Passage for the rest of the Canadian fur trade's reign.

CHAPTER 10

ROOM
TO FEED

FALL 1811–SUMMER 1812

W HEN WILLIAM HENRY arrived at Boat
Encampment with Thompson's fresh trade goods, he
brought word from the North West Company's annual meeting three months earlier. There the partners had decided to
send out a new agent to handle the business of the Columbia
Department, "intending by this arrangement that Mr. David
Thompson should be left to prosecute his plans of discovery
on the west side of the Rocky Mountains towards the Pacific."
Thompson did not record his reaction to the news that now
that he had surveyed the entire course of the Columbia, the
company was going to give him time to do it.

Winter was coming on as he began his first trip downstream from Boat Encampment on October 19. Two days
later he came upon a herd of eight caribou resting beside
the river: "They were not at all shy and had the place been
good we might have killed several." His hunters had told him
that these animals lived in the area, and he had noticed some
of their tracks in the sand on his way upstream but had not
actually seen what he called "reindeer" since his posting on

Hudson Bay. He thought this herd must be a different species, and his intuition turned out to be correct: he was looking
at woodland caribou, close cousins to the barren ground species of the far north.

The furmen arrived back at Kettle Falls without incident
on October 30. The native village there, so full of life when
Thompson had passed through on his way to Astoria, was
now entirely deserted, and there was no sign of the horses he
had sent ahead for, either. He waited one day, then walked the
seventy miles south through the Colville Valley to Spokane
House. There he left the Hawaiian Coxe with Jaco Finlay
and set off with packhorses for the Flathead country. Near
Kullyspel House he met Bercier, who reported that the Flat
Bows were doing more gambling than trapping and that there
had been another Piegan raid near Kootanae House—this
time two Kootenais had been killed and three Iroquois hunters robbed and left naked on the trail. Word had it that the
Piegans had been planning to ambush Thompson's supply
canoes, which they had expected to come by the southern
route over Howse Pass, but had gotten tired of waiting.

Thompson pushed on through snow and sleet to Saleesh
House, and when he arrived on November 19, he found the
post "in a Ruinous condition." The roofs and floors all needed
repairing, and the men's house was such a mess that they had
to pitch a tent inside in order to stay dry. There was nothing to eat. Finan McDonald had left a note saying that he
had gone to the Flathead camp for food, but he didn't come
back for days and days, and in his journal entries Thompson
sounds a bit testy about the whole situation. A week later his
clerk did return with an ample supply of provisions, and on
the same day James McMillan arrived from the Saskatchewan
with John George McTavish, the man slated to succeed
Thompson as supervisor of the Columbia Department.
Within two days the supplies they brought had been sorted
and McTavish was headed west to Spokane House to assume
his duties. On his own again, Thompson concentrated on

repairing the buildings at Saleesh House so they'd last, especially the roof. Le Bon Vieux brought in a nice *chevreuil* at an opportune moment and loaned Thompson three horses to take a short trip up the Clark Fork. The weather was a sloppy "glush" that made a mess out of everything.

January of 1812 began cold and clear, with only a skiff of snow on the ground, and Thompson took sick with a sore throat and feverish cold. Too puny to work for a couple of days, he couldn't eat or sleep, and measured his pulse rate at 120. As he began to mend, he laid out plans for a sledge with wheels on it and designed a mousetrap. A very sore eye troubled him through the latter part of January, but did not keep him from using his wood-bending skills to craft some snowshoes for Finan McDonald. The men started work on a cargo canoe, and Le Bon Vieux's wife braided seventy fathoms of cordage to sew it together. When cold weather stalled the boat project, two of the voyageurs set up a kettle of ashes and boiled them with water to make lye, which they then mixed with animal fat for a supply of soap.

In mid-February the surveyor and Finan McDonald pointed two canoes upriver, intending to trade at the various winter camps for furs and provisions. There was strong shore ice in many places along the Clark Fork, and at one point they had to plow through eighty yards of frozen river. Their first stop was at the tents of the Kalispel chief Cartier, who provided them with some dried meat. Next day, hungry again, they shot "a poor Chevreuil that was run down and much torn by the Wolves," and Cartier followed along with them to the large Flathead camp at the junction of the Flathead and Clark Fork Rivers. Here Thompson counted sixty tents of families and noted that so many of the men had been killed in recent battles with the Piegans that there were another twenty tents of widows.

While Finan McDonald handled the trade, Thompson hired the Gauche, a Kootenai who had hunted for him in the past, to guide him on an excursion. The Gauche led him from

WINTER JOURNEYS AROUND SALEESH HOUSE

the Flathead River south along a ridge trail and down into the
valley where the modern town of Missoula lies. The day was
clear and good for viewing; Thompson climbed the round hill
now called Mount Jumbo and looked out at the surrounding
valleys. With information he had gathered from local people
and his knowledge of Lewis and Clark's journey, he was able
to retrace the Americans' path along the Bitterroot Valley
to Traveler's Rest, then across the mountains through Lolo
Pass. It was a lot of geography to take in, but the surveyor
knew exactly what he was looking at: "The route Capn. Lewis
& Party were from the Misserourie, behind those blue Hills
to the above Branch & down it to the Brook of the Defile
that leads to the Salmon." With that vision Thompson closed
one long seam in the scheme of his big map, and from the
mountaintop it all made sense.

Thompson made a rough sketch of the rivers and hills, then he and the Gauche climbed down from Mount Jumbo into the narrow river canyon known as the Hell Gate, a favorite rendezvous spot for Piegan war parties gathering to attack the Flatheads. Thompson called this cleft "the Defiles of Courter" in memory of the American trapper who had been killed two years before somewhere in the vicinity. He would have liked to look around some more, but their horses were worn out from struggling through the deep snow and it was beginning to storm: "Very bad Weather all of the Evening & Night & no shelter, I passed much of the Night standing leaning against a Tree – Kingfishers about."

On their way home the next day, they passed the bones of a horse beside the trail. Thompson noticed that the skull was carefully positioned in the center of the skeleton, and the Gauche told him that its nose pointed to the grave of its master—both warrior and horse had been killed in a battle on this spot. "The ridge of the Nose was marked with 7 Stripes of red signifying the number of Enemies he had slain with his own hand in Combat, on one side of the Head were marked 1 red Stripe, on the other side 3 red Stripes, signifying the number of Wounds he had received in former Battles. The Nose was all marked with red, signifying his End."

The pair made it back to the Flathead camp by noon, where Finan McDonald had been trying unsuccessfully to dry some meat underneath a linen tent. Two days later Thompson was invited to a council of the Flatheads and their allies, who had gathered to discuss a recent peace offer from the Piegans. As he related the story in his *Narrative*, not everyone thought peace was a good idea; one old man said he felt much safer with the Piegans as enemies than as friends:

> Who is there among us that has not cut off his hair several times, and mourned over our relations and friends, their flesh devoured, and their bones gnawed, by Wolves and Dogs. A state of peace has always been a

> time of anxiety, we were willing to trust and sure to
> be deceived . . . Do as you please, I now sleep all night,
> but-if you make peace I shall sleep in the day, and watch
> all night.

Some of the other elders spoke in favor of calling a truce,
while many of the younger men wanted to use their new
guns to avenge their dead. When the chief Cartier asked
Thompson for his opinion, he listed the different tribes east
of the mountains and their approximate sizes. He pointed out
that the bands and allies of the Piegans were numerous and
not under a single chief's control: "My advice is, that you do
not make peace with only one Tribe, and leave yourselves exposed to the inroads of all the others, and let your Answer
[be] that you claim by ancient rights the freedom of hunting
the Bison, that you will not make War upon any of them but
shall always be ready to defend yourselves." After much discussion the tribes at the parley decided not to make peace,
but to cross the Divide only in parties large enough to defend
themselves. If harassed by the Piegans again, they vowed to
fight, and the chiefs dispatched messengers telling all of their
allies to prepare for war the next-summer.

Directly after the council, the surveyor reengaged his
guide the Gauche and rode north. They passed the Old
Chief's winter camp and then "came smartly on trot & hard
Gallop to 1:25 P.M., when we alighted on the top of a bare
Knowl, commanding a very extensive View of the Lake &
Country far around." They were looking across Flathead
Lake, "a fine sheet of water . . . the haunt in all seasons of
aquatic fowl." While the surveyor sketched the lake and some
of the surrounding landscape, the Gauche pointed out a wide
gap in the mountains to the east; he said that his people and
many other west-side tribes used to follow a trail through this
gap on their way to the plains to hunt buffalo, but no one had
gone that way for several years because of their fear of the
Piegans.

Back at the Flathead camp the next day, Thompson loaded his canoe with the meat and furs he and Finan McDonald had traded from the various hunters and started for Saleesh House with his voyageurs. On their way they camped through a violent storm: "Heavy gust of Wind about Midnight tore up the Tent, tossed the Canoe over & over, split it in several places & we often thought to be buried under the trees." They were able to repair the canoe and get to the post the next morning, where they started packing for the long haul across the mountains.

By March 12 everything was ready, and while the men gummed two canoes, Thompson made a last-minute sketch of the view of plains and hills to the north. The next day they started downriver and immediately damaged both boats in the rapids of Thompson Falls. After half a day for repairs, they continued on through sleet and snow. At another big rapid they passed a cluster of wooden crosses that the voyageurs had erected in memory of a free hunter and his family who had drowned there the previous summer. They stopped for a barrel of gum at Kullyspel House, then took the overland route to the Spokane post. The pelts collected there amounted to 122 fur packs, weighing almost 11,000 pounds. The Columbia trade was steadily increasing, much as Thompson had hoped it would in the letter he had written to the partners four years before.

He and his crew started north toward Kettle Falls on horseback and a few days later camped near a stand of decent cedar along the Colville River. While they split out timbers for canoes, a steady flow of visitors came and went: a group of free hunters who had been trapping on the Okanogan River; Bercier, leading eighteen horses loaded with gum and furs; Jaco Finlay, who stayed to help build four new boats; a voyageur with ten rolls of watap; Martin, the Iroquois who-had helped Thompson dislocate his thumb two years before; three-fingered James McMillan and newcomer John George McTavish. By the evening of April 21, Thompson had collected six canoes at the falls, gummed and ready to go. He divided the baggage and then went out to observe for the latitude and longitude of the Ilthkoyape Falls one more time (48° 37' 22" N, 117° 54' 58" W). At noon the next day, the heavily laden Columbia brigade moved upstream. They portaged around the Dalles des Morts, negotiated the Columbia's hairpin loop at Boat Encampment, then switched to horses for the climb over Athabasca Pass. Thompson, walking ahead on bearpaw snowshoes in ice-crusted snow, sprained his right ankle and limped to the summit.

"AH, ATHABASCA PASS," said the park guide when I asked him about the trail. "Gonna make a slog for yourself, eh?"

"It's nice up top," he allowed. "They have the brass plaque at the Committee's Punchbowl, where the fur traders used to clink a toast every time they crossed. And you'll get a good look at Scott Glacier. But down in the woods, it's just a lot of walking. And you won't see much game. Elk OK. Goat. Moose here and there. A few sheep if you glass the slopes. Maybe caribou up on the ridges. Grizzly, of course. If you're lucky a wolf—there was a wolf pack working that area when I made my wildlife count. But mostly it's a long slog."

A long slog was just fine with me that day. I started up a hill on a wide gravel track that wound through some boglands, then narrowed to a horse trail and took to the trees away from the noisy course of the Whirlpool River. Mosquitoes wafted up in clouds from a rich understory of berry bushes and ferns, and there were miles to put in with only occasional glimpses of river. Old-growth spruce and lodgepole pine blotted out the sky, and the trail turned soggy as the gravel faded to sodden hoofprints. But even with the skin curling off my toes from the constant wetness, I could see how this path made sense to David Thompson. The river lay far to the north of his Piegan troubles, and the rolling benches made for a gradual ascent.

About halfway through the thirty-mile trek up to Athabasca Pass, the trail breaks out of the timber onto the wide, silvery promenade of the Whirlpool River's floodplain. A few miles ahead, the icy jumble of Scott Glacier pours from a saddle between two massive peaks. Buffalo of former times ascended this drainage during their late-summer searches for cool air and fresh grass, marking out a course that hunters could follow, then Thompson and his voyageurs. Bison and furmen liked those long, even slogs.

The open flat beside the river ends in a steep, wooded headwall; after that it's all rocks and intricately carved cascades as the trail climbs through a dense subalpine forest to top the Divide. It was somewhere around here that David Thompson had seen that big set of footprints on his first trip over this pass—the tracks his hunters had insisted belonged to a "large unknown animal." During his next trip the men reminded him of the tracks and pointed out a mountain where the creature was supposed to live: "On the top of the eminence, there was a Lake of several miles around which was deep moss, with much coarse grass in places, and rushes; that these animals fed there, they were sure from the great quantity of moss torn up, with grass and rushes; the hunters all agreed this animal was not carnivorous, but fed on moss, and vegetables."

It's hard not to be intrigued by this account. The Whirlpool drainage does have an Ice Age look about it, and it has the room, the vast empty spaces that it would take to harbor an outsized relic. Rich bogs and lakes lie pocked all along the watercourse, many of them surrounded by dense, wetland vegetation. The thought of such good coarse grass, of sedges and rushes torn up by roving tusks, of sphagnum moss trunk-fed by the bucketload into some gaping maw . . . but Thompson never saw a mammoth, and his hunters admitted that not one of them had ever seen one either.

I reached the incline late in the afternoon and didn't feel

like getting swallowed up by the woods again, so I set up my tent at a campsite right there. I wandered around a little bit, in and out of the trees, until I stepped in a huge, berry-rich bear flop. I returned to the tent, unlaced my pack, and gobbled everything I could find inside it to eat. After supper I was still filled with the restless exhaustion that had dogged me all the way up the trail. I wanted to be looking for some of those fourteen-inch footprints, but I couldn't seem to keep my mind focused on the ground.

Three days before, on another steep trail in the woods, a Frenchman walking ten feet in front of me had keeled over with a heart attack. I hadn't known the man—we were part of a group of tourists on the way up to look at some fossil beds—but I couldn't shake the image of the awkward twist in his shoulder as he had turned to speak, or the way dribbles of liquid had leaked from his red plastic water bottle as it rolled down the hill into my hand.

My campsite on the Whirlpool stared straight at Scott Glacier, and I thought I would ford the river and hike over for a closer look. The water didn't look more than waist deep, but it was running fast enough that I could see round rocks rolling along its bed. I took off my boots and pants and knelt down on the bank to test the water, so loud and cold. My knees nestled into the smooth skipper rocks along its edge.

He had seemed healthy enough, a middle-aged man on vacation. He had brought along his tripod to take pictures of the fossils. He had a thin, curved nose, and porcelain skin that looked almost translucent. After he collapsed onto the ground, the dirt and needles that stuck to his face had made it seem as if he were sinking into the forest; his last breaths had drained away into the vast mountains, and within a few minutes he was gone.

Down on my knees by the Whirlpool, gooseflesh covered my legs. I stood up and stepped into the current, feeling for the rocks with my toes. The water rushed about my knees. My arms flapped in the air, grasping for balance. As I worked my way across, the crags of Scott Peak hovered directly before me. "The passage to the other World, the Indians suppose to be by a high Crag. Their grandfather lends them a hand up it – if good he brings them safe to the top. If bad, he when half way up lets them fall to the bottom, where a mist forever blinds their Eyes." So reads a brief note in the back of the daybook that David Thompson carried with him across Athabasca Pass in 1812.

On my way back down from the pass, I was caught in a violent hailstorm and took refuge on the front porch of a forestry work cabin. Propped up against the wall was a neat cross-section from an old lodgepole pine. The tree slice, about as big around as a logger's chest, had 206 tight little growth rings, and someone had counted backwards from the outside of the circle, marking dates and events with an ink pen in a long winter count. Thin blue lines showed the year of Canada's independence from the Crown, World Wars II and I, and the bad winter of 1886–87. Near the center was a dot for the year Thompson first passed this way. The tree had been a mere sapling then, not even big enough to chop for firewood. I ran my finger around the little ridge of raised grain, barely a hair's thickness, and then followed the circles on out, feeling the layers that had gradually buried the winter of 1811 inside the tree. I thought about how David Thompson had struggled that season, and during most of his others, with the elements and with the Piegans; I thought about his close calls with rapids and blizzards, starvation and sickness. Yet as far as I could tell, during all of his distant expeditions, the surveyor never lost a single man under his command.

"MAY 8TH FRIDAY A very fine Night & Day – did not freeze much. At 3½ A.M. set off – held on up the Banks, very bad walking . . . could find no water 'till 8½ A.M. when we breakfasted – At Height of Land tried to observe, but the Sun was past the Meridian. Took a pipe [with] men." The surveyor worked his way down from Athabasca Pass for the last time and steered his canoes east, picking up Charlotte and the children, including a year-old boy he had never seen, somewhere along the way. Upon retirement many of the furmen left their native wives and offspring in the field and married again in eastern Canada or England, but Thompson was taking his family with him.

By the time they arrived at Fort William in July, war had been declared between the United States and Great Britain. Although this was obviously a subject of great concern, the partners had hopes that the conflict would not completely disrupt their business. William McGillivray was in London, where he was fitting out a merchant vessel for the mouth of the Columbia; in a letter that his emissary Donald McTavish delivered to Fort William, he wrote that he was waiting to launch the ship until he heard whether David Thompson had found a practical route for transporting the supplies to his interior posts. Thompson indeed had, and the partners at the rendezvous recognized how much he had accomplished during his five years of unbroken work. After setting in motion a range of plans to develop the surveyor's new Athabasca-Columbia route, they placed before the meeting "a resolve entered into that David Thompson now going down on Rotation shall be allowed his full share of the Company's profits for three years . . . that he is to finish his Charts, Maps, etc. and deliver them to the agents in that time."

A couple of days after the wintering partners approved the measure, a vessel arrived at the fort carrying news that the American fort at Mackinaw had fallen. Fearing live action on the Great Lakes, Thompson and his family got back in their canoe and dashed along the north shore of Lake Superior to the narrow straits that lead into Lake Huron, where they had to scrape the U.S. border. Once through, they were safe to cut north for the Ottawa River and float on to Montreal.

CHAPTER ELEVEN

THE SMELL OF CAMAS ROOT

1812–1857

W HEN THOMPSON arrived in Montreal in the fall
of 1812, he walked down a city street for the first
time in twenty-seven years. He seemed to take to the settled
lifestyle straightaway, purchasing a house and a farm in the
village of Terrebonne, north of the city. He was still arranging his family in their new home when he resumed his daily
journal, using the same fur company format that he had
learned as a teenager on the Saskatchewan. "October 20th
Tuesday A white frosty morning, but charming day . . . engaged a House Keeper at 10 Dollars per month . . . Sent for
writing desk Hinges." In early entries, he recorded the latest
news of the War of 1812 and observed for the latitude of his
new abode (45° 40' 59" N). On October 30 he called in a
minister and solemnized his vows with Charlotte. The next
day he was commissioned as an ensign major in the
Sedentary Militia under former North West partner
Roderick Mackenzie and immediately set about getting the
guns in good order for the local troops. There were several
retired furmen living in the area, and the rest of the fall reads

like a typical Thompson blur of work mixed up with an established couple's social schedule: the surveyor bought a milk
cow and danced till midnight; he built wooden bedsteads for
the children and dined at the priest's house after attending
high mass; he copied out his Columbia journals and took in
a holiday ball; he was rousted out of bed by a troop alert and
went for a ride in his new cariole. Just before Christmas he
made the four-hour drive to Montreal, where he had dinner
with William McGillivray and then brought Fanny home
from boarding school for the holidays. During January he
nursed Charlotte and two of the children through a bad case
of the measles and made a model of a cannon cart for the war
effort. But what Thompson really concentrated on, from the
moment he was settled in Terrebone, was his map work.

Building on the sheets he had begun to ink in years
before, and adding information forwarded to him from other
traders, Thompson settled down to his ambitious cartography project. Within seven months he had sent McGillivray a
sketch of the Oregon Country, and soon afterward he mailed
a representation that incorporated all of the territory from
Hudson Bay west to the Pacific. This second large map was
hung in the dining hall at Fort William, on a blank wall
across from oil paintings of Admiral Nelson and the Battle of
Trafalgar. For many seasons Thompson's map guided travelers who passed through on their way west. On the Pacific
Slope of these first two maps, he penned in a watercourse
he called the Caledonia River, which he showed rising just
west of his Boat Encampment and curling southwest to enter
the Pacific between the Fraser and the Columbia. No such
river exists, and Thompson corrected this mistake in the next
version of his work. But the original maps were reproduced
several times without his permission, and the phantom river
serves as a marker that traces uncredited editions of the surveyor's work. In 1814, Thompson delivered yet another chart
of the West to his partners, an even more accurate version
that didn't get a public viewing for another thirty-five years.

THOMPSON'S BIG map of 1814 is on permanent display at the Provincial Archives of Ontario in Toronto. At ten by six-and-a-half feet, the chart covers an entire wall at the entrance of the archive's reading room. It is enclosed in a specially designed glass case and further protected by a dark curtain that rolls away when you press a button. To prevent excessive light from damaging the paper and ink, the drape automatically rolls back after one minute.

The first thing I saw as the curtain opened was color: the sheets of rag linen paper have darkened with age to a varied, autumnal hue that in another two centuries might approach the orange back side of good birch rind. The writing ink of Thompson's day was rendered from oak apple galls, boiled together in a recipe that included lumps of iron sulfate and gum arabic. It flowed jet black from the goose quill, but over time mellowed into its original oaken tones, and now spreads a web of sepia across the linen continent. Around the periphery of his chart, the heavily inked squares that delineate degrees of latitude and longitude glow with the umbers of a deep forest night.

When he assembled the twenty-five individual sheets of his project, Thompson allowed himself plenty of overlap; where the folios join, his mucilage glue forms a wide strip that's lighter than the single layers and often damaged or blurred. One of these glue strips follows the 49th parallel, and there are tears and gaps along the crease; light brown repair marks obscure parts of the upper Okanogan country, Kettle Falls, the Kootenay River between Bonner's Ferry and Kootenay Lake, and the territory east of the Tobacco Plains.

Thompson used several sizes and styles of script to conjure different levels of information from the map. All-capital block letters designate mountain ranges and major rivers. Brooks, rivulets, and native trails he labeled in smaller, cursive script. A swirled "NWCo" appears wherever a trade house existed. There are snippets of information, the sounds of the surveyor whispering to himself: he deems the Colville River "Unnavigable," and at the mouth of the mighty Fraser he remarks, "To this place white men have come from the sea." He laid neat feather plumes beside each watercourse to denote the direction of flow, and along these arrows the furmen's journeys of discovery move again. Alexander Mackenzie's short portage across the upper Rockies makes sense. Ram Rivulet is clearly delineated, and no matter what a charlatan the Rook turned out to be as a guide, you can see that he was very close to being on the mark. Thompson used the local names for many of the rivers; Howse Pass and Athabasca Pass are simply "Heights of Land."

It's an amazingly accurate and at the same time idiosyncratic piece of cartography. Thompson laid the ink on as an artist might, with delicate nuances of shade and texture that indicate the width of a river oxbow or the elevation of the Eagle Hills in the midst of the prairies. The Rocky Mountains look like a twisted chain, with separate loops linking the big peaks north and south in an effort to convey timberline, glaciers, height, and mass all in an instant. Thompson deviated from this bird's-eye perspective only once, right above his Kootanae House at the headwaters of the Columbia. During the two winters he spent there, he developed a special regard for the peak he named Mount Nelson, "which stands alone in native grandeur." He went outside over and over again to measure its height and sketch its profile, and on his big map he inscribed a circle in the range west of Kootanae House, then drew in a side view of the peak. It's the only construction like it on the whole chart, one nod to the mountain that stood at the center of all his western movements.

AS THOMPSON sat in Terrebonne, tending his garden and transcribing points and courses from his field notebooks onto his maps, the situation on the Columbia was anything but calm. In August of 1812 a visitor to Fort Astoria told the Americans that their supply ship *Tonquin* had been overwhelmed by angry natives off the coast of Vancouver Island and blown to smithereens. The vessel's loss left the American post defenseless in a time of war, and when Thompson's successor John George McTavish paddled down the Columbia from Spokane House in the summer of 1813, he negotiated a deal with Duncan McDougall to buy Fort Astoria for the North West Company and place its men under British protection. The following March the Nor'Westers' merchant ship *Isaac Todd* arrived from Portsmouth, accompanied by a frigate from the Royal Navy that had orders to wipe out any American settlements in the region, but the Union Jack was already flying over Astoria. The *Isaac Todd* provided the post with all the trade goods it needed and offered some company veterans an opportunity for a comfortable ride back around the Horn to civilization. On a sloppy May evening in 1814, two of Thompson's old cohorts, Alexander Henry and Donald McTavish, left a farewell party and stepped into the dory that would ferry them out to the vessel, which lay anchored off Tongue Point. The Columbia's dark currents capsized the little boat, drowning all hands on board.

That same year David Thompson was visited by personal tragedy.

> January 11th Tuesday. A fine cloudy day. My poor dear little John passed the Night with great difficulty of breathing, but quiet thro' extreme weakness, and at 7 A.M. it pleased the Almighty God to take him from this World – had a Coffin of Oak made for him. He is 5 years 4½ months old – measures 3 ft. 9 in. and still appears a beautiful Boy. This loss has plunged us in deep affliction, especially his poor Mother.

A few weeks after John's death, Thompson traveled to Quebec to obtain a license as a land surveyor. When he returned to Terrebonne after riding all night, he found two of his daughters ill with roundworms, a common affliction of that time. Twelve-year-old Fanny soon recovered, but seven-year-old Emma grew worse. For the next week Thompson tirelessly nursed the little girl who had crossed Howse Pass with him as a toddler, dosing her with calomel, Carolina pink root, and castor oil. On February 20 he recorded hopes of her recovery. Over the next two days, however, she relapsed, and on the evening of February 22, she died. "February 24 Thursday. A very fine Morning - at 10½ A.M. smart Rain came on & continued with Sleet all day - at 9 A.M. sent off the Body of my poor Emma. At 10 set off myself and at 1½ P.M. buried my poor little Daughter close touching her little Brother John in the same Grave. God Almighty the Saviour of the World, bless them both."

In 1815 the family moved to Glengarry County, Ontario, and the next year Thompson mailed a prospectus to a London bookmaker that described an ambitious atlas he had in mind. It stretched "from the east side of Lake Superior, and Hudson's Bay, quite across the continent to the Pacific Ocean." It would include the territory of each of the Indian nations, and all the trading posts as set out by the Hudson's Bay and North West Companies. It would be accompanied by a sister chart, marked with the important mountains and drainages, on which he would superimpose the "position and extent of the Coal Mines; of the various Beds of different kinds of Stone and Rock; of the great Meadows and Forests; the limits of the countries on which the Bison, Elk, Red Deer, Wild Sheep, etc. are found; the line of the position of the Countries, over which, is the most constant appearance and greatest brightness of the Aurora Borealis."

Referring to himself in the third person, Thompson strived to give his potential buyer some idea of what had gone into the making of such a project, and promised delivery within three years: "Nothing less than an unremitting perseverance bordering on enthusiasm could have enabled him to have brought these maps to their present state; in early life he

THE SMELL OF CAMAS ROOT

conceived the idea of this work, and Providence has given him to complete, amidst various dangers, all that one man could hope to perform." The publisher was not so impressed, and turned down the proposal.

Around this time Thompson accepted a post as astronomer with the International Boundary Commission. From his new position he guided the official U.S.-Canadian survey of the 49th parallel from Saint-Régis, Quebec, west through Lake of the Woods, then down to the southeastern corner of Manitoba. This kind of baseline survey constituted a life's work in itself, and he traveled many of the routes exactly as he had during his days with the North West Company, directing a handful of voyageurs in a small boat and recording his positions neatly in a daily journal. On the Great Lakes they fought heat and mosquitoes, wind and heavy surf. In many areas flat land and thick woods made observation points hard to establish; the men would fell trees and erect pole stations, then clamber up live trees at the next stop and try to spot the poles.

In the summer of 1819, on the western end of Lake Erie, the surveyor and his crew entered an area of miasmic swamp and soon all came down with sweats and fever. One of the men lay delirious in the bottom of the boat, and the rest of the crew had trouble getting up the strength to row. "August 8th Heavy showers with close sultry weather and we camped on a wet sand with everything dripping wet. Myself in fever: pulse 101 to the minute. 2 men very ill of the fever and the rest complaining at times." His daybook entries for the month sound a lot like those from his first difficult summer on Windermere Lake, except that in this case the local inhabitants were Dutchmen who sold the party milk and loaves of bread, and when Thompson's crew pulled out of the field in early fall, they ferried across Lake Erie in a steamboat: "The rolling of the vessel and working of the engine, made us all sick."

In 1820 William McGillivray held a dinner for all present

and former North West Company partners at his palatial house in Montreal. It was a gala affair, attended by many members of Montreal society. One of the guests was a young scientist named J. J. Bigsby, who found himself seated beside the explorer David Thompson: "He was plainly dressed, quiet and observant. His figure was short and compact, and his black hair was worn short all around, and cut square, as if by one stroke of the shears, just above the eyebrows. His complexion was of a gardener's ruddy brown, while the expression of deeply furrowed features was friendly and intelligent, but his cut-short nose gave him an odd look . . . "

Since there are no known photographs or portraits of Thompson, this description is the closest contemporary likeness of him that exists. At the time of McGillivray's dinner, the surveyor was fifty years old, still at work in the field for the Boundary Commission. Bigsby later got a job with the commission himself and, while traveling with Thompson, had the chance to hear some of the surveyor's tales: "He can create a wilderness and people it . . . or climb the Rocky Mountains with you in a snowstorm, so clearly and palpably, that only shut your eyes and you hear the crack of a rifle shot, or feel the snow-flakes melt on your cheeks as he talks." Bigsby also recorded Thompson's practice of reading, "in the most extraordinary French," three chapters each of the Old and New Testaments to his men during their spare time.

David Thompson served ten years on the Boundary Commission, the last four as sole chief astronomer—his calculations were one of the few things agreed upon by both sides. When the project degenerated into a political dispute in 1826, he resigned and retired back to Glengarry County to live as a farmer and businessman. His neighbors included some of his former fur-trading partners, but by this time William McGillivray's North West empire had collapsed. The Hudson's Bay Company had merged with its former nemesis in 1821, and the terms of amalgamation were not at all favorable to the North West Company. McGillivray died in 1825, and two months later his company declared bank-ruptcy; its substantial debts included the sum of four hundred pounds owed to David Thompson.

At the end of 1826, Finan McDonald joined the enclave of retired Nor'Westers in Glengarry County. His career had extended all over the Northwest, where he had become known as a faithful family man and good-hearted giant with a quick temper; every traveler of the period tells a story about him. Jaco Finlay kept a lower profile, taking over Spokane House when it was abandoned by the Hudson's Bay Company shortly after it assumed control of the business. Jaco lived there peacefully with his family until his death in 1828.

Another of Thompson's former acquaintances did not fade so quietly. The Kootenai berdache Qánqon, the messen-ger-prophetess who had paced Thompson and the Astorians up the Columbia in 1812, apparently told her story of white men who would come bearing gifts as far north as the Shuswap Indian territory in New Caledonia. Despite rumors of her death there, Qánqon reappeared some years later in the Kootenai country as a translator and shaman. Her fame spread south, and trade journals from western Montana's Flathead Post make mention of her in 1825 and again in 1837, when, according to a missionary's account, her attempt to broker peace between some Flatheads and a Blackfeet raid-ing party finally led to her demise.

Modern Kootenai people provided anthropologist Claude Schaeffer with a fuller version of the berdache's death. Apparently Qánqon, though no longer a young woman, had gone out with a raiding party of young Kootenai warriors. As on her first raid, the party was unable to locate any enemy bands and was returning to its home camp under relaxed guard when it walked right into a Blackfeet ambush. One brave, traveling toward the rear of Qánqon's party, managed to hide himself in thick brush, where he listened to the suc-cessive war whoops of the Blackfeet, each one signaling the end of another Kootenai warrior. He heard a woman's yell and recognized Qánqon's voice. Her screams seemed to continue for a long time before he heard a final Blackfeet whoop.

Over time, details of Qánqon's death filtered back to her people. Members of the war party said that she sustained several gunshot wounds before they could subdue her. Then she was held in a seated position while the warriors methodically slashed at her midsection with knives. But each new wound closed up as soon as the knife was withdrawn. Apparently this healing occurred several times, but Qánqon gave no more cries. Finally one warrior opened up her chest and ate a piece of her heart, a coup de grace that was reserved for the most tenacious enemies. Qánqon was unable to heal this wound and died, after half a day of torture—a measure of the great strength of her spirit protector. It was said that when the Kootenai burial party arrived some time later, no wild animals or birds had disturbed her body.

BETWEEN HIS SHARES in the North West Company and his position with the International Boundary Commission, David Thompson made considerable money over the course of his career. But in the years after his retirement, it began to slip away. William McGillivray's bankruptcy hurt, and several of Thompson's children made poor business decisions with their father's backing. The collection of petty local debts, which within the scheme of the fur trade he had accomplished so efficiently, proved more difficult back in civilization; even the town church defaulted on a note to Thompson. The last of David and Charlotte's thirteen children was born in Glengarry County in 1829, and that winter he made an unfortunate contract to supply the British army with cordwood that cost him the rest of his capital. His notebook for 1833 begins with a page entitled "A List of Accounts due to D. Thompson, 30th January 1833," but the debts were for paltry sums, and by the end of the year, he had lost all his land-holdings to creditors. At about the time his personal finances dwindled to nothing, his journal comments were concerned with a dry summer that seemed to reflect his own situation: "No Pigeons and very few Ducks Geese etc. very few Rooks or Birds of any kind except in the depth of the Forest in July, and August, almost all the Wells dried up and the Fields were destitute of Herbage even the Clover when cut had no undergrass but appeared as if the ground had been exposed to a burning sun. Butter very scarce and fever – frequent winds."

Over the next three years Thompson undertook a variety of routine surveying jobs, measuring out canals, township boundaries, and land grants. May of 1837 found him interviewing, at age sixty-seven, for the job of clarifying the Muskoka-Madawaska River route from Georgian Bay to the Ottawa River. A Captain Baddely was a member of the government panel who heard the interview, and he wrote to the Surveyor General about it:

> Mr. Thompson dined with me yesterday . . . he is highly qualified for the duty in point of scientific and professional requirements . . . I think it is necessary, however, from the confidence which has been placed in me, and my desire to see the service properly conducted, to acquaint you that there are rumours abroad that Mr. T. is not trustworthy as to reporting of facts. This I mention without knowing what degree of credit to attach, although I must confess that there is something in his conversation which I do not like and which makes me suspect his candour.

Apparently the rumors that clouded the surveyor's reputation involved Canadian resentment over several decisions made by the International Boundary Commission, on which he had held a prominent position—an ironic smear, since Thompson was highly critical of some of the political decisions that were being made concerning Canada's boundary with the United States. In any case, the commission hired Thompson for the Muskoka job.

The surveyor began by rejecting Captain Baddely's rec-
ommendation for a tin canoe, listening instead to his voyageurs and spending two weeks in the construction of a more
seaworthy cedar vessel. Once out, he searched the somewhat
barren landscape for more than simple points on the map,
thinking, as he often had in the West, of the possibilities
for human settlement. In a vigorous stand of hardwoods he
"bored the Soil for 2 feet a good dark grey loam, with about
2 or 3 in. of rich vegetable Mould on the top. Appears very
good for Agriculture."

When he had time apart from his surveying work,
Thompson kept tinkering with his sheaf of maps, and in 1843
he mailed the final, perfected set of his atlas to officials in
England. These five large sheets, each one four feet by ten
feet, contain much of the detailed information promised in
his 1816 proposal. That same year the Canadian government
decided to purchase a version of all his maps of the country.
Arrowsmith of London, still the world's premier cartographer,
was asked to set a fair price. It was decreed that Thompson
would receive 150 pounds, a pittance for the amount of work
he had invested in the project. Arrowsmith then borrowed
from the set to clarify its own maps, which were soon published as a Hudson's Bay pamphlet without any credit to
Thompson.

Thompson's maps were important documents—Britain
and the United States were still arguing about the location
of their border, and his explorations and surveys constituted
a legitimate stake to a large part of the Oregon Territory.
During the negotiations Thompson wrote several letters to
the officials involved, once suggesting a boundary along the
47th parallel from the Rocky Mountains to the Columbia,
then down the center of that river to the sea. This would have
awarded to Canada what is now northwestern Montana, the
Idaho panhandle, and most of Washington State. In another
letter Thompson described how he had crossed the Rocky
Mountains in 1801 and 1802 to begin the exploration of the

region. Whether he misremembered the date by five years or was fudging to establish precedence, his efforts came to nothing. The Americans held firm in their demands for the entire region, and in 1846 the British government ceded its claim to all lands south of the 49th parallel. Thompson was outraged, and for the rest of his life he felt that "blockhead" politicians had given away to the Americans some of the best of the country he had explored—especially his old trade route from Saleesh House west to Kullyspel and Spokane Houses.

Shortly after the 1846 boundary settlement, Thompson's vision failed. Apparently the eye that he had damaged as a teenager, during his frantic winter of learning with Philip Turnor, had never fully recovered, and finally his other eye weakened enough to leave him unable to practice his trade. Thompson and Charlotte moved in with one of their daughters, and this was the time when he decided to write an account of his adventures in the fur trade. A decade earlier, the American writer Washington Irving had tried to purchase the rights to all of Thompson's personal notebooks for use in writing *Astoria*, but Thompson had refused to sell, preferring to tell his own story. Certain that the public would be interested in his far-ranging travels, he began paging through his old field journals.

DAVID THOMPSON'S surviving notebooks, all seventy-seven of them, are grouped by number in a series of green archival boxes in Toronto. They are old and fragile, and before I could look at them I had to slip on a pair of soft cotton gloves. Each of the daybooks is ten inches wide and fourteen inches tall, large enough that it took a lot of steady writing to fill one up. Inside their marbled covers, some of the pages are smeared with mud and marked with dark splotches of lamp oil. Circles of mold range in color from dove brown to a beautiful mauve. A note fell out of one journal volume into my gloved hand; it had been written by a conservator who had inspected the molds and decided that they had probably stopped growing some time ago.

The script in Thompson's western field journals does not have the elegance and versatility of the lettering on his maps, but it is for the most part still clear and readable. As I sat in the reading room of the Provincial Archives, within sight of the curtain that hides his monumental map, I could see how his writing clenched up as he grew old. By the time he had penned four drafts of the *Narrative*, his fluid stroke had grown very shaky. Some historians have tried to connect Thompson's faltering hand with a dimming of thought, in the way that his brother-in-law, John McDonald of Garth, expressed it when he tried to dictate his own adventures at age eighty-five: "It may naturally be expected that, at that age, the memory is gone." But David Thompson's memory was far from shot. He had nursed the idea of a book about his travels for many years, perhaps ever since he copied out pages of Samuel Hearne's explorations at the frigid trade depot in Churchill when he was fourteen years old. While working on the *Narrative* he had his copious diaries before him, and they formed a mother lode of original data. For long stretches Thompson stuck right with the daybooks, reeling off events almost exactly as he had originally set them down. At other times a simple journal entry sparked deeper memories.

On a fall day in 1809, Thompson had stopped at a bend in the Pend Oreille River to smoke with a small group of Kalispel Indians led by a good-natured old chief. In his diary it amounts to nothing more than a brief exchange: "The oldest man according to custom made a speech & a Present of 2 Cakes of Root Bread about 12 lb. of Roots & 2½ dried Salmon . . . " The Kalispel chief had presented the surveyor with his first basket of roasted camas bulbs. They would become one of his trail staples, a food that made his belly grumble but kept it full. Thompson had saved some of these roots, and from his desk in 1847, when he was seventy-seven years old, he could take time to savor the moment, to focus his rheumy eye on a few small tubers.

> These Roots are about the size of a Nutmeg, they are near the surface, and are turned up with a pointed Stick, they are farinaceous, of a pleasant taste, easily masticated, and nutritive, they are found in the small meadows of short grass, in a rich soil, and a short exposure to the Sun dries them sufficiently to keep for years. I have some beside me which were dug up in 1811 and are now thirty-six years old and are in good preservation . . . but they have lost their fine aromatic smell.
>
> *Narrative*

As he sniffed the camas roots, Thompson transported himself back to the blue-petaled meadows of the Pend Oreille, and the shriveled relics on his desk brought back the taste of the whole place.

STORIES HAVE BEEN passed down about David Thompson's pitiable later life—how at age seventy he applied for a clerk's position with the Hudson's Bay Company, only to be rejected; how, blind and penniless, he was forced to pawn the instruments of his trade and on one occasion even his winter coat. But there are other stories, such as the one about him taking his grandchildren out at night and teaching them the names of the stars. His daughter Mary also set down a series of memories from this period that don't sound so terrible. She said that a Montreal oculist, much to everyone's amazement, managed to restore clear vision to both of her aged father's eyes. She remembered how Thompson remained particularly neat in his dress and appearance, his only complaint being a pair of very tender feet, and his only indulgence being the accumulation of a great variety of slippers and shoes. At the age of seventy-five, when he was immersed in writing his

Narrative, "he seemed to live his life over in talking to himself aloud over some anecdotes and jokes they played on each other in his travels with his companions. We would hear him laugh heartily over them with tears streaming down his cheeks." She remembered one story that he delighted in telling, about a particularly hungry winter journey across the mountains. He and his men became so desperate, he said, that they decided they would have to kill one of their dogs for breakfast the next day. But when they awoke in the morning, all their dogs had disappeared, and they didn't see them again until they were twenty miles down the trail. Mary said that her father became quite absent-minded and once completely filled his niece's house with smoke when he left his sealskin cap and gloves on a hot woodstove. On another occasion he drove home from a friend's house with the wrong horse harnessed to his buggy, wondering all the way why his steed was acting so strangely. When everyone laughed at his mistake, "he enjoyed it himself and thought it a good joke."

Thompson died on February 10, 1857, two months before his eighty-seventh birthday. Charlotte followed him within three months and was buried beside him in the Mount Royal cemetery in Montreal. One of their sons sold the unpublished *Narrative* to a lawyer, and for years it languished in a drawer. Thompson's name faded altogether for thirty years, until the Canadian explorer and geologist J. B. Tyrrell plotted courses off some surprisingly accurate old maps during a survey of the Rocky Mountains. When he found out who had drawn them, Tyrrell researched David Thompson's original reports. He located and purchased the pages of the *Narrative,* then put together a manuscript from the four drafts that Thompson had never completely finished. In 1916 it was published in a limited edition by Canada's Champlain Society, causing a great stir among history buffs on both sides of the border. In 1927, J. B. Tyrrell raised a fluted column, with a sextant riding on top, as a monument over Thompson's grave.

EPILOGUE

THE SIXTY-MILE section of the Columbia River that courses downstream from Priest Rapids Dam is known as Hanford Reach. It is the last free-flowing stretch of the river in the United States, unchanged by dams or dredging. On the morning we chose to paddle through it, we had quite a load in our tubby canoe. I sat in the lookout seat in the bow and Gene Hunn took the stern, an unlikely steersman surrounded by books and binoculars. James Selam's son Willie, a coach at Wapato High School, took the middle seat alongside two coolers and a pile of life jackets. We had shoehorned James into a space directly in front of Willie, with his feet stuck straight out under my seat in the bow. The elder Selam remained motionless as we pushed cautiously out into the Columbia, negotiated the pilings of Vernita Bridge at a bit of an angle, then straightened out and glided smartly down into a landscape dominated on the west by Hanford's nuclear ziggurats. The huge compounds galvanized everyone's attention at first, and James said they reminded him of the mythical Swallowing Monster that according to Sahaptin lore dwells in the depths of the Big River.

In contrast with the complex structures on the nuclear reserve, the river's east bank stands absolutely empty. It was toward the east that Gene started looking as he leafed through Click Relander's book about the Wanapam people, trying to get James to help identify the local landmarks. "That ridge of hills that begins above Priest Rapids: Wahluke, 'rising up.' That means leaping or jumping, right James? You can see how it rises up off the plain."

James shook his head. "More like the rising of your spirit when you are dead, moving from stage to stage as it ascends." He let his outstretched hand float up from waist to shoulder.

"OK. And here Relander calls these points Na Nook? Ya Nook? Wa Nook? Does any of that make sense, James?"

"To me, maybe. I don't think to you."

Willie spotted some geese on a gravel bar downstream, and we ruddered to drift quietly toward them. The geese spooked while we were still well away, honking low and then taking off. Willie told us that when he was a kid, he would spend hours stalking honkers as they fed, moving a little ways on his belly, never looking at them directly with his eyes. When the sentry bird lifted its neck, Willie would pause and flatten himself on the ground until the birds all put their heads back down. He would shake his hair out over his face and peer at them through the strands until he thought it was safe to move another few feet.

As we drifted closer, we realized that the bar fluttered with other life as well. Stationary blue herons, horned larks, a mule deer nibbling at grass, mergansers in a backwater, spotted sandpipers at the waterline, cormorants bunched up along the point, and—what was that? Four white pelicans.

James had never seen a white pelican, so we paddled hard across the current to land on the lower tip of the gravel bar and sneak back for a look. James's feet had gone fast asleep, and Willie and I had to hoist him out of the canoe, then send him stumbling stiff-legged toward the birds. Much calmer than the geese, the pelicans contorted their necks and tucked their bills up under their wings. From hopelessly far away, James snapped a couple of pictures of the white bumps. The birds took off, and in slow motion one wheeled its black wingtips close around us. James whirled with his camera and caught it flat against the sun.

As we approached Coyote Rapids, James told how the Wanapam prophet Smohalla had led his dream and dance sessions at this site over a hundred years ago. Straight downstream we could see the point of the sacred hill, Laliik, where the Oriole came to Smoholla and infused him with the idea that the Plateau peoples should resist white encroachment and stick to the old ways; that a day would eventually come when the whole world would turn over, swallowing all the whites and those who followed their path. Then all the generations of honorable dead would resurface to live as people should live.

Gene had spoken often of the great paradox of this spot in the river, where Smohalla's prophecy of extermination might be bearing fruit on the nuclear reserve. We were hoping for a wild, frothy ride across the shoal, but the height of the water had reduced Coyote Rapids to a riffle, and we glided through with only a few burbles to waver our bow. "Those who are true shall pass through the earth," chanted Willie. "So spoke Smohalla."

Next we entered waters where some years before James and Willie had fished for salmon at night. For the rest of the afternoon Willie would spot a certain gravel bar or swirl of water and remember exactly how they had set their net and each fish that came over the side as they reeled it in. He said it had not been a profitable trip.

And yet on this day the fish were moving. *Whack!* A series of well-spaced, chinook-sized splashes kept our heads turning, but never quite in time to make out what they were. We eased through a left bend of the river, past a shoestring of an island, and headed straight for a line of creamy cliffs marked by strata of volcanic ash.

"The White Bluffs," said James. "My father camped here, and told me how they would look. Just like this. But I've only been here at night before, on our fishing boat."

We decided to stop as close to the cliffs as we could. The air temperature was 105 degrees, and Gene, Willie, and I flopped into the river as soon as we got the boat ashore. While the rest of us swam in the cool water, James waded gingerly in the shallows, trying to get some feeling back into his feet.

When we returned, he was picking up fist-sized river rocks and pitching them straight down on the shore one by one. After each toss he would bend stiffly down to retrieve the rock and feel the broken edge. He did this over and over, until finally he bobbed up with one that had cracked ragged and keen but kept a smooth round end that nested in his palm. "See?" he said. "Just right for scraping hides." A cursory search turned up several piles of similarly knapped flint along the shore, mixed up with iron wagon-wheel hoops and hubs, oak spokes, and the rings of many campsites. The bend at the White Cliffs had been a river ford since prehistoric times, and then the regular route of a cattle drive that pushed north to feed the prospectors in the gold rush on the Kootenay River. James picked up an iron rod, oddly curled at one end, and used it as a shepherd's crook while he patrolled the shore. It was at just such a place as this, he said, that Heron would stretch out his foot, farther and farther, until his toes reached the opposite shore, forming a bridge that his smaller animal kin could walk across.

After lunch we drifted downstream, and James nodded off in the parboiling heat. We entered a wide part of the river where for the first time we could see amber rocks on the bottom as we moved along at four or five miles an hour. I tumbled off the bow and floated on my back, toes forward, letting the current whisk me over the rocks. As I bobbed downstream, I kept thinking of how David Thompson recorded only cool, cloudy days on this stretch of the desert, whereas here we were, in the same month, under a most relentless sun.

A roar of voices went up from the canoe, an explosion that seemed to lift the pattern of sunlight off the surface of the water. Stunned, almost afraid, I rolled over on my belly to stroke a wide circle, searching across the water's surface for a sign. The river seemed to have turned black and opaque. Willie was hollering to me about a big fish; Gene suggested with much laughter that the Swallowing Monster was after me and I might want to get out of the river. I curled my toes under and swam for the canoe, hard, trying to keep my eyes peeled all round. There was nothing to see, but when Willie leaned forward to give me a hand up out of the water, he reeled me in with the extra strength of adrenaline.

"It was a sturgeon," he stammered."It came up head first. I could see its nose, and then its eyes, those beady eyes, and then its mouth—it had a big mouth. And then those plates on-its back, it came up so slow, and it just kept rising and rising . . ." With his hands Willie tried to describe the head of a man-sized fish. When he got to its mouth, he opened his fingers up wide.

"I think it was a whale," offered Gene. "Spyhopping."

"Spying on us."

"Looking," said James. "Looking for the Wanapam."

"It was right next to the boat. It was three feet from the boat. It could have eaten a paddle."

"A sturgeon," said Willie. "They live on the bottom. Sturgeon don't do that. I've been fishing all my life and I've never seen a sturgeon roll up to the top like that."

THE SUN WAS mercifully setting by the time we landed and shuttled the canoe back around to Vernita Bridge. Everyone was tired and hungry, but James asked that we form a small circle before we drove away. "Let us stand together here for just a minute," he said, "and think about what we have seen today."

He pointed away from the hazy sunset. "Today the fathers were talking to me, telling me the old things because when I heard them the first time, as a child, I was listening. I couldn't see them outside today, but I could hear them inside. I could feel that they were there. You talk about David Thompson. I've seen what he said. I've read Lewis and Clark. These men saw how the Indian had stored up food, and could provide for their needs. You think about the things that your explorers did not see."

James lifted his head, and said it again. "Think about these things."

CHRONOLOGY

DATE	EVENT
1607	English colonists found Jamestown, Virginia
1608	Samuel de Champlain and French colonists found Quebec
	Telescope invented
1610	Henry Hudson explores Hudson Bay
1670	Hudson's Bay Company chartered in London
1673	French explorers explore Mississippi River, reach mouth of Missouri River
1730	Mirror sextant invented
1752	Benjamin Franklin flies kite in electrical storm
1754	Anthony Henday travels west from Hudson Bay onto Plains, meets natives on horseback and sees Rocky Mountains
1763	Treaty of Paris officially ends French and Indian Wars and gives Great Britain control of Canada
1770	David Thompson born in London
	William Wordsworth born in Cockermouth, England
1771	Captain James Cook completes his first voyage around the world
1772	Samuel Hearne explores Coppermine River to Arctic Ocean
1775	Daniel Boone leads party of settlers into Kentucky
1776	American Revolution begins
	Spanish establish mission at San Francisco
1777	David Thompson enters Grey Coat School
1778	Spinning mule invented to spin multiple strands of yarn
	James Cook trades for sea otter pelts in Nootka Sound
1779	James Cook killed by Hawaiian natives, cutting short his search for Northwest Passage
1781	Smallpox epidemic begins to sweep northern Plains
1783	Treaty of Paris ends American Revolution
	North West Fur Company established in Montreal
1784	David Thompson begins apprenticeship on Hudson Bay
	Dr. Samuel Johnson dies in London
	James Cook's journal of his last voyage published in London
1785	Introduction of power loom in England for weaving cloth
1787	David Thompson winters with Piegans near Rocky Mountains

1789   French Revolution begins
        Alexander Mackenzie reaches Arctic Ocean
        David Thompson learns surveying from Philip Turnor
1790   Benjamin Franklin dies in Philadelphia
        British Captain George Vancouver begins his three-year
            survey of northwest coast of North America
1792   American Captain Robert Gray discovers mouth of
            Columbia River
        George Vancouver's Lieutenant William Broughton
            explores Columbia 100 miles upriver
1793   Alexander Mackenzie reaches Pacific Ocean at Bella Coola
        David Thompson surveys Muskrat Country west of
            Hudson Bay
1794   Jay Treaty establishes neutral commission to settle border
            disputes between United States and Canada
1796   Scottish explorer Mungo Park reaches headwaters of Niger
            River in what is now Mali, West Africa
1797   David Thompson leaves Hudson's Bay Company to join
            North West Company
1798   David Thompson travels to Mandan villages and charts
            headwaters of Mississippi River
        Napoleon invades Egypt; Horatio Nelson and British Navy
            defeat French at Battle of the Nile
1799   David Thompson marries Charlotte Small
        Alexander Mackenzie resigns from North West Company
        George Vancouver's *Journeys to the North Pacific Ocean*
            published in London
1800   Alexander Mackenzie joins XY Fur Company
1801   David Thompson attempts to cross Rocky Mountains
        Alexander Mackenzie's *Voyages to the Frozen and Pacific
            Oceans* published in London; Mackenzie knighted in
            honor of his explorations
        1803   Thomas Jefferson completes Louisiana Purchase
1804   David Thompson works in Peace River country
        Lewis and Clark start up Missouri River
        Merger of the Northwest and XY Fur Companies
1805   Admiral Nelson defeats French at Battle of Trafalgar
        Lewis and Clark reach Pacific Ocean
1806   Russian-American Fur Company collects otter pelts from
            Alaska to Spanish California
        Mungo Park killed by natives on Niger River

1807	David Thompson crosses Rockies and builds trading post at headwaters of Columbia River
	Manuel Lisa winters on Yellowstone River
	Zebulon Pike explores Southwest into Colorado
	Great Britain abolishes institution of slavery
	Thomas Jefferson signs bill banning all foreign trade following British attacks on American shipping
1808	David Thompson explores Kootenai River
	Simon Fraser follows Fraser River to the Pacific
	Napoleon invades Spain
1809	President James Madison reinstates embargo on British trade
	Jean-Baptiste Lamarck's theory of evolution based on acquired characteristics published in Paris
	Tecumseh and the Prophet campaign to unite all native Americans east of the Mississippi
	Charles Darwin born
1810	David Thompson builds trade houses on Pend Oreille Lake and Flathead River
	Sir Walter Scott publishes *The Lady of the Lake*
1811	John Jacob Astor's Pacific Fur Company establishes post at mouth of Columbia River
	David Thompson follows Columbia to Pacific and finishes charting entire length of the river
	William Price Hunt, leading Astor's overland party, explores Snake River Valley and much of future Oregon Trail
1812	David Thompson retires to Montreal
	War declared between United States and Great Britain
	Napoleon retreats from Russia after burning Moscow
	Baron Cuvier publishes first volume of his *Researches on the Bones of Fossil Vertebrates*
1813	Jane Austen publishes *Pride and Prejudice* anonymously in London
1814	David Thompson delivers his map of western North America to partners of North West Company
	Treaty of Ghent ends War of 1812
1815	Wellington defeats Napoleon at Waterloo
1817	David Thompson takes post as chief surveyor for International Boundary Commission
1821	Amalgamation of North West and Hudson's Bay Companies

1823   James Fenimore Cooper's *The Pioneer,* first volume of his
          Leatherstocking series, published in United States
1825   Spokane House closed; Fort Colville built at Kettle Falls
1836   Washington Irving's *Astoria* published
1839   American Elkanah Walker builds mission for Spokane
          Indians north of Spokane House
1843   David Thompson sends a set of refined maps to London
          The first of 300,000 American settlers follow Oregon
          Trail west
1846   David Thompson begins compiling a book about his
travels
          Great Britain and United States settle long-disputed
             boundary of Oregon Territory
          United States annexes California after war with Mexico
1849   Alexander Ross's *Adventures of the First Settlers on the
          Columbia River* published in United States
1851   Gabriel Franchère's *Narrative of a Voyage to the
          Northwest Coast of America* published in Montreal
1853   Isaac Stevens surveys route for railroad across northern
          Rockies
1855   Stevens persuades tribes of Columbia Plateau to sign treaty
          ceding their lands and to move to reservations
          Flatheads, Kootenais, and Pend Oreilles sign treaty ceding
             25,000 square miles of territory
          Gold discovered on Pend Oreille River
1856   Bessemer furnace used to make steel in England
1857   David Thompson dies in Montreal
1916   Thompson's *Narrative of Travels in Western North America,
          1784–1812* published by Champlain Society in Toronto

FURTHER READING

PRIMARY SOURCES

Baxter, James P. *A Memoir of Jacques Cartier, Sieur de Limoilou: His Voyages to the St. Lawrence.* New York: Dodd, Mead & Co., 1906.

Belyea, Barbara, ed. *Columbia Journals.* Montreal: McGill-Queen's University Press, 1994.

Bigsby, John Jeremiah. *The Shoe and Canoe, or Pictures of Travel in Canada.* 2 vols. London: Chapman & Hall, 1850.

Bridgewater, Dorothy. "John Jacob Astor Relative to his Settlement on the Columbia River." *Yale University Gazette* 24 (1949): 47–69.

Burpee, Lawrence J., ed. "Some Letters of David Thompson." *Canadian Historical Review* 4 (1923): 105–26.

Coues, Elliott, ed. *New Light on the Early History of the Greater Northwest: The Manuscript Journals of Alexander Henry and of David Thompson.* 3 vols. New York: Francis P. Harper, 1897; reprint, 2 vols. Minneapolis: Ross and Haines, 1965.

Cox, Ross. *The Columbia River.* Edited by Edgar I. Stewart and Jane K. Stewart. Norman: University of Oklahoma Press, 1957.

Dempsey, Hugh, ed. "David Thompson's Journey to the Bow River." *Alberta Historical Review* 13 (Spring 1965): 7–14.

———. "David Thompson's Journey to the Red Deer River." *Alberta Historical Review* 13 (Winter 1965): 1–8.

———. "David Thompson on the Peace River." *Alberta Historical Review* 14 (1966).

DeVoto, Bernard, ed. *The Journals of Lewis and Clark.* Boston: Houghton Mifflin Company, 1953.

Elliott, T. C., ed. "Journal of David Thompson." *Oregon Historical Quarterly* 15 (1914): 39–63, 104–25, 216.

———. "David Thompson's Journeys in the Spokane Country." *Washington Historical Quarterly* 8 (1917): 183–87; 9 (1918): 11–16, 103–106, 169–73, 284–87; 10 (1919): 97–103.

———. "David Thompson's Journeys in Idaho." *Washington Historical Quarterly* 11 (1920): 97–103.

———. "David Thompson and Beginnings in Idaho." *Oregon Historical Quarterly* 21 (1920): 49–61.

———. "The Discovery of the Source of the Columbia River." *Oregon Historical Quarterly* 26 (1925): 23–49.

———. "David Thompson's Journeys in the Pend Oreille Country." *Washington Historical Quarterly* 23 (1932): 18–24, 88–93, 173–176.

Franchere, Gabriel. *Journal of a Voyage to the Northwest Coast of America.* Edited by W. Kaye Lamb. Toronto: Champlain Society, 1969.

Franks, C. E. S., ed. "David Thompson's Explorations of the Muskoka and Madawaska Rivers, 1837." *Queens Quarterly* 92 (1985): 348–363.

Fraser, Simon. *Letters and Journals.* Edited by W. Kaye Lamb. Toronto: Macmillan, 1960.

Glover, Richard, ed. *David Thompson's Narrative*. Toronto: Champlain Society, 1962.

Grey Coat School minutes. City of Westminster Archives. Westminster, England.

Henry, Alexander. *The Journal of Alexander Henry the Younger, 1799–1814*. 2 vols. Edited by Barry M. Gough. Toronto: The Champlain Society, 1992.

————. Letter to Duncan Cameron, February 1, 1809. National Archives of Canada, MG 19, E1, Vol. 29.

Hopwood, Victor, ed. *David Thompson: Travels in Western North America, 1784–1812*. Toronto: Macmillan, 1971.

Howay, Frederick W., ed. *"David Thompson's Account of his First Attempt to Cross the Rockies."* Queen's Quarterly 40 (1933): 333–56.

————. *Voyages of the* Columbia *to the Northwest Coast*. Portland: Oregon Historical Society Press, 1990.

Hudson's Bay Company Archives. Provincial Archives of Manitoba, Winnipeg.

Jackson, Donald, ed. *Letters of the Lewis and Clark Expedition*. 2 vols. Urbana: University of Illinois Press, 1978.

Johnson, Alice, ed. *Saskatchewan Journals and Corrrespondence*. London: Hudson's Bay Record Society, 1967.

Jones, Robert F., ed.*Annals of Astoria: The Headquarters Log of the Pacific Fur Company of the Columbia River, 1811–13*. New York: Fordham University Press, 1999.

Kane, Paul. *Wanderings of an Artist among the Indians of North America*. 1859; reprint, Edmonton: M. G. Hurtig, 1986.

Leverette, Clarke E., ed. *"David Thompson's Journal of the IBC Survey 1817–27 of Lake Erie."* Inland Seas 44 (1988): 32–45.

McDougall, Duncan. "Astoria Journal, 1810–1813." Manuscript. Rosenbach Museum and Library, Philadelphia.

McGillivray, Duncan. "Account of the North American Wild Sheep." *Medical Repository VI*, 1803.

————. *Journal*. Edited by A. S. Morton. Toronto: Macmillan Company, 1929.

————. "Some Account of the Trade Carried on by the North West Company." In *Report of the Public Archives of Canada (1928)*. Ottawa: King's Printer, 1929.

Mackenzie, Alexander. *Journals and Letters*. Edited by W. Kaye Lamb. Toronto: Macmillan Company, 1970.

————. *Voyages from Montreal, on the River St. Laurence, through the Continent of North America, to the Frozen and Pacific Oceans*. London, 1801. Reprint. Edmonton: M. G. Hurtig, 1971.

"Map Drawn by Jean Findley 1806." Hudson's Bay Company Archive, E.3/4 fos. 16d–17.

Moreau, William. *The Writings of David Thompson*. 3 vols. Toronto: McGill-Queen's University Press, and Seattle: University of Washington Press (in press).

Moulton, Gary E., ed. *The Journals of Lewis and Clark Expedition*. Lincoln: University of Nebraska Press, 1983–1993.

Mourning Dove. *Mourning Dove: A Salishan Autobiography*. Edited by Jay Miller. Lincoln: University of Nebraska Press, 1990.

Ross, Alexander. *Adventures of the First Settlers on the Oregon or Columbia River,*

1810–1813. Edited by Kenneth Spaulding. London, 1849. Reprint, Lincoln: University of Nebraska Press, 1986.

Schaeffer, Claude. "The Kutenai." Manuscript. Special Collections, Glenbow Museum Archives, Calgary.

Thompson, David. "Account of an Attempt to Cross the Rocky Mountains by Mr. James Hughes, nine Men & Myself, on the Part of the N. W. Company, 1800." Journal. Vancouver Public Library, Vancouver, British Columbia.

_____. Bend of the Missouri. Map, Library of Congress, Washington, D.C.

_____. "Extract from *A Voyage of Discovery Round the World* by Captain George Vancouver, regarding the North West Coast of America." Journal. Vancouver Public Library, Vancouver, British Columbia.

_____. Notebooks. David Thompson Collection, F 443, Provincial Archives of Ontario, Toronto.

_____. "Journey to the Rocky Mountain." 1801. National Archives of Canada, Ottawa, Ontario.

_____. Letter to Alexander Fraser, December 21, 1810. In Masson, *Les Bourgeois*, 2:41–42 (fn).

_____. Letter to Anthony Barclay, December 9, 1843. PRO.FO 5/412. fos. 62–63.

_____. Letter to Donald McTavish, March 3, 1808. HBCA, A.67/1, fos. 12–13d.

_____. Letter to North West Company partners, March 4, 1808. HBCA, A.67/1, fo. 8.

_____. Letter to Sir James Alexander, June 10, 1845, PRO FO5/441. In "Letters and Reports Relating to the Oregon Territory" as "Remarks on the Oregon Territory."

_____. Letters, 1839–1843. National Archives of Canada, Ottawa, Ontario.

_____. "Letters and Reports Relating to the Oregon Territory." *Report of the Provincial Archives Department of the Province of British Columbia for the Year Ended December 31st, 1913.* Victoria, B.C., 1914.

_____. "Map of North America from 84° West." FO 925/4622, sheets 1–10. The National Archives, Kew, England.

_____. "Map of North America from 110° West." FO 925/4622, sheets 11–18. The National Archives, Kew, England.

_____. "Map of the North-West Territory." Archives of Ontario, Toronto.

_____. "Narrative of the Establishment on the Scources of the Columbia, addressed to Mr. Duncan McGillivray, Director of the N. W. Company, and the Gentlemen of the upper Fort des Prairies." 1807. Royal Commonwealth Society Library, Cambridge, England.

_____. "Oregon Territory from Actual Survey." British Library, London, England.

_____. "Remarks on the Countries Westward of the Rocky Mountains, with References to the Rough Chart, by D. T., Terrebonne. 19 April 1813." Royal Commonwealth Society Library, Cambridge, England.

_____. "Sketch of Capt. Lewis's Voyage to the Pacific Ocean by the Missesourii & Columbia Rivers from the States of America." Journal. Vancouver Public Library. Vancouver, British Columbia.

_____. "Travels manuscripts." David Thompson Papers, MS 21, Thomas Fisher Rare Book Library, University of Toronto.

Tyrrell, Joseph B., ed. *David Thompson's Narrative of His Explorations in Western America, 1784–1812*. Toronto: Champlain Society, 1916.

_____. *The Journals of Samuel Hearne and Philip Turnor*. Toronto: Champlain Society, 1934.

_____. "Letter of Roseman and Perch." Oregon Historical Quarterly, 38 (1937): 392–397.

_____. J. B. Tyrrell Papers. Special Collections, National Archives of Canada.

_____. J. B. Tyrrell Papers. Thomas Fisher Rare Book Library, University of Toronto.

Vancouver, George. *A Voyage of Discovery to the North Pacific Ocean and Round the World*. Edited by W. Kaye Lamb. 4 vols. London: Hakluyt Society, 1984.

Wallace, W. S., ed. *Documents Relating to the Northwest Company*. Toronto: Champlain Society, 1934.

White, M. Catherine, ed. *David Thompson's Journals Relating to Montana and Adjacent Regions, 1808–1812*. Missoula: Montana State University Press, 1950.

Wood, W. Raymond, ed. "David Thompson at the Mandan-Hidatsa Villages, 1797–98: The Original Journals." *Ethnohistory* 24 (1977): 329–42.

SECONDARY SOURCES

Allen, John Logan. *Passage Through the Garden: Lewis and Clark and the Image of the American Northwest*. Urbana: University of Chicago Press, 1975.

Archives of Ontario. "Conservation of the David Thompson Map." *Archives Newsletter '79*, October 1979, pp. 7–9.

Arima, E. Y. *Blackfeet and Palefaces: The Pikani and Rocky Mountain House*. Ottawa, Ont.: The Golden Dog Press, 1995.

Belyea, Barbara. "The 'Columbian Enterprise' and A. S. Morton: A Historical Exemplum." *BC Studies* 86 (1990): 3–27.

Bemis, S. F. "Jay's Treaty and the Northwest Boundary Gap," *American Historical Review* 27 (1922): 465–484.

Boyd, Robert T. *The Coming of the Spirit of Pestilence*. Vancouver: University of British Columbia Press, 1999.

_____. "The Introduction of Infectious Diseases Among the Indians of the Pacific Northwest, 1774–1874." Ph.D. dissertation, University of Washington, 1985.

Braunberger, A. Barry, and Thain White. "Howse's House." *Washington Archaeologist* 8 (April & July 1964): 1–89.

Brown, Jennifer S. H. *Strangers in the Blood: Fur Trade Company Families in Indian Country*. Vancouver: University of British Columbia Press, 1980.

_____. "Charlotte Small Personified: Identities in Motion." Paper presented to American Society of Ethnohistory, Williamsburg, Virginia, 2006.

Campbell, M. W. *The North West Company*. New York: St. Martin's Press, 1957.

Carriker, Robert C. *The Kalispel People*. Phoenix: Indian Tribal Series, 1973.

Carroll, Francis M. *A Good and Wise Measure*. Toronto: University of Toronto Press, 2001.

Chance, David. *People of the Falls*. Kettle Falls, Wa.: Kettle Falls Historical Center, 1986.

Clark, Ella E. "The Bridge of the Gods in Fact and Fantasy." *Oregon Historical Quarterly* 53 (March 1952): 29–38.

Clark, Robert C. *History of the Willamette Valley*. Chicago, 1927.

Day, Elsie. "An Old Westminster Endowment." *Journal of Education*, 1 September 1885: 359–363.

Dempsey, Hugh. *The Amazing Death of Calf Shirt and other Blackfoot Stories*. Saskatoon: Fifth House Publishers, 1994.

_____. *A History of Rocky Mountain House*. Ottawa: Canadian Historic Sites: Occasional Papers in Archaeology and History, No. 6, 1973.

_____. *The Indians of Alberta*. Calgary: Glenbow Museum, 1988.

DeVoto, Bernard. *The Course of Empire*. Boston: Houghton-Mifflin Company, 1952.

Eaton, Diane and Sheila Urbanek. *Paul Kane's Great Nor West*. Vancouver: University of British Columbia Press, 1996.

Elliott, T. C. "The Strange Case of David Thompson and Jeremy Pinch." *Oregon Historical Quarterly* 40 (1939): 188–99.

Ewers, John C. *The Blackfeet: Raiders on the Northwestern Plains*. Norman: University of Oklahoma Press, 1958.

_____. *The Story of the Blackfeet*. Washington, D.C.: Bureau of Indian Affairs, 1959.

_____. *The Horse in Blackfoot Indian Culture*. Smithsonian Institution, Bureau of American Ethnology, Bulletin 159. Washington: U. S. Government Printing Office, 1955.

Fahey, John. *The Kalispel Indians*. Norman: University of Oklahoma Press, 1986.

Fenn, Elizabeth A. *Pox Americana*. New York: Farrar, Strauss and Giroux, 2001.

Ferris, Joel E. "David Thompson in Washington: Spokane House." David Thompson Sesquicentennial Symposium, Sandpoint, Idaho, 1959.

Gallagher, Tim. "David Thompson's Detour: A B.C. Man Rediscovers Rocky Mountain Trade Route." *British Columbia Report*, December 3, 1990.

Gottfred, J. "How David Thompson Navigated." *Northwest Journal*. www.north westjournal.ca/dtnav.html.2005.

_____. "The Location of David Thompson's 'Goods Shed' on the Athabasca River." *Northwest Journal* IX: 7–14.

Gough, Barry. *The Royal Navy and the Northwest Coast of North America*. Vancouver: University of British Columbia Press, 1971.

Harper, J. Russell. *Paul Kane's Frontier, including Wanderings of an Artist among the Indians of North America by Paul Kane*. Fort Worth: Amon Carter Museum, 1971.

Hawkes, Arthur. "The World's Greatest Geographer." *Toronto Star Weekly*, May 29, 1927.

Hopwood, Victor. "David Thompson and his Maps." *Proceedings of the Seventh Annual Conference of the Association of Canadian Map Librarians (1973)*. Ottawa: Association of Canadian Map Librarians, 1974.

Howard, Henry. *Anatomy, Physiology and Pathology of the Eye*. Montreal: Armour and Ramsay, 1850.

Hunn, Eugene S. *Nch'I-Wana: The Big River: Mid-Columbia Indians and Their Land*. Seattle: University of Washington Press, 1990.

Innis, Harold A. *The Fur Trade in Canada: An Introduction to Canadian Economic History*. New Haven: Yale University Press, 1956.

Irving, Washington. *Astoria, or Anecdotes of an Enterprise Beyond the Rocky Mountains*. Norman: University of Oklahoma Press, 1964.

Jackson, John C. *Children of the Fur Trade*. Missoula: Mountain Press Publishing, 1996.

_____. "Old Rivet." *Columbia: The Magazine of Northwest History*, Summer 2004, pp. 17–23.

Jennings, John. *The Canoe: A Living Tradition*. Toronto: Firefly Books, 2002.

Jenish, D'Arcy. *Epic Wanderer: David Thompson & the Mapping of the Canadian West*. Toronto: Doubleday of Canada; Lincoln: University of Nebraska Press, 2003.

_____. "The Fall and Rise of David Thompson." *The Beaver*. February 2004.

_____. "The Great Map." *The Beaver*, December 2006.

Josephy, Alvin M., Jr. *The Nez Perce Indians and the Opening of the Northwest*. New Haven: Yale University Press, 1965.

Karamanski, Theodore J. "The Iroquois and the Fur Trade of the Far West." *The Beaver*, Spring 1982.

Layman, William D. "Hawkbells: David Thompson in North Central Washington." *Columbia Magazine*, Winter 1991/1992, pp. 12–19.

_____. *Native River: The Columbia Remembered*. Pullman: Washington State University Press, 2002.

Lewis, W. S. and Jacob A. Meyers, eds. "The Daughter of Angus McDonald." *Washington Historical Quarterly* 13 (1922): 107–117.

McCart, Joyce and Peter. *On the Road with David Thompson*. Calgary: Fifth House, 2000.

MacDonald, Graham A. "Aspects of the Life and Work of David Thompson: with Special Reference to Rocky Mountain House," Cultural and Resource Management, Western Canada Service Centre, Calgary, Alberta, April 2001.

McDonald, Ross. "Images of David Thompson." Paper presented to American Society of Ethnohistory, Williamsburg, Virginia, 2006.

McGregor, J. G. *Peter Fidler: Canada's Forgotten Surveyor, 1769–1822*. Toronto: McClelland and Stewart Ltd., 1966.

MacLaren, I.S. "David Thompson's Imaginative Mapping of the Canadian Northwest, 1784–1812." *Ariel*, April 1984.

_____, ed. "Journal of Paul Kane's Western Travels." *American Art Journal* XXI (No. 2), 1989.

Majors, Harry M. "John McClellan in the Mountain Rockies, 1807." *Northwest Discovery* 2, No. 9 (November–December 1981).

Malaher, David G. "David Thompson's Surveys of the Missouri/Mississippi Territory in 1797–98." Paper presented to the 9th North American Fur Trade Conference & Ruperts Land Colloquium, St. Louis, Missouri, May 25, 2006.

Masson, L. R., ed. *Les Bourgeois de la Compagnie du Nord-Quest*. 2 vols. 1889. Reprint. New York: Antiquarian Press, 1960.

Mattina, Anthony, and Allan Taylor. "The Salish Vocabularies of David Thompson." *International Journal of American Linguistics* 50 (1984): 48–83.

Meyers, J. A. "Finan McDonald—Explorer, Fur Trader, and Legislator." *Washington Historical Quarterly* 13 (1922): 196–208.

_____. "Jacques Raphael Finlay." *Washington Historical Quarterly* 10 (1919): 163–67.

Mirkwood Ecological Consultants. *Athabasca Pass Heritage Trail: Resource and Heritage Information.* Ministry of Forests, Golden Forest District Recreation Program. 1993.

Moreau, William. "David Thompson's Claims," *Columbia* 15 (Summer 2001): 38–43.

_____. "David Thompson's Writing of His *Travels*: The Genetics of an Emerging Exploration Text." PhD Thesis, University of Toronto, 1997.

_____. "Thought, Genesis, Mirage: Editing David Thompson's Travels." Presentation to the Champlain Society, Toronto, 1999.

Morse, Eric W. *Fur Trade Routes of Canada: Then and Now.* Toronto: University of Toronto Press, 1973.

Morton, A. S. "The North West Company's Columbian Enterprise and David Thompson." *Canadian Historical Review* 17 (1936): 266–88.

Newman, Peter C. *Company of Adventurers.* New York: Viking, 1985.

_____. *Caesars of the Wilderness.* New York: Viking, 1987.

Nisbet, Jack. *Visible Bones: Journeys across Time in the Columbia River Country.* Seattle: Sasquatch Books, 2003.

_____. *The Mapmaker's Eye: David Thompson on the Columbia Plateau.* Pullman: Washington State University Press, 2005.

_____. "Mammoths and People in the Upper Columbia." *North Columbia Monthly,* January 2005.

_____. "Quills." *Pacific Northwest Inlander,* February 9, 2006.

_____. "Breaking a Leg." *North Columbia Monthly,* December 2006.

Nute, Grace Lee. *The Voyageur.* St. Paul: Minnesota Historical Society, 1951.

Peltier, Jerome. "Neglected Spokane House." In *Northwest History: Articles from the Pacific Northwest Quarterly.* Fairfield, WA: Ye Galleon Press, 1996, pp. 7–15.

Plaskett, J. S. "The Astronomy of the Explorers." *British Columbia Historical Quarterly* 4 (April 1940): 63–76.

Relander, Click. *Drummers and Dreamers.* Seattle: Pacific North West Parks and Forest Association, 1986.

Rich, E. E. *The Fur Trade and the Northwest to 1857.* Canadian Centenary Series. Toronto: McClelland and Steward, 1967.

_____. *History of the Hudson's Bay Company, 1670–1870.* 2 vols. London: Hudson's Bay Record Society, 1960.

Rocheleau, J. E. "The Hills & Scenery Were the Principal Object." Thompson Falls, Montana: Clark's Fork Forge, 2001.

Ronda, James. *Astoria and Empire.* Lincoln: University of Nebraska Press, 1990.

_____. *Lewis and Clark among the Indians.* Lincoln: University of Nebraska Press, 1984.

Ruby, Robert H., and John A. Brown. *The Spokane Indians: Children of the Sun.* Norman: University of Oklahoma Press, 1970.

Ruggles, Richard I. "Hospital Boys of the Bay." *The Beaver* 308 (Autumn 1977): 4–11.

Schaeffer, Claude. "The Kutenai Female Berdache." *Ethnohistory* 12 (1965): 193–236.

_____. *Le Blanc and La Gasse: Predecessors of David Thompson in the Columbian Plateau.* Browning, MT.: Museum of the Plains Indian, 1966.

_____. "Plains Kutenai: An Ethnological Evaluation." *Alberta Historical Review* 30 (1982): 1–9.

Schalk, Randall F., and Robert R. Mierendorf, eds. *Cultural Resources of the Rocky Reach of the Columbia River.* Vol. 1. Project Report No. 1, Center for Northwest Anthropology, WSU, Pullman, 1983.

Seavy, Nathaniel E. and Aaron J. Baker. "Observations of Black-billed Magpies (Pica pica) 'Ice Fishing' for Aquatic Insects." *Northwestern Naturalist* 77 (Spring 1996): 22.

Smith, Allan H. "An Ethnohistorical Analysis of David Thompson's 1809–1811 Journeys in the Lower Pend Oreille Valley, Northeastern Washington." *Ethnohistory* 8 (1961): 309–381.

Smyth, David. "David Thompson's Surveying Instruments and Methods in the Northwest 1790–1812." *Cartographica* 18 (1981): 1–17.

Thomson, Don W. *Men and Meridians: The History of Surveying and Mapping in Canada.* 3 vols. Ottawa: R. Dumahel, 1966–69.

Turner, Nancy. *Food Plants of Interior First Peoples.* Royal British Columbia Museum, 1997.

Tyrrell, J. B. "David Thompson and the Columbia River." *Canadian Historical Review* 18 (1937): 12–13.

_____. "Letter of Roseman and Perch, July 10, 1807." *Oregon Historical Quarterly* 38 (December 1937): 391–97.

_____. "The Re-Discovery of David Thompson." *Transactions of the Royal Society of Canada*, 3rd series, 22 (1928): 233–47.

USFDA. "Bad Bug Book" (*Ascaris lumbricoides*). http://vm.cfsan.fda.gov.

Von Kirk, Sylvia. *Many Tender Ties: Women in Fur-Trade Society in Western Canada, 1670–1870.* Winnipeg: Watson & Dwyer Publishing, 1981.

Ward, Fred J. "Duncan McDonald Endeavored to Find Site of Salish House." Montana News Association, May 24, 1934.

Wheat, Carl I. *Mapping the Transmississippi West.* 2 vols. San Francisco: Institute of Historical Cartography, 1957.

White, Compton I. "Old Trade Post Is Found Again: M'Donald Helps." *Missoulian* September 16, 1923.

White, M. Catherine. "Saleesh House: The First Trading Post among the Flathead." *Pacific Northwest Quarterly* July 1942, pp. 251–263.

www.DavidThompson200.ca

CHAPTER NOTES

Archives and works frequently cited are identified by the following abbreviations:
AO: Archives of Ontario, Toronto
DCB: Dictionary of Canadian Biography
DT: David Thompson
HBC: Hudson's Bay Company
HBCA: Hudson's Bay Company Archives, Winnipeg
PRO: Public Record Office
TFL: Thomas Fisher Rare Book Library, University of Toronto
VPL: Vancouver Public Library

PROLOGUE
p. 2: "The ground of the day...": DT, June 18, 1811, AO Notebook 25.
p. 3: Historic photographs of Kettle Falls: Layman, *Native River*, 149–59.
p. 3: Archaeology of Kettle Falls: Chance, *People of the Falls.*

CHAPTER 1: IN THE COUNTRY OF SAUKAMAPPEE
Unless specified otherwise, Thompson quotes were taken from Tyrrell: *David Thompson's Narrative.*
p. 9: Grey Coat School: Grey Coat School Minutes; Day, "Old Westminster Endowment"; Ruggles, "Hospital Boys."
"mathematical education": DT to Sir James Alexander, May 9, 1845, in "Letters and Reports Relating to the Oregon Territory," 122.
p. 10: transatlantic voyage: Log of the Prince Rupert, 1784, HBCA, C.1/906.
p. 11: Early fur trade history: Innis, *Fur Trade in Canada*; Rich, *History of the Hudson's Bay Company.*
"They bartered all they had": Baxter, *Memoir of Jacques Cartier.*
p. 13: North West Company: Campbell, *North West Company.*
p. 14: a glowing letter: HBC Governors to Samuel Hearne, May 19, 1784, HBCA, A.6/13.
p. 17: South Branch House journal, 1786–1787: HBCA, B.205/a/1.
p. 19–26: Piegan Blackfeet: Ewers, *Blackfeet: Raiders on the Northwestern Plains*; *Story of the Blackfeet*; Horse in Blackfoot Indian Culture; Dempsey, *Amazing Death of Calf Shirt.*
p. 23–24: Smallpox epidemic of 1780–81: Boyd, *Coming of the Spirit*; "Introduction of Infectious Diseases"; Fenn, *Pox Americana*; Nisbet, *Visible Bones*, 94–108.

CHAPTER 2: A WELL-REGULATED WATCH
p. 31: William Tomison: DCB
p. 31–32: Manchester House journal, 1787–1789: HBCA, B.121/a/3.
Medical viewpoint on DT's broken leg: Nisbet, "Breaking a Leg."
p. 33: Malcolm Ross: DCB; Tyrrell, *Hearne and Turnor Journals*, Appendix C.
Cumberland House journal, 1789–1790: HBCA, B.49/a/20–21.
DT's first journal: AO Notebook 1.
Philip Turnor: DCB.

18th century surveying: Gottfred, "How David Thompson Navigated"; Plaskett, "Astronomy of the Explorers"; Smyth, "David Thompson's Surveying Instruments"; Thomson, *Men and Meridians*, Vol. 1.

p. 34: "The mean of the foregoing": 1790, AO Notebook 1.

p. 35: "I have inserted some Observations": Turnor to HBC Governors, HBCA, A.11/117.

Peter Fidler: DCB; McGregor, *Peter Fidler*.

p. 36: DT letter to HBC Governors: HBCA, A.11/117, fo. 108.

gift of brass sextant: Letter from Alexander Lean, May 1791, HBCA, A.5/3.

p. 37: "a reward for your assiduity": Letter from Alexander Lean, May 25, 1792, ibid.

supply order to London: Officers and Servants' Account Book, HBCA, A.16/111.

substantial sum of sixty pounds per year: Letter from Alexander Lean, May 25, 1794, HBCA, A.5/3.

p. 39: Summer of 1796: AO Notebooks 4 & 5.

p. 40: Malcolm Ross's journal, May 21, 1797: Bedford House journal, HBCA, B.14/a/1.

"May 22 Monday": AO Notebook 5.

Visit of Alexander Fraser to Ross & Thompson: Bedford House journal, April 6, 1797, HBCA, B/14/a/1.

Letter berating chief factor at York Factory: AO Notebook 5, fo. 237.

p. 41: "Gentlemen—As I am now in the employ": AO Notebook 5, fo. 237.

"so base a man": William Tomison to Joseph Colen, August 6, 1797, HBCA, B.239/b/60.

Grand Portage: Campbell, *North West Company*.

p. 42: Thompson's 1799 salary: Masson, *Les Bourgeois*, p. 63.

U.S./Canadian border: Bemis, "Jay's Treaty"; Malaher, "David Thompson's Surveys."

p. 43: Voyageurs: Nute, *The Voyageur*.

Survey from Lake Winnipeg to Assiniboine River: AO Notebooks 8, 9, 10.

Visit to Mandan villages: AO Notebooks 7 & 8; Wood, "David Thompson at the Mandan-Hidatsa Villages."

p. 45: "They appeared to be very intelligent": January 5, 1798, AO Notebook 7.

"their Amusements of Dancing Singing etc.": January 9, 1798, ibid.

p. 48: Journey to Mississippi headwaters: AO Notebook 9 & 11.

p. 49: Mackenzie's credit to DT: Mackenzie, *Voyages from Montreal*, lviii.

Journey to Athabasca: AO Notebooks 6, 10 & 12.

Charlotte Small: Brown, "Charlotte Small Personified."

Country wives: Brown, *Strangers in the Blood*; Von Kirk, *Many Tender Ties*.

Thompson family Bible: Tyrrell, *David Thompson's Narrative*, lv.

p. 50: Posting at Fort George: AO Notebooks 6 & 10.

John McDonald of Garth: DCB, 482; Masson, *Les Bourgeois*, 20–59.

Early encounters with Kootenai Indians: Edmonton House Journal (March 12, 1798; September 26, 1799; October 4, 1799), HBCA, B.239/a; McGillivray, *Journal*, 56–57; Nisbet, *Mapmaker's Eye*, 25–27.

Chapter 3: Smoking with Eagles

p. 51: Rocky Mountain House: Dempsey, *History of Rocky Mountain House*; MacDonald, "Aspects of the Life and Work." Rocky Mountain House is a National Historic Site that has undergone an extensive renovation for the David Thompson Bicentennial.

p. 53: fur trade canoes: Jennings, *Canoe*; Morse, *Fur Trade Routes*.

p. 55: tribes in vicinity of Rocky Mountain House: Arima, *Blackfeet and Palefaces*; Dempsey, *Indians of Alberta*.

Retracing of DT's routes in Alberta: McCart, *On the Road*.

p. 57–62: DT's excursion to meet Kootenais: AO Notebook 13, fos. 90–97; 106–109; Dempsey, "Thompson's Journey to the Red Deer River."

p. 58: Fidler's 1792 meeting with Kootenais: Fidler Journal (December 29, 1792–January 4, 1793), HBCA, E.3/2, fos. 28–40.

p. 62: Duncan McGillivray: DCB; McGillivray, *Journal*.

p. 63: Mackenzie's explorations: Mackenzie, *Voyages from Montreal*.

Robert Gray: Howay, *Voyages of the Columbia*.

George Vancouver & William Broughton: Vancouver, *Voyage of Discovery*.

Mackenzie & Tacoutche Tesse: Map in Mackenzie, *Voyages from Montreal*.

p. 65–66: Thompson & McGillivray scouting expedition: AO Notebook 13, fos. 97–105; Dempsey, "David Thompson's Journey to the Bow River."

p. 66: relocation of Iroquois: Karamanski, "Iroquois and the Fur Trade."

p. 67: McGillivray's exploration of Brazeau: AO Notebook 13, fos. 133–136.

"rheumatism or some other vile disorder": McGillivray, *Journal*, 51.

Extracts from Vancouver's Voyages: VPL journal, fos. 2–49.

p. 68: La Gasse, Le Blanc & Kootenai guide: Fidler journal, HBCA, E.3/2, fos. 36–38.

p. 68–72: DT's 1801 report to McGillivray brothers: VPL journal, fos. 50–62.

p. 72: Birth of Fanny Thompson: Tyrrell, *David Thompson's Narrative*, lv.

p. 73: La Gasse & Le Blanc: Schaeffer, *Le Blanc and La Gasse*; Ruby and Brown, *Spokane Indians*, 35.

p. 75: Mackenzie & XY Company: Rich, *History of the Hudson's Bay Company*, Vol. 2: 216–231.

DT in Peace River region: Dempsey, "David Thompson on the Peace River."

DT's election as N. W. Co. partner: Wallace, *Documents*, 183.

p. 76: DT's chart of Mandan villages: Thompson, "Bend of the Missouri map"; Nisbet, *Mapmaker's Eye*, 33–34.

Arrowsmith chart: Wheat, *Mapping the Transmississippi West*, 178.

Jefferson's instructions to Lewis and Clark: DeVoto, *Journals*, xxxvii.

Simon Fraser and New Caledonia: Fraser, *Letters and Journals*.

p. 77–78: Lewis's encounter with Piegans: Moulton, *Journals*, Vol. 8: 127–133.

p. 78: Side Hill Calf: Ronda, *Lewis and Clark among the Indians*, 238–243.

CHAPTER 4: NEUTRAL GROUND

AO Notebooks 18, 19 & 20, and "Narrative of the Establishment on the Sources of the Columbia."

p. 79: 1806 summer rendezvous at Fort William: Wallace, *Documents*, 210–31.

Jacques Raphael Finlay: Jackson, J. C., *Children of the Fur Trade*; Meyers, "Jacques Raphael Finlay"; Nisbet, *Visible Bones*, 204–29.

p. 79–81: Rocky Mountain House, Fall 1806–Spring 1807: AO Notebook 18

Map "drawn by Jean Findley 1806": HBCA, E.3/4 fos. 16d–17; Nisbet, *Mapmaker's Eye*, 7.

p. 81: "May 10th Sunday": AO Notebook 20.

p. 83: Finan McDonald: Meyers, "Finan McDonald"; White, *David Thompson's Journals*, 234–36.

"The greatest hardship": "Narrative of the Establishment."

p. 84: "as this was the last & only place": "Narrative of the Establishment."

"I observed near the foot of the rocks": Henry, *Journal*, Vol. 2, 507–9.

p. 87: "June 15 Monday": AO Notebook 18.

"where the Springs send their Rills": "Narrative of the Establishment."

p. 88: "was obliged to keep hold": June 25, 1807, AO Notebook 20.

"The water descending in innumerable Rills": "Narrative of the Establishment."

p. 89: "Gave the men a large Dog": June 26, 1807, AO Notebook 18.

"From what has been said of the Road": "Narrative of the Establishment."

p. 91–92: "Beaulieu has been these 10 days": AO Notebook 20.

Medical comment on porcupine quill: Nisbet, "Quills."

p. 92: "shared the last morsel": July 10, 1807, AO Notebook 18.

"Two of them went a hunting": July 16, 1807, ibid.

p. 93: "having left all the others behind": July 18, 1807, ibid.

"From the state of the country": "Narrative of the Establishment."

"a strong taint": ibid.

p. 94: "shared a small piece": ibid.

"Sleep at last": ibid.

"July 22nd Wednesday": AO Notebook 18.

p. 95: plans for Kootanae House: ibid, fo. 267.

Fur post construction: Nisbet, *Mapmaker's Eye*, 44.

p. 96: "a military Post of the Americans": "Narrative of the Establishment."

p. 97: "This establishment of the Americans": ibid.

"to see the Truth of the Matter.": August 27, 1807, AO Notebook 19.

"What their future intentions are": ibid.

p. 98: "They sang around him all night": September 2, 1807, ibid.

"he is useful in many respects": September 11, 1807, ibid.

"What I say in French": DT letter to NWC partners, March 8, 1808.

p. 99: "I told them that we were well prepared.": "Narrative of the Establishment."

"spoke much to the purpose": ibid.

p. 100: "as he alone was capable": September 18, 1807, AO Notebook 19.

"always lying down in some lonely place": September 18, 1807, AO Notebook 20.

Zachery Perch letter: Edmonton House journal, November 10, 1807. HBCA, B.60/a/7.

p. 101: Flat Bow chief Ugly Head: Nisbet, *Mapmaker's Eye*, 47.

p. 104: Nurses Fables: September 28, 1807, AO Notebook 20.

p. 105: "give them battle": October 26, 1807, AO Notebook 19.

DT's supply order: Order for the Columbia Department, 1807–1808, AO Notebook 18, fo. 266.

p. 106: "Transcribed Capn Lewis's account": VPL journal, fos. 63–70. Also see Jackson, *Letters*, 335–343.

Barrel organ: Nisbet, *Mapmaker's Eye*, 51.

Winter of 1807–1808 at Kootanae House: AO Notebooks 19 & 20.

p. 107: Letter from Jeremy Pinch: Elliott, "Strange Case."

calm reply to "your polite favor of the 29th Sept.": ibid.

p. 108: "not one of these petty officers": ibid.

Theories regarding Perch and Pinch letters: Elliott, "Strange Case"; Josephy, *Nez Perce Indians*, 40–49; Majors, "John McClellan in the Mountain Rockies"; Tyrrell, "Letter of Roseman and Perch."

"arranged the desk for papers": January 14, 1808, AO Notebook 19.

Making snowshoes: Nisbet, *Mapmaker's Eye*, 130.

p. 110: "Febry 6th Saturday": AO Notebook 19.

Public letter to Hughes, McTavish, McDonald: March 4, 1808. HBCA, A.67/1, fo. 8.

p. 111: Letter to Donald McTavish: March 3, 1808. HBCA, A.67/1, fos. 12–13d.

CHAPTER 5: BORDER CROSSING

AO Notebooks 19, 21 & 23.

p. 113: "April 22 Friday": AO Notebook 21.

p. 115: "a hissing noise": April 24, 1808, ibid.

Bitterroot bulbs: Turner, *Food Plants*, 136–39.

"This is the place": April 25, 1808, Notebook 21.

Tobacco cultivation: Nisbet, *Visible Bones*, 132–152.

p. 116: "April 30th Saturday": AO Notebook 19.

"His Tail 2 ft. 10 in.": May 3, 1808, ibid.

p. 117: "The least slip": May 6, 1808, AO Notebook 21.

"it was with difficulty": May 7, 1808, ibid.

p. 123: "violent Eddies that threatened": May 7, 1808, AO Notebook 19.

"It smelt strongly": ibid.

p. 124: Moss bread: Turner, *Food Plants*, 33–36.

p. 125: "it was too much putrified": May 13, 1808, AO Notebook 19.

p. 126: "but my time and the weakness of my men": draft of letter, ibid, fos. 339–341.

"& thus all my fine hopes are ruined": May 17, 1808, ibid.

p. 127: decided to leave sextant behind: AO Notebook 24, fo. 65.

"May 19 Thursday": AO Notebook 19.

"the broken rocks has cut the Legs of the Horses": May 26, 1808, ibid.

"bid a kind adieu to our humane Guide": June 5, 1808, ibid.

p. 128: "they have fared but poorly at times": June 8, 1808, ibid.

"One of my horses nearly crushing my children": June 19, 1808, ibid.

"June 20th Monday": ibid.

p. 129 Iroquois trappers: Nisbet, *Mapmaker's Eye*, 67.

p. 130: McGillivray's petitions to British government: McGillivray, "Some Account of the Trade."

"in honor of the family": draft of letter, AO Notebook 19, fos. 339–341.

p. 131: Birth of baby John: (August 25, 1808), Tyrrell, lv.

p. 132: "unwieldy Masses of Snow and Ice": October 20, 1808, AO Notebook 23.

p. 133: "they drank and fought": November 12, 1808, ibid.

Winter of 1808–1809 at Kootanae House: AO Notebook 23.

drawings of the east slope of the Rockies: Thomas Fisher Rare Book Library, F2417–2418.

Magpies "ice fishing": Seavy, "Observations of Black-billed Magpies."

p. 134–137: Lodge Pole Woman, Qanqon: Schaeffer, "Kutenai Female Berdache."

p. 137: "The expedition across the mountains": James Bird to James McNab, Edmonton House journal, August 1, 1808, HBCA B.60/a/8.

p. 138: "We have not heard": Alexander Henry to Duncan Cameron.

CHAPTER 6: TOUCHING THE CIRCLE

p. 139–45: Events from March 1809–September 26,1809: AO Notebook 23.

p. 139: Drawing of Mount Nelson: Thomas Fisher Rare Book Library, F2417–2418.

p. 141: Simon Fraser & Tacoutche Tesse: Fraser, *Letters and Journals.*
"1809. The Partners of the Co.": AO Notebook 28, fos. 16–17.

p. 143: Joseph Howse: DCB, Vol. 8: 411–414.

p. 144: Kalispel and Pend Oreille Indians: Carriker, *Kalispel People*; Fahey, *Kalispel Indians*; Smith, "An Ethnohistorical Analysis."
Kullypel House: White, Compton I. "Old Trade Post"; Nisbet, *Mapmaker's Eye*, 75.
Finan McDonald's marriage: White, *David Thompson's Journals*, 235.

p. 145: Camas: Turner, *Food Plants*, 66–7.

p. 149: Events from September 27, 1809–July 22, 1810: AO Notebook 22.
Saleesh House: Rocheleau, "The Hills & Scenery"; White, "Saleesh House."

p. 151: DT's Salish vocabulary: Mattina and Taylor, "Salish Vocabularies."

p. 152: white free hunters: Jackson, John C., "Old Rivet." Nisbet, *Mapmaker's Eye*, 81.
American trapper named Courter: Josephy, *Nez Perce Indians*, p. 660, 663; Majors, "John McClellan"; Nisbet, *Mapmaker's Eye*, 80–82; Tyrrell, "Letter of Roseman and Perch."

p. 157: Duncan McDonald interview: Ward, "Duncan McDonald Endeavored."
Christine McDonald interview: Lewis and Meyers, "Daughter of Angus McDonald."

CHAPTER 7: OMEN OF THE RED STICK

p. 163–166: Events through July 22, 1810: AO Notebook 22.

p. 163: Henry and Hughes had passed a rough winter: Henry, *Journal*, 414–451.

p. 164: "We got an alarm": June 24, 1810, ibid, 452.
"They fell upon a party of Americans": ibid, 545.

p. 165: "Mr. Thompson embarked": ibid, 452.

p. 166: Annual meeting in Fort William, 1810: Wallace, *Documents*, 264–65.
"the critical situation of our affairs": DT letter to Alexander Fraser.
John Jacob Astor: Bridgewater, "John Jacob Astor"; Ronda, *Astoria and Empire.*
Some historians have inferred: Belyea, "The 'Columbian Enterprise'"; Morton, "The North West Company's Columbian Enterprise."

p. 167: "At 2 O'Clock Mr. Thompson arrived": Henry, *Journal*, 470.

p. 169–173: Henry's account of events at Rocky Mountain House, October 5–November 7, 1810: ibid, 480–94.

p. 171–81: Thompson's Athabasca Pass journey: AO Notebook 25.

p. 173: Route to Brule Lake: Gottfred, "Location of David Thompson's 'Goods Shed.'"
My Dear Fraser: DT letter to Alexander Fraser, December 21, 1810.

p. 175: stopped to cache a third of their goods: see List of Goods, 29 December 1810.

p. 175–76: Athabasca Pass trail: Gallagher, "David Thompson's Detour"; Mirkwood Ecological Consultants, Athabasca Pass Heritage Trail.

p. 178: Thompson's cedar canoe: Nisbet, *Mapmaker's Eye*, 94–95.

p. 180: Howse's activities west of Divide: Braunberger and White, "Howse's House."

"that if they again meet with a white man": Edmonton House journal, May 13, 1811. HBCA, B.60/a/9.

p. 181: Spokane House: Ferris, "Spokane House"; Peltier, "Neglected Spokane House."

CHAPTER 8: WANAPUM

p. 183–87: June 19–July 2, 1811: AO Notebook 25.

p. 185: Paul Kane: Eaton and Urbanek, *Paul Kane's Great Nor-West*, 124–26; Harper, *Paul Kane's Frontier*, 90, 122–25; MacLaren, "Journal of Paul Kane," 42.

p. 186: *Mourning Dove: A Salishan Autobiography*, 99–113.

p. 187–206: July 3–July 15, 1811: AO Notebook 27.

Journey down Columbia: Moreau, "David Thompson's Claims."

p. 190–91: Schalk and Mierendorf, *Cultural Resources*.

p. 201: Relander, *Drummers and Dreamers*.

p. 203: Yellepit and Lewis & Clark: Moulton, *Journals*, Vol. 5: 296–307.

p. 204: "in the greatest agutation": ibid., 305–307.

p. 204–206: The Dalles: Ronda, Lewis and Clark among the Indians, 169–74.

p. 206: Point Vancouver: Vancouver: *A Voyage of Discovery*.

CHAPTER 9: SITTING IN THE WATER

AO Notebook 27

p. 207–210: Pacific Fur Company: Bridgewater, "John Jacob Astor"; Franchere, *Journal of a Voyage*; McDougall, "Astoria Journal"; Ronda, *Astoria and Empire*; Ross, *Adventures of the First Settlers*.

p. 209: "two strange Indians": Franchere, *Journal of a Voyage*, 53.

p. 211: resolution passed by North West partners: Bridgewater, "John Jacob Astor," 53.

p. 212: Thompson's letter to Astorians: ibid, 52–53.

McDougall & Stuarts' letter to Thompson: ibid, 53.

"How could we account": Ross, *Adventures*, 102.

p. 213: "The description this gentleman gave": Franchere, *Journal of a Voyage*, 55.

"Mr. Thompson at once recognized": Ross, *Adventures*, 101.

"He recognized the two Indians": Franchere, *Journal of a Voyage*, 55.

p. 217: "for the sake of mutual protection and safety" & "After our canoes were laden": Ross, *Adventures*, 115.

p. 219: "Down came the mast, sail, and rigging": ibid, 116.

p. 221: Bridge of the Gods myth: Clark, "Bridge of the Gods."

p. 224: Coxe "was looked upon by Mr. Thompson": Ross, *Adventures*, 126.

p. 226: "what did we see waving triumphantly" & "saying that Koo Koo Sint": ibid, 139.

p. 227–28: "bold adventurous amazons": ibid, 153.

CHAPTER 10: ROOM TO FEED

AO Notebook 30

p. 231: "intending by this arrangement": Wallace, *Documents*, 265–67.

p. 236: Thompson's sketch of "Saleesh [Flathead] Lake & Mountains": TFL.

p. 242: "a resolve entered into": Wallace, *Documents*, 270–72.

CHAPTER 11: THE SMELL OF CAMAS ROOT

p. 243–248: October 1812–June 1814: AO Notebook 28

p. 244: Thompson's ambitious cartography project: Belyea, *Columbia Journals*, 294–316; Hopwood, "David Thompson and his Maps."

a sketch of the Oregon country: DT: "Remarks on the Countries Westward."

map hung in dining hall at Fort William: Cox, *Columbia River*, 332.

p. 244–45: 1814 chart: Archives of Ontario, "Conservation of the David Thompson Map."

p. 247: Tonquin incident: Irving, *Astoria*; Ronda,*Astoria and Empire*, 235–37.

North West Company's purchase of Fort Astoria: Ronda, *Astoria and Empire*, 288–91.

Isaac Todd, death of Henry & McTavish: Gough, *Royal Navy and the Northwest Coast*; Henry, Journal, Vol. 1: liv–lxi; Vol. 2: 618–744; Ronda, *Astoria and Empire*, 278–94.

p. 248: prospectus for atlas: Burpee, "Some Letters of David Thompson," 108–9.

p. 249: International Boundary Commission: Carroll, *A Good and Wise Measure*; Lerette, "David Thompson's Journal of the IBC Survey."

p. 250: William McGillivray's dinner, 1820: Bigsby,*The Shoe and Canoe*, I:114–15.

p. 251: Finan McDonald's retirement: Meyers, "Finan McDonald."

Jaco Finlay and Spokane House: Nisbet, *Visible Bones*, 215–18.

Qanqon's death: Schaeffer, "The Kutenai Female Berdache."

p. 252: Thompson's notebook for 1833: AO Notebook 70A.

p. 253: "Mr. Thompson dined with me yesterday": Franks, "David Thompson's Explorations," 253.

p. 254: "bored the soil for 2 feet": ibid, 255.

final, perfected set of his atlas: DT, Map of North America, PRO; DT to Anthony Barclay, December 9, 1843.

purchase of Thompson's maps: DT, "Letters and Reports Relating to the Oregon Territory," 121–22.

Thompson letters re: Oregon boundary: ibid, 112–135.

description of crossing Rocky Mountains in 1801: DT to Sir James Alexander, May 9, 1845. In "Letters and Reports Relating to the Oregon Territory," p. 122–23.

p. 256: four drafts of the "Travels": Moreau, "David Thompson's Writing"; "Thought, Genesis, Mirage."

"It may naturally be expected": John McDonald, "Autobiographical Notes" in Masson, *Les Bourgeois*, I: 59.

"The oldest man according to custom": September 29, 1809, AO Notebook 22.

p. 257: taking his grandchildren out at night: Tyrrell, "Rediscovery", 245.

daughter's memories: Charlotte Thompson to Tyrrell, 1889, Tyrrell Papers, TFL.

Montreal oculist: Howard, *Anatomy, Physiology and Pathology of the Eye*, 357–58.

J. B. Tyrrell & DT: Tyrrell, "The Re-Discovery of David Thompson."

Tyrrell's monument: Hawkes, "The World's Greatest Geographer."

EPILOGUE

Ethnography of Hanford Reach: Hunn, *Nch'I-Wana*.

INDEX

Ignace (Iroquois), 179, 197, 190
Île á la Crosse, 49
Ilthkoyape Falls. *See* Kettle Falls
Interior Salish, 187
International Boundary Commission, 249,
  250, 252, 253
Iroquois Indians, 66, 111, 129, 132, 168,
  232
Irving, Washington, 255
Issac Todd (ship), 247

Jacques (Iroquois), 140
Jefferson, Thomas, 76, 202
John Day River, 204, 225
Jolly watch, 37, 52
Journals, Thompson's field, 5, 33, 255–56

Kalispel Indians, 144, 145, 150, 180, 187,
  228, 256
Kane, Paul, 185
Kettle Falls, 6, 183, 184, 186, 187, 228,
  237, 238; present–day, 2, 3, 4
Kingfishers, 235
Koo-Koo-Sint, 151, 226
Kootanae Appee, 25–26, 27, 80–81, 97
Kootanae House, 94–102, 105, 133, 143,
  161, 246
Kootanae Pound, 88
Kootenai Falls, 117, 118, 119, 123, 144, 161
Kootenai Indians, 50, 57, 58, 62, 65, 67,
  77, 105, 115, 150; lore, 73–75, 100,
  104, 147; and Piegans, 57–61, 97–98,
  107, 124
Kootenai/Kootenay River, 103, 113, 117,
  119, 126, 228, 262; spelling of, vii, 102
Kootenay Lake, 124, 125–26, 133
Kootenay Plains, 83–84, 85–86, 87, 129,
  132, 143, 170
Kullyspel House, 144–45, 159, 180, 237,
  255
Kullyspel Indians. *See* Kalispel Indians
Kulsmayuk (Kootenai), 74

La Chaudière. *See* Kettle Falls
La Gasse (voyageur), 57, 62, 67, 72, 73
Lake Athabasca, 13, 35, 39, 62, 63, 75, 76
Lake Indians. *See* Flat Bow Indians
Lake la Pluie. *See* Rainy Lake
Lake Superior, 41, 42, 48, 62, 75, 242
Lake Winnipeg, 13, 15, 37, 43, 129

Lake of the Woods, 42, 129, 249
Lamprey eels, 223
Larches. *See* Tamarack
Large Kidney, 150
Latitude and longitude, 38, 90, 108, 202,
  215, 238, 243; calculation of, 33–35
Le Blanc (voyageur), 62, 67, 72, 73
Le Bon Vieux, 150, 159, 161, 181, 228, 233
Le Camble (voyageur), 83
Le Monde (Kootenai), 116
Lewis and Clark expedition, 76–78, 96,
  202, 234, 264; accounts of journey,
  106, 165, 186
Line-hauling, 15, 83
Lisa, Manual, 108
Lolo Pass, 234
London, England, 9, 10, 242, 248,
  254; headquarters of Hudson's Bay
  Company, 4, 35, 37, 39, 40
Loons, 105, 179
Louisiana Territory, 44, 76
Lussier (voyageur), 83, 127, 139–40
Lynx pelts, 17

MacDonald, Christine & Duncan, 157
McDonald, Finan, 81–84, 88, 144, 209–
  14, 227, 251; at Kootanae House, 91,
  97, 105, 113, 128, 133; at Kullyspel
  House, 144, 149; at Saleesh House,
  159, 165, 180, 232, 233, 237; at
  Spokane House, 181, 209
McDonald of Garth, John, 50, 51, 77,
  79–80, 101, 256
McDougall, Duncan, 209–15, 217, 224,
  247
McGillivray, Duncan, 65, 67, 126, 130–
  31; and western expansion, 62, 76, 205
McGillivray, William, 42, 62, 65,
  244, 249–51; head of North West
  Company, 76, 166, 242
McGillivrays River, 103, 131, 228
Mackenzie, Alexander, 42, 48, 49, 75, 76,
  141; explorations, 42, 63–65, 77, 90
Mackenzie, Roderick, 243
McMillan, James, 112, 129, 132, 163, 237;
  at Saleesh House, 149–50, 232
McTavish, Donald, 110, 111–12, 130,
  242, 247
McTavish, John George, 232, 237, 247
Magpies, 1, 133

ABOUT THE AUTHOR AND THE ILLUSTRATOR

JACK NISBET is a teacher, naturalist, and writer who explores human and natural history in the greater Northwest. Since the publication of *Sources of the River* in 1994, he has written *Purple Flat Top*; *Singing Grass, Burning Sage*; *Visible Bones*; and *The Mapmaker's Eye*, an illustrated version of David Thompson's work on the Columbia Plateau. Nisbet lives with his wife and two children in Spokane.

JACK MCMASTER is an illustrator and graphic designer. His works include the re-creation of David Thompson's 1814 map, the "North-West Territories of the Province of Canada," which is on display in the Great Hall of Old Fort William, Thunder Bay, Ontario. Jack lives with his family in Nova Scotia.